Ratio Decidendi and Obiter Dictum

Daniel Mitidiero

Ratio Decidendi and Obiter Dictum

A Curious Case

Springer

Daniel Mitidiero
Faculdade de Direito
Universidade Federal do Rio Grande do Sul
Porto Alegre, Rio Grande do Sul, Brazil

ISBN 978-3-031-93151-2 ISBN 978-3-031-93152-9 (eBook)
https://doi.org/10.1007/978-3-031-93152-9

English translation of the Portuguese language edition: "Ratio Decidendi" Published by Thomson Reuters, 2023. Translated by Aline Lampert and Regina Fleck Bergmüller. Revised by Laura Wilde and Augusto Caballero Fleck.

This Springer imprint is published by the registered company Springer Nature Switzerland AG
The registered company address is: Gewerbestrasse 11, 6330 Cham, Switzerland

To Cláudio Michelon,
for the bridge between Porto Alegre and Edinburgh—
and for showing me the lost steps.

To Victória,
for walking every step of the way together—
from one end of Chambers Street to the other.

Foreword

The past twenty years have seen a groundswell of interest in the theory and practice of judicial law-creation and, in particular, in the doctrine of judicial precedent. This renewed interest has not only meant that much more has been written about precedents than ever before, but also that our understanding of precedent-based judicial reasoning and decision-making is now much more sophisticated and nuanced than it was just a few decades ago. These advances in our comprehension of the doctrine of precedent, in turn, allowed for a more productive dialogue between different practices of precedent-following across different jurisdictions in a process of mutual learning that has influenced judicial practice in many a national and international court.

Ratio Decidendi and Obiter Dictum is the latest addition to this body of literature that is reshaping our understanding of precedent-based reasoning and decision-making. The book creatively utilizes an analytical framework of great conceptual clarity, whose threads were originally developed by lawyers and theorists working primarily within the common law tradition, but which were woven together by the author to shed light on the practice of judicial law-creation in a Civilian legal system (Brazilian Law). But its interest does not lie simply in its illumination of Brazilian judicial practice (the book does that admiringly, of course). The application of the framework to the Brazilian context helps to demonstrate, more generally, how it can help us understand precedent-like practices in other civilian jurisdictions.

This analytical framework is carefully laid out in the book, in dialogue with the history of our conceptions of the *Ratio* and of *Obiter*. In fact, the book addresses some of the main changes in our understanding of judicial precedent over the past few hundred years (and especially since the 1930s) and in doing so, it provides a concise, but very useful, history of the two related concepts it set out to elucidate. The endgame, however, is not primarily historical, but conceptual. What we learn from history is mobilized in the service of our understanding of judicial law-creation in Brazil (and, as mentioned above, on practices belonging to other civilian systems).

But the book the reader has in hands is not only a new book; it is also a new *kind* of book. For decades, many legal academics have been trying to write serious scholarship in a more informal manner, but have consistently failed to combine academic rigour with colloquiality of expression. To the best of my knowledge, this is the first book in the English language to have achieved this and that is not a mean feat. Daniel Mitidiero's innovative style has been recognized in his native Brazil by the award to one of his previous books of the Jabuti Prize (the most prestigious literary prize in Brazil) for legal writing.

For all these reasons, I am delighted to present *Ratio Decidendi and Obiter Dictum* to English speaking audiences. A friend once wrote that contributing a foreword for someone else's book is like welcoming someone to a house that is not yours. But any possible awkwardness that might arise from this situation dissipates if one has witnessed that house being built and furnished. Daniel spent much of the winter of 2023 as a visiting scholar at Edinburgh Law School and I have fond memories of long conversations about many of the arguments in the book in Edinburgh's dim winter sun.

The upsurge in academic writing on precedents shows no sign on waning anytime soon. In that body of literature, more particularly on the sub-field of comparative study of precedent-based judicial decision-making, *Ratio Decidendi and Obiter Dictum* has a distinctive place, and anyone interested or curious about it, should take the time to read it. I certainly benefited immensely from doing so.

The University of Edinburgh, Edinburgh Law School, Edinburgh, UK
Winter 2025

Claudio Michelon

Preface

A book about the *ratio decidendi* and *obiter dictum* written by a Brazilian scholar? Not so long ago, this may have been dismissed as amateurish, exhibitionist, or the folly of an artist safe in fortuitous marriage. The historical development of Brazilian Law, however, has brought it closer to the Common Law tradition. As such, the need to promote legal certainty, freedom, and equality through precedents counters the above prejudices. The *ratio* and *obiter* have practical implications to the Brazilian legal system. To not familiarize oneself with the basic definitions, to understand how they work or have adapted to Brazilian Law, means that one may find it difficult to rise to the daily demands of legal practice.

Whilst these reasons can explain why the topic must be studied in Brazil, they are not in themselves enough to explain the publication of this book; that is where the role of tradition comes into play. My writing delves into English and American Law and introduces this to Brazilian legal literature; it seems fitting to publish the result in the language of Stevenson, the Beatles, and Oasis. This is nothing short of being accountable; I'm glad I did it and I hope I don't let you down.

I would like to thank once again my dear friend, Professor Claudio Michelon, from the University of Edinburgh, for his hospitality, for accepting to write the preface of this book, and for the extraordinary moments we shared. I have endless appreciation for Claudio's affectionate reception, generosity, the coffee meetings in which we discussed the ideas of this book, his constructive criticism and for the Sunday afternoons in which we spent time together as if we were a family—with Laila, Laura, Gabriel, and Victória. Speaking of whom, I wish to express gratitude to Laila for all her affection and attention; you made all the difference, and I carry our days of Edinburgh in my heart. I also thank the translators: Aline Lampert and Regina Fleck Bergmüller, and the proofreader Laura Wilde—I am sure that the English version is much better than the original Portuguese. I am also grateful to Augusto Fleck for preparing the English manuscript. I thank Springer and Karol Araújo as well, for believing in the book's publication. Finally, on *Chambers Street*, in Edinburgh, on the corner of 24 de Outubro Avenue and Quintino Street, in Porto Alegre—in short, here, there, and everywhere—I thank Victória: *you're my wonderwall.*

Res severa verum gaudium.

Porto Alegre, RS, Brazil
Spring 2024

Daniel Mitidiero

Competing Interests The author has no competing interests to declare that are relevant to the content of this manuscript.

Contents

About the Author

Daniel Mitidiero is an Associate Professor of Civil Procedure at the Federal University of Rio Grande do Sul (since 2011). He holds a PhD in Law (UFRGS) (2007) and is a Visiting Scholar at the University of Edinburgh, Scotland (2023), University of La Plata, Argentina (since 2015) and the University of Pavia, Italy (2013). He is a member of the Council of the International Association of Procedural Law (IAPL), member of the Instituto Iberoamericano de Derecho Procesal (IIDP), of the Associazione Italiana fra gli Studiosi del Processo Civile (AISPC), of the Associación Argentina de Derecho Process (AADP), and member of the Board of the Instituto Brasileiro de Direito Processual (IBDP). He is the author of multiple books and works published in several countries. Daniel is also a practising lawyer in Brazil.

Chapter 1
Introduction

In 1934, in an essay that became a classic on the distinction between precedent in *Common Law* and caselaw in *Civil Law*, Arthur Goodhart noted that the main difference between the two traditions is precedents were binding for the former while caselaw was persuasive for the latter.[1] In 1961, in a book that was for a long time the main reference on precedents in *Common Law*, Rupert Cross stated that the search for the *ratio decidendi* was one of the peculiarities of Anglo-American Law, having no parallel in the Roman-Canonical rooted legal system.[2]

If you cracked a smile reading this first paragraph, you know that these observations belong to the history books—at least, the Brazilian Law history books. Anyone familiar with Brazilian courts knows that we have mandatory precedents—and this has more to do with the way law is approached from a logical-argumentative perspective and with the transformation of the Supreme Courts undertaken from there than with the Code of 2015—and that we must know what they say to live in accordance with the Law.

This has dominated the past decade. The matter now, however, is no longer about rebuilding the authority of the courts and the source system of sources, but about understanding how the determines the administration of the day-to-day judicial matters. How we deal with precedents is, therefore, a top priority; this is where the *ratio decidendi* takes center stage.

In light of this, three goals encouraged me to write the first part of this book. The first is to show the history of *ratio decidendi,* to explore the debate about its definitions and purposes. The second is to learn from its development in the *Common Law* and, thus, suggest an understanding of the *ratio* capable of dealing with identical, similar and distinct issues in the Brazilian legal system. The third is to demonstrate how this context is useful in our journey along the road of legal

[1] Goodhart (1934), p. 42, vol. L.

[2] Cross and Harris (1991), p. 49.

D. Mitidiero, *Ratio Decidendi and Obiter Dictum*,
https://doi.org/10.1007/978-3-031-93152-9_1

procedure. Each of the three first chapters has been written to reach each of those goals.

After the completion of the first part, however, I realized that the *ratio* was haunted. It was a new concern and the path was clear. I had to draw attention to the fact—a little recognised fact indeed—that a considerable danger was on the loose. The ghost of the *obiter dictum* plagued the *ratio* and had the potential to improperly obscure or usurp it. My concern arose: how to protect the *ratio* from *obitering*. Is it possible to devise a formula capable of architecting the peaceful coexistence of the *ratio* and *obiter*? That is the impetus of the second part of this book. My endeavours are tripartite. Perhaps a more conventional path could have been taken, but that is not my way. I apologise in advance for my extravagances; I will not omit them, but I can, however, explain them.

The first chapter of the second part, "by the side of the road" starts with an attempt to characterise *obiter dictum*. Within this, three more steps: its definition ("just chit-chatting?"), classification ("ancient trees") and, finally, the attempts to erase it by obliterating the demarcations that separate it from the *ratio* ("without borders?").

In the second, "the wind-up bird chronicle", I address its twofold abilities: the lawful and nefarious. In the first, I argue that the *obiter* is a signal, as to the development of the Law and, in case of interpretative doubts, the determination of the *ratio*. Properly conceived, it is a cue (*"creeeak"*). However, it is vulnerable to corruption; not unlike the *Stange Case of Dr. Jekyll and Mr. Hyde*. It may illegitimately supersede or conceal the *ratio* (*"obitering"*). One must know how to prevent it: how to discern the potion and how to destroy it ("how to avoid it?"). If we fail, labels operating merely as smoke screens may triumph over the Law.

In the third, "may the force be with you", I examine the effects of the *obiter*. Only the *ratio* is mandatory, of course, but not all *obiter* is created equal. Some merely illustrate the law and do not need to be considered. Others, have a persuasive pull and, therefore, must be debated in court ("illustrating, persuading"). But what distinguishes one *obiter* from the other? Why are some considered, whilst others left to languish? Various criteria are drawn upon to answer these questions ("connect the dots"). Finally, we discern where the force is strong—what makes an obiter valuable—and how it progresses from Padawan to Jedi ("the empire strikes back").

I hope you will enjoy the ride.

References

Cross R, Harris J (1991) Precedent in English Law, 4th edn. Oxford University Press, Oxford

Goodhart A (1934) Precedent in English and Continental Law. Law Q Rev 50:40–65

Part I
Ratio Decidendi: When Is an Issue Identical, Similar, or Distinct?

Chapter 2
Ratio Decidendi

Debates of definitions have always been part of legal life, and some reoccur with greater frequency than others. Every now and then, a perspective arises which transforms the orthodoxy. As such is the case with the notion of precedent. Outlining its contours means establishing a continuity between disparate and temporally distinct traditions. It requires theoretical-philosophical speculation, historical-comparative sense, and attention to the particularities of Brazilian Law. The ratio is a challenging concept to demarcate. But it is not simply a matter of taste, although the possession of a refined palate certainly helps. If it had a flavour, I could not say it is that of an aged cheese, say a *grana* or a *cheddar*, but nor would it be akin to a mint tea or *mojito*. It is a concept that alludes a precise and unquestioned definition.

Settle in; take a piece of *grana*, a sip of *mojito*. We shall begin.

The debate around precedent is far from new ground for me. In 2016[1] I discussed its authority, and, in 2013, I considered the role of the Supreme Courts.[2] Here, I turn my attention to the *ratio decidendi* within Brazilian Law. I seek to explore and clarify how our various understandings of the *ratio* relate to the nature of interpretation. The theories of the ratio can be encapsulated in three verbs: declare, create, and rebuild. But before we proceed to these competing definitions, we must first attend to the foundational matter and distinguish *ratio decidendi* from the conceptions with which it has been increasingly treated as synonymous with under Brazilian Law.

I use the term *ratio decidendi* as a synonym for precedent.[3] Precedents are necessary and sufficient reasons for the solution of a duly particularised issue from a factual-legal point of view obtained by a logical-argumentative rebuilding

---

[1] Mitidiero (2023).

[2] Mitidiero (2022a).

[3] Mitidiero (2023). By the way, the expression *ratio decidendi* is traditional in English Law, while the expression *holding* is more common in US Law (Atiyah and Summers 1987, p. 124). To inventory and critique the different senses in which the word "precedent" is used is outside my concerns at this time. If you are interested in the topic, I suggest you consult Chiassoni (2019),

D. Mitidiero, *Ratio Decidendi and Obiter Dictum*,
https://doi.org/10.1007/978-3-031-93152-9_2

undertaken from the decision of cases by the unanimity or majority of a panel of Supreme Court judges.[4]

Precedents are distinct from both decisions and summulas. Although related concepts, they exist at different discursive levels.[5] A decision is a discourse designed to resolve a case. The precedent is a discourse arising from the rebuilding of certain briefs used to decide a case, duly contextualised by the corresponding facts. The summula is a statement derived from the precedent with the abstraction of the facts. There is a discourse, a metadiscourse, and a meta-metadiscourse. But these divergences do not structure a normative hierarchy; rather this escalation represents a growing abstraction of the case. The decision, precedent and summula are distinct concepts, with differing functions.

A decision resolves a delimited case; this may involve a concrete or abstract controversy.[6] A decision has a particularised object: either the facts debated in court in light of the interpretation and application of certain norms or abstractly considered norms. Simply put, decisions determine a concrete case or a law in theory. In either situation, the debate is established and resolved with its *provision*. A decision is rendered over a particularly characterised controversy.

Conversely, precedents do not resolve cases. A decision resolves a specific controversy from the past, whereas precedents determine a general direction for the future.[7] By consubstantiating themselves in a discourse elaborated from a rebuilding of certain briefs, precedents seek to give unity to legal order.[8] Features of the controversy which are pivotal in a decision—certain aspects of the concrete case or the specific law that was abstractly considered[9]—are irrelevant to the precedent, as it is the provision that resolves it. What truly matters are the *facts*—which function as *briefs*—that grant meaning to the Law. The basis for rebuilding is the constant *justification* of the case decision, thus establishing the meaning of the

---

p. 202, in which the three main meanings of the term (*"precedent-judgement", "precedent-ratio" and "precedent-order")* are listed.

[4]I will return to this definition later, but I immediately note that I used the broader expression "logical-argumentative reconstruction" instead of "generalisations": generalisation is one of the activities that can be carried out as reconstruction (*infra*, items 2.1 and 2.2).

[5]By the way, I quote below some paragraphs of *Reclamação*.

[6]When referring to "abstract" controversies, I have in mind those related to the abstract control of constitutionality. For a broad view on it, with the appropriate bibliographical references, Mitidiero (2022b).

[7]In fact, the precedent can only be understood as an orientation figuratively. Technically, the precedents constitute legally protected conclusive reasons, that is, legal norms: in this condition, they oblige their recipients. It is not, therefore, a simple guideline. It is a prescription that links someone's behavior in a mandatory way, regardless of the correctness of the solution covered. On the subject, with the appropriate bibliographic indications, Mitidiero (2023).

[8]I would like to point out that in *Common Law* the distinction between decision (*"judgment"*) and *ratio decidendi* (*"precedent"*) was elaborated precisely to highlight these two discursive levels, their different objects and different objectives, which I intend to make clear by exposing their historical development (*infra*, item 1.1).

[9]*Infra*, item 2.1.

Law in a given context. Following this line of reasoning, precedents indicate the direction of the Law when identical or similar issues arise. In other words, the precedent is the Law itself duly interpreted by the Supreme Courts from a given case.[10] *Legis interpretatio legis vim obtinet.*[11]

On the other hand, summulas are abstract statements which derive from precedent. Precedents are cities walled by facts, but summulas are merely outposts.[12] The facts-reasons that led to the decision are omitted from the precedent and, likewise, the summulas is only a "summary-statement"[13] of the precedent. Due to its abstract nature, a summula is not binding.[14] Only the underlying precedent is binding and, consequently, in the absence of accompanying facts, summulas are not enforceable.[15] Thus, even when a summula is treated as binding, the weight of this imperative comes from is its underlying precedent. Summulas represent an *interna corporis* work method but have been erroneously conflated with the precedents that they represent. It is a mistake to treat these two concepts as tantamount.[16]

Alongside these three concepts, Brazilian Law also has *theses*, a close relative of the summulas. Like summulas, *theses* do not constitute precedents, rather they are answers to the *themes*, which constitute a way of indexing issues under the appreciation of the Supreme Courts. A *thesis* is given by the Supreme Court to the precedent.[17] However, this does not exempt the assessment of its congruence with the facts-reasons it seeks to portray. What binds, therefore, is not the thesis itself, but the precedent from which it derives. However, as with the summulas, the precedent—or the *ratio decidendi*—can be mistaken for the theses. Brazilian Law

[10] Mitidiero (2023). By the way, I made this point based on Tarello (1980), Guastini (2011), Chiassoni (2007). In the same vein, Alexander (2023), p. 18.

[11] Brocardo quoted by Brian Garner in Thomas Branch, *Principia Legis et Aequitatis*, 1753, which means that the interpretation of the law has the force of law (Garner 2016, p. 333).

[12] Mitidiero (2024), p. 320.

[13] Mello (2008), p. 147.

[14] Cramer (2016) pp. 85–86; Câmara (2018), p. 221; Viana and Nunes (2018), p. 214.

[15] According to art. 926, § 2°, CPC.

[16] As I have already written in my book *Precedentes*, "in 1963, by amending the Internal Regulations of the Federal Supreme Court, the caselaw summulas of the Federal Supreme Court were created. These summulas were originally conceived as general and abstract statements that aimed to quickly inform the Federal Supreme Court Ministers about the Court's orientation on a given issue. It is for this reason that they were initially thought of as a 'working method' for the Federal Supreme Court: they aimed to help identify how this court interpreted a certain norm to let them control the interpretation made by ordinary instances. In this vein, the summulas constituted a 'caselaw horizon' for the Federal Supreme Court to guide its own Ministers." With the institution of binding summulas in 2004 (art. 103-A, CRFB), "the summulas – whose initial role was to facilitate the task of controlling then exercised by the Federal Supreme Court and later to avoid the admission of appeals – began to have the role of determining the content of judicial decisions. Summulas would no longer contain guidelines solely directed to the Ministers of the Federal Supreme Court itself. They began to convey rules for the entire Judiciary and for the entire Public Administration" (Mitidiero 2023).

[17] I will return to the topic later (*infra*, item 2.1).

confuses the two terms in several passages of *soft law*.[18] Where the *ratio* is rebuilt by the interpreter's activity before the issue that must be judged, the *theses* is the formulation panel of judges that assessed the issue that will serve as a precedent. It is entirely possible that the *thesis* is indistinguishable from the *ratio* in the absence of its facts. However, it is important to recognise that these are, technically, distinct concepts.

Now we are clear on the distinct nature of the *ratio decidendi*, we can now move to analyse its history and the three verbs that have been attributed to its interpretative activity: declare, build, and rebuild. Legal literature has presented a number of ways to characterise the *ratio,* but the search for an element capable of reassembling them to a common core has generally been renounced.[19] Here I aim to contextualise the history of the *ratio* with the theories of its interpretation. Not only is this an engaging method of navigating its story, but much is revealed between the lines. I hope this becomes apparent as we progress.

2.1 The Search for the Spirit: Declaring the *Ratio*

In my book *Precedentes*, I traced the history of the precedent in English Law and the three functions it has performed over time: illustrating, persuading, and binding. Although my focus here is different, a brief recap of this can help our understanding of the *ratio's* emergence.

Initially, the precedent merely *illustrated* the principles of the *Common Law* without the judges feeling obliged to mention or follow them in their decisions.[20] The earliest formulation of the maxim of *stare decisis* and of *treat like cases alike* can be found in Bracton in the thirteenth century.[21] But that is not to say that the

---

[18] In the 2015 Civil Procedure Code, there are passages in which it can be seen that the precedent is being correctly understood as *ratio decidendi* (such as, for example, when art. 489, § 1, item V, states that the precedent shall be observed due to its "determining grounds"), but others which might be mistaken with the decisions (for example, art. 927, item I), with the summulas (for example, art. 927, item II) and with the interpretations (for example, arts. 927, item III, 1,039 and 1,040). It's a fruit salad (Mitidiero 2024, p. 321). The confusion between *ratio decidendi* and interpretation is explicit; however, in Recommendation No. 134, of 2022, of the CNJ (art. 14, §§ 1 and 2—in several other passages, in fact, the interpretation is clearly taken as a precedent, as, for example, in arts. 4, 5, 11, 13, 14, 19 and 48). Characterising the CNJ Recommendations as *soft law*, Didier Júnior and Fernandez (2022), pp. 70–75.

[19] A good and succinct attempt to do so, however, can be found in Chiassoni (2019), p. 211, which will be analysed in due course (*infra,* items 1.1 and 1.3).

[20] Lewis (1930a), p. 215, n. 46; Micheli (1938), pp. 22–23; Postema (2002), p. 161; Berman (2003), p. 273; Duxbury (2008), p. 32. For a broad view on precedents with illustrative function, Mitidiero (2023).

[21] Henry de Bracton (1210?–1268?), *De legibus et consuetudinibus Angliae*, quoted by Hogue (1986). Indianapolis: Liberty Fund, p. 200: *"if any new and unwonted circumstances... shall arise, then if anything analogous has happened before, let the case be adjudged in like manner (si tamen similia evenerint per simile iudicentur) since it is a good opportunity for proceeding from like to like (a similibus ad similia)*".

precedent was as we know it today.[22] Rather, the precedent was simply the decisions contained in the *pleas rolls*.[23] The precarious writing of the *Year Books*—private repertoires for the collection of cases and their dissemination—prevented a more accurate comparison between cases.[24] As such, the role of the precedent was naturally limited and, between the thirteenth and sixteenth centuries (when we have the first record of a case used as a precedent in England[25]), there was no such differentiation between the *ratio decidendi* and *obiter dictum*.

This distinction began to emerge in the seventeenth century as precedents took a more significant role in the practice of law. Characterised as the "*best proof*"[26] of a principle capable of determining the decision of a case, the ratio started to perform a *persuasive* function. As such, interest arose regarding what is effectively binding in a decision.[27] Concurrently, the *Year Books* were surpassed by Edward Coke's *Named Reports*.[28] These recordings offered greater accuracy as to the facts, the debates and

---

[22] Hogue (1986), p. 201.

[23] Duxbury (2008), p. 32. The *pleas rolls* were the court records that contained the decisions. Apparently, they were very difficult to access even for those who judged cases (Allen 1939, pp. 189–190).

[24] Dawson (1986), pp. 64–65, notes that the first printed version of the *Year Book* appeared in the fifteenth century (1495), being attributed to Staham. The *Year Books* were precarious because they reported only fragments of the cases, often with vague allusions (Allen 1939, pp. 178–181). At the time of the *Year Books*, moreover, the term *"precedent"* (or *"president"*) was already popularised: in Dyer, one of the pioneers of *private reports*, it appears in a case tried as early as in 1557 (Allen 1939, p. 192).

[25] The case *Maulay v. Abbot of Whitby*, tried by the *King's Bench* in 1281, cited a 1274 case between Edmund Lancaster and Robert de Ferrers (Brand 2006, p. 67). By the way, the *King's Bench* was one of the central courts of *Common Law* (also known as Westminster courts), alongside *Common Pleas* and *Exchequer* (on the subject, Baker 2002, pp. 17–22; Langbein et al. 2009, pp. 118–122). Next to the *Common Law* courts, there was also the *Court of Chancery* in Westminster, which had been judging cases in *Equity* since as early as the 14th century. In the nineteenth century in England, and in the twentieth century in the United States, *Common Law* and *Equity* merged into a single system. On the subject, Baker (2002); Langbein et al. (2009).

[26] The characterization of the precedent as *evidence* or *proof* of the existence of the *Common Law*—and therefore not as a right per se—is one of the hallmarks of the classic doctrine of the precedent. In 1628, Edward Coke (1552–1634) subtitled his *The First Part of the Institutes of the Laws of England. Or, a Commentary upon Littleton*, the emblematic and always repeated phrase: *"our book cases are the best proofs what Law is"* (Neil Duxbury 2008, p. 34). Still in the seventeenth century, Hale (1971), p. 45, wrote that *"judicial decisions (...) have a great Weight and Authority in Expounding, Declaring, and Publishing what the Law of this Kingdom is"*, noting shortly thereafter that *"such Decisions are less than a Law, yet they are a greater Evidence"*. Finally, in the eighteenth century, Blackstone (1979), p. 69, said that *"judicial decisions are the main and most authoritative evidence, can be given, of the existence of such a custom as shall form a part of the common law"*.

[27] For a broad view on precedents with illustrative function, Mitidiero (2023).

[28] In general, it is possible to periodise the evolutionary stages of judicial repositories into four: (i) *Year Books* (1290–1535); (ii) *Named Reports* (1535–1765); (iii) *Authorized Reports* (1765–1865); and (iv) *Law Reports* (1865 onwards) (Lewis 1930a, p. 207, n. 46). As the relationship between *reports* and precedents is significant, several authors have even tried to tell the history of the precedent taking into account these different stages of the *reports* (such as, for example, Lewis 1930a, 1930b, 1931, 1932 and John Dawson 1986, pp. 50 et seq.).

the legal solutions given to the cases.[29] The foundations for the modern *ratio's* development were set.

The first differentiation of the *ratio decidendi* from the *obiter dictum* has been attributed to William Fulbeck in 1600.[30] Fulbeck noted that it was necessary to distinguish between the "principal points" and the "bye-matters".[31] In 1673 this distinction penetrated the Common Pleas at the hands of Chief Justice Sir John Vaughan in *Bole v. Horton*.[32] Vaughan followed a similar line of reasoning to Fulbeck, distinguishing "judicial opinion" from "gratis dictum". He states that "an opinion given in Court, if not necessary to the judgement given of record", is not "judicial opinion, nor more than a gratis dictum", but that "an opinion, though erroneous, concluding to the judgement, is a judicial opinion because delivered under the sanction of the judge's oath, upon deliberation".[33]

The emerging emphasis on what was effectively decided and, thus, should serve as precedent, developed alongside the imperative that the ratio obey due process. Consequently, the practise of citing previous cases that were unconnected to the case on trial was eliminated. Vaughan also notes that precedents "are useful to decide questions, but in such cases as these which depend upon fundamental principles, from which demonstrations may be drawn, millions of precedents are to no purpose".[34]

The development of the *ratio* was well underway. Bracton emphasised *case law* and coined the maxim *a similibus ad similia*. Coke remodelled the *Reports* and insisted on precedent as *the best proof* of *Common Law*. Fulbeck and Vaughan severed the decision from the precedent, distinguishing "judicial opinion" from *"gratis dictum"*. And, gradually, the "judicial opinion" became increasingly identified with the "general principles" underlying the decision.[35] It was even said that "the reason and spirit of cases make law, not the letter of precedents"[36]—

[29] Allen (1939), p. 197. Of course, the task of collecting cases did not cease to be precarious overnight. Even with the *Named Reports* a lot has happened. Sometimes, the importance of a case ends up being rescued only many, many years later. The example given by Claudio Michelon is eloquent: to properly solve a case involving illicit enrichment in Scottish law (*Morgan Guarantee*, decided in 1995 by the *Court of Session*), it was necessary to rebuild the *ratio* of a timidly reported case, including with the help of legal historians (*Stirling*, decided in 1733). Only by appealing to the forensic files, containing the manifestations of the parties and the succinct judicial decision, was it possible to rebuild *Stirling* and overrule *Glasgow*, decided in 1959 by the same court (Michelon 2023, pp. 121–122).

[30] Fulbeck (1829) (the recollection of Fulbeck's name appears, for example, in Duxbury 2008, p. 67).

[31] Fulbeck (1829), pp. 237–238. Fulbeck dealt with the subject in the last chapter of his book (Chapter IX, whose title is *"what method is to be used in handling and disposing matters of law"*, pp. 221 et seq., specifically by way of *"observations upon the analysis"*, pp. 235 et seq.).

[32] Sir John Vaughan (1603–1674), *Bole v. Horton* (1673) (Allen 1939, p. 198).

[33] Allen (1939), p. 198 (which removed the passages quoted from *Vaughan's Reports*, p. 382).

[34] Allen (1939), p. 199 (which removed the passage quoted from *Vaughan's Reports*, p. 419).

[35] Lord Mansfield (1705–1793) in *Rust v. Cooper* (1777) (Allen 1939, p. 207).

[36] Lord Mansfield in *Fisher v. Prince* (1762) (Allen 1939, p. 207).

adjustments made by Lord Mansfield in the eighteenth century as Chief of Justice of the King's Bench. Mansfield insisted that the mere citation of decisions, without explaining their principles, would not constitute a valid working method for the law. He echoes this sentiment in *Jones v. Randall:* "the law of England would be a strange science if indeed it were decided upon precedents only".[37] Likewise, in *Rust v. Cooper* that "the law does not consist in particular cases, but in general principles, which run through the cases and govern the decision of them".[38] The decision was now distinct from the precedent. The precedent constituted only the "judicial opinion" which could be identified with the general principles, that is, with the reason and the spirit of the case.

The nineteenth century saw the further development of this emphasis on general principles. James Ram[39] in his "universal practical guide"[40] identified a "judicial opinion" as the "main part of the argument",[41] noting that it could not be "void of principle".[42] Subsequently, John Austin defined the *ratio decidendi*—perhaps the first to use the expression[43]—as "the general reasons or principles of a judicial decision", abstracted "from any peculiarities of the case".[44] Consequently, at the beginning of the twentieth century, John Salmond established both the *binding* nature of the precedent and solidified the link between the "principle"[45] and *ratio decidendi.*

To say that the *ratio* is the principle underpinning a decision has become a common and "safe" place.[46] As a tool created to demonstrate that precedents and decisions are different things, this has served its purpose. However, this is observation was, and continues to be, marred by its indefinite nature. Whilst the differentiation of the decision and precedent laid the groundwork for developing *methods* to find the *ration,* the declaration of the "spirit" saw the search for the particular of the

[37] Lord Mansfield in *Jones v. Randall* (1774) (Allen 1939, p. 207).

[38] Lord Mansfield in *Rust v. Cooper* (1777) (Allen 1939, p. 207).

[39] Ram (1871) (the first edition was published in London by Maxwell—this second edition has John Townshend's additions and notes). According to Freda (2012), p. 18, James Ram's work represents the first explicit defence of the doctrine of the binding character of precedent in England. Also highlighting the importance of Ram's book, not so much for the analysis undertaken, but for the reported cases and the clear link between precedent and legal certainty, Evans (1987), p. 46.

[40] Ram (1871), p. 102.

[41] Ram (1871), p. 102.

[42] Ram (1871), p. 104.

[43] It is unclear to me whether Montrose (1957b), p. 588, in that passage, attributed the expression *"ratio decidendi"* to Austin or if it only highlighted the novelty of its definition. It is also unclear whether Geoffrey Marshall (1929–2003) attributed it to Austin or not in Marshall (1997), p. 511. Anyway, as Giovanni Tarello noted (Tarello 1962, p. 209), this is strongly related to the "rational" company typical of Bentham and Austin (in which "rational" appears as the search for the principle on which the decision was based). For that reason, it doesn't seem difficult to me that he actually coined it.

[44] Austin (1873), p. 97.

[45] Salmond (1913), p. 173.

[46] Goodhart (1937b), p. 2.

elements that compose it. Now defined, legal theorists where quick to add to their agenda, the matter of formulating a guide for the *ratio's* determination.[47] This pursuit emerged in nineteenth century with Wambaugh and was then taken up by Goodhart and Cross in the twentieth century.

In 1892 Eugene Wambaugh published his *The Study of Cases* to teach students the methods to detect the *ratio decidendi.*[48] In a chapter entitled "how to find the doctrine of a case," Wambaugh defined the *ratio decidendi* as the "general proposition of law that, connected with the circumstances of the case, logically leads to the decision.[49]" The best guide for this would be the decision of the Court,[50] which should be read under the light of four keys.[51] Accordingly, Wambaugh outlined tools to navigate the "circumstances of the case" and the "general proposition" to identify the *ratio decidendi.* With reference to the facts, he noted that no two cases would ever be identical.[52] Therefore, to properly compare them, it is necessary to eliminate their inessential circumstances.[53] At a minimum, the people involved, the time and place of the facts, would be different and thus, in principle, irrelevant.[54] Concerning the Law, he argued—and here is the heart of his method[55]—that a proposition could only be considered "precedent" if the introduction of a word inverting its meaning could also change the solution of the case.[56] It was necessary

---

[47] Highlighting the difference between the problems of "defining" and "determining" the *ratio decidendi*, Simpson (1961), p. 168; Duxbury (2008), p. 75.

[48] Wambaugh (1894), pp. V and VII. As Neil Duxbury observes (Duxbury 2021, pp. 65–66), the publication of *The Study of Cases* occurred in the same year that Wambaugh began teaching at Harvard—which, not by chance, already lived under the didactic empire of the "case method" proposed by Christopher Columbus Langdell (1826–1906) (according to Friedman 2005, p. 468). This circumstance perhaps explains the primacy of American legal scholarship in examining the problem of determining the *ratio decidendi.*

[49] Wambaugh (1894), p. 29. Although I do not quote it in this passage, it is a definition most likely inspired by Austin (1873), pp. 93–98, whose work Wambaugh knew and appreciated (Op. cit., pp. 77–79).

[50] Wambaugh (1894), p. 28.

[51] Wambaugh (1894), pp. 13–15, 24 and 29: for the search for the *ratio* to be fruitful, one should work only with the material "contained in" and "necessary for" the decision, supported by a "general rule", all expressly or implicitly "deliberated" by the Court (I took the liberty of reorganising the order of *"principles"*—of *"keys"*—proposed by Wambaugh to assist in the discovery of the *"doctrine of the case"*).

[52] Wambaugh (1894), p. 14.

[53] Wambaugh, (1894), pp. 15–16.

[54] Wambaugh, (1894), pp. 14–15.

[55] Marinoni (2022), p. 159.

[56] Wambaugh (1894), p. 17. Under the heading "a test for determining whether a case is precedent for a given doctrine", Wambaugh wrote that "yet by experiment even the beginner can determine whether it is possible for a given proposition of law to be involved in a given case. In order to make the test, let him first frame carefully the supposed proposition of law. Let him then insert in the proposition a word reversing its meaning. Let him then inquire whether, if the court had it in mind, the decision could have been the same. If the answer be affirmative, then, however excellent the original proposition may be, the case is not a precedent for that proposition, but if the answer be negative the case is a precedent for the original proposition and possibly for other propositions also".

to survive the "test" of inversion so that the proposition could be considered a precedent.

Arthur Goodhart subsequently tackled the identification of the *ratio* in three seminal essays: "Three Cases on Possession" (1928),[57] "Determining the Ratio Decidendi" (1930),[58] and "The Ratio Decidendi of a Case" (1959).[59] His arguments were met with both radical criticism[60] and important reformulations[61] and, thus, significantly contributed to the ongoing debate around the search for the *ratio*. In "Three Cases", he sought to define the ratio, stating that the *ratio* would be the "material grounds" for solving an issue.[62] Following Wambaugh's observations of the relevant facts, he observed that only what was considered by the Court could be considered material ground.[63] Consequently, he criticised the judgements of Lord Russell of Killowen, Holmes, Pollock, Wright and Salmond in *Bridges v. Hawkesworth*, arguing both alterations in the facts and improper elaboration of principles.[64] Likewise, he denounced the unsound explanations[65] given by Salmond in *Elwes v. Brigg Gas Company* and *South Staffordshire Walter Company v. Sharman*.

In his second essay,[66] Goodhart outlines three steps and several rules to identify the "principle of the case" and thus, the ratio. He defines the *ratio decidendi*—or the "principle of the case"—as the conclusion reached by the Court based on the material facts of the case.[67] The *ratio* would, therefore, not be in the "reason" (or "reasoning")[68] in the "proposition of law",[69] or in all the facts of the case,[70]

[57] Goodhart (1937a), pp. 75–90.

[58] Goodhart (1937b), pp. 1–26.

[59] Goodhart (1959), pp. 117–124.

[60] *Infra*, item 1.2.

[61] *Infra*, item 1.3.

[62] Goodhart (1937a), p. 75.

[63] Goodhart (1937a), pp. 75 and 84. In these passages, Goodhart invokes Wambaugh's "fourth principle" ("doctrine in mind of the court"), according to which the "doctrine of the case must be a doctrine that is in the mind of the court", that is, it must be that one considered and deliberated—expressly or implicitly—by the court (Wambaugh 1894, pp. 24–27 and 29).

[64] Goodhart (1937a), pp. 76–84.

[65] Goodhart (1937a), pp. 84–90.

[66] Goodhart (1937b), pp. 25–26, in which the rules for the definition of the *ratio* (five) and especially for the definition of the facts and separation between the material and the immaterial (ten) are summarised by way of conclusion.

[67] Goodhart (1937b), p. 22.

[68] Goodhart (1937b), pp. 2–4 and 25. The expressions "reason" and "reasoning" are used by Goodhart throughout the text interchangeably (Goodhart 1937b, pp. 2–3).

[69] Goodhart (1937b), pp. 9 and 25. The term "proposition of law" is used as a synonym for legal rule (Goodhart 1937b, pp. 5–9).

[70] Goodhart (1937b), pp. 9–10.

but in the "conclusion" formulated based on certain facts.[71] Here Goodhart builds upon the work of Wambaugh, outlining specific steps to identify the facts relevant to the determination of the *ratio* and proposing rules for its characterisation.

Goodhart's first step involves defining the facts of a case, this is characterised by two particularities of the English Law from that time: the absence of exposition of the facts in some decisions and any differences between the facts contained in the decisions and those in the *reports*. The difficulties in defining the facts of the case and the rules for the respective solution of the problems arising therefrom are interesting from a historical-comparative point of view but irrelevant to Brazilian Law—because here, all decisions have a report of the facts, which must also be expressly analysed in the statement of reasoning.[72] Therefore, we can exclude this from our analysis.[73]

His second step is to use the reasoning of the decision to identify the relevant facts.[74] Goodhart proposed six rules to identify them, which I have condensed into five:[75] (i) in principle, the facts related to people, time, place, kind, and amount would be irrelevant;[76] (ii) the facts expressly or implicitly treated as irrelevant in the decision would be irrelevant;[77] (iii) the facts expressly treated as relevant would be relevant;[78] (iv) if the decision does not distinguish between relevant and irrelevant facts, all should be considered relevant;[79] and (v) if the decision is composed of

---

[71] Goodhart (1937b), pp. 2–9, 22 and 25. In presenting his definition of *ratio* in *"Determining,"* Goodhart talks about "conclusion" based on "material facts". Of course, the purpose of the text is to draw a map so that you can find the facts of the case and, among them, the facts relevant to the decision. The definition of "conclusion", therefore, makes only one point, playing a supporting role in it. Throughout the text, however, Goodhart implies in several passages that this "conclusion" can be identified with a "decision" involving a "principle" or a "general rule", which makes perfect sense not only in the light of "Determining" in general, but also because of the observations made in "Three Cases" and "The Ratio Decidendi of a Case". His step forward with "Determining" is precisely in the idea to compare cases based on their "material facts". It is not possible to eliminate from the definition of the *ratio* in Goodhart, however, the normative element, which appears not only to illuminate what are the material facts and what are the immaterial ones (Goodhart 1937b, p. 18), but also to forge the Court's "conclusion" (Goodhart 1937b, pp. 2–9 and 25).

[72] Art. 489, items I and II, and § 1, CPC.

[73] If you are interested in the topic, you can consult Goodhart (1937b), pp. 11–15. I note that in the essay's conclusions, rules 2, 3 and 4 concern the definition of the facts of the case (Op. cit., p. 26).

[74] Goodhart (1937b), p. 18. Referring to the problem of defining the relevance of facts, Goodhart wrote: "the reasons given by the judge in his opinion, or his statement of the rule of law which he is following, are of peculiar importance, for they may furnish us with a guide for determining which facts he considered material and which immaterial." Although in 1930 Goodhart did not summarise this rule in his conclusions, in 1959 he highlighted it as the "most important" for determining "material facts" (Goodhart 1959, p. 119). Sometimes we need time to be clear about our own ideas.

[75] Goodhart (1937b), pp. 25–26.

[76] Goodhart (1937b), pp. 11, 16, and 25. It is, of course, a rule inspired by Wambaugh (1894), pp. 14–15.

[77] Goodhart (1937b), pp. 16–20 and 26.

[78] Goodhart (1937b), pp. 20 and 26.

[79] Goodhart (1937b), pp. 21 and 26.

votes that agree in the provision, but differ in the reasoning, only the facts so considered unanimously or by the majority of the board would be relevant.[80]

To illustrate these rules, Goodhart analysed two cases: *People v. Vandewater*, 1928, and *Rylands v. Fletcher*, 1868. In the first case, *Vandewater,* a purveyor of alcoholic beverages—a banned activity in the United States at that time—was charged with public nuisance. Among the facts of the case were the maintenance of the place of sale of alcoholic beverages, the rioting, the discomfort and the noise in the neighbourhood resulting from it. The *New York Court of Appeals* held that the mere maintenance of a place for the illicit sale of beverages constituted a source of social disturbance. As such, Goodhart argued that the Court understood that the relevant fact for the decision was the maintenance of this "illicit drinking place". The effect of this activity on the neighbourhood was irrelevant.[81] In the second case, *Fletcher* hired a contractor to build a reservoir on his land. The contractor, acting negligently, built a reservoir that subsequently leaked water and, thus, caused damage to *Rylands* by flooding a mining field on his property. Among the facts of the case were *Fletcher's* reservoir, the contractor's negligent construction, the water leakage, and the damage caused to *Rylands*. The *House of Lords* took *Fletcher's* strict liability to *Rylands*, condemning him to compensate for the damages. As such, Goodhart proposed that the relevant fact of the decision was the water leakage and the occurrence of damages; the contractor's negligent performance was irrelevant.[82]

Goodhart's third and final step involved comparing cases to determine if the *ratio* of the first would apply to the second. If the relevant facts are identical, then the answer is yes. If, in the second case, any material fact is missing, then the precedent would not apply. If there is a fact not considered in the first, the application of the precedent would depend on its characterisation as relevant or not.[83] His ideas generated enormous debate in the legal literature.[84]

---

[80] Goodhart (1937b), pp. 21–22 and 26.

[81] Goodhart (1937b), pp. 16–17.

[82] Goodhart (1937b), pp. 17–18.

[83] Goodhart (1937b), pp. 23–24.

[84] The essay *"Determining"* generated a well-known and heated debate between James Montrose and Brian Simpson about Goodhart's proposal. While Montrose saw in it a mistaken alternative to the "classical theory" of *Common Law* to define the *ratio decidendi* (Montrose 1957a, pp. 124–130; Montrose 1957b, pp. 587–595), Simpson saw no difference between classical theory and Goodhart's (Simpson 1958, pp. 155–160; Simpson 1959, pp. 453–457). Both, however, agreed that his ideas were unsatisfactory for the solution of the problem, which led him to write *"The Ratio Decidendi of a Case"*, mainly to clarify the meaning of his proposals. Although not very conclusive, the debate is always referred to in the works on the subject, and it is worth checking if you are curious about the subject, but deviates from the purpose of my presentation (I anticipate, however, that some authors may find my "not very conclusive" an understatement—in the opinion of Larry Alexander, for example, the debate is "tiring and infamous", according to Alexander 1989, p. 18, footnote no. 21).

In response to this emanating discourse, Goodhart penned his final essay: "The Ratio Decidendi of a Case".[85] He reiterates the ideas of "Determining",[86] pointing to *Donoghue v. Stevenson* as a "striking illustration".[87] Additionally, he clarifies that he did not intend to impose "fixed rules" to determine the *ratio*, rather he sought to offer a "guide" for doing so.[88] It would be a "vain hope" to[89] imagine—observed Goodhart—the existence of an infallible method to identify the *ratio*. Finally, he concluded that the task of the judges charged with enforcing the *ratio* is to simply declare the pre-existing rule; it is not their role to build it.[90]

In 1961, Rupert Cross published his *Precedent in English Law*, which was quickly established as the most influential textbook on the subject in England.[91] Following the emphasis placed on the facts by Wambaugh and Goodhart, Cross sought to bring the rules to the forefront in the search for the ratio. He observed that Goodhart gave a "scarce" treatment to how matters of law are alleged and decided and gave little attention to the reasoning and any subsequent cases that also dealt with the same theme.[92] Unlike Goodhart, Cross did not explicitly propose a method for determining the *ratio* but offered an alternative definition that implied a criterion for doing so.

For Cross, the *ratio decidendi* would consist of any legal rule treated explicitly or implicitly by the Court as a "necessary step" towards its conclusion.[93] The facts of the case would serve to guide its identification.[94] This "necessary step" indicates a test for the *ratio*—to know if a certain rule composes it would be enough to remove it from the rationale.[95] Determining the *ratio* would involve investigating the rule, the

---

[85] Goodhart (1959), pp. 117–124. In this essay, Goodhart sought to clarify his ideas in the face of criticism formulated not only by Montrose and Simpson, but also by Stone (1946), pp. 186–189. This essay by Goodhart led to another essay by Stone in response to it (*infra*, item 1.2).

[86] Goodhart (1959), pp. 118–119.

[87] Goodhart (1959), p. 120. *Donoghue v. Stevenson* is a famous case tried by the *House of Lords* in 1932. It will soon reappear (*infra*, item 1.2).

[88] Goodhart (1959), p. 123.

[89] Goodhart (1959), p. 124.

[90] Goodhart (1959), p. 123.

[91] Cross (1961). From the 4th edition onwards, published in 1991, the book was updated by Jim Harris—it is his, by the way, the observation that Cross's book, throughout its three editions (1961, 1968 and 1977), constituted the basic and fundamental work on precedents in English *Common Law* (Cross and Harris 1991, p. V). I venture to say that this role today is played by Duxbury (2008).

[92] Cross and Harris (1991), p. 67.

[93] Cross and Harris (1991), p. 72. I note that the idea of accentuating the *ratio* as a "necessary step" is undoubtedly Cross's, but in a way it was already possible to foresee it in Wambaugh in 1892 (*ratio* as the legal statement from which "the decision logically follows", Wambaugh 1894, p. 29). In the same vein, Abramowicz and Stearns (2005), p. 1,056.

[94] Cross (1977), p. 153.

[95] Speaking of which, legal scholars later came to call it the "test of necessity" (for a representative view on this matter, Duxbury 2008, p. 78, which—by the way—also criticises him based on Neil MacCormick, *infra*, item 1.3).

facts, and any subsequent cases and formulating a "rule" capable of covering all these aspects.[96]

We have transversed four centuries of history—Fulbeck, Vaughan, Mansfield, Ram, Austin, Wambaugh, Goodhart, and Cross—in a whistlestop fashion. Through this development of definition and identification of the *ratio*, common threads can be observed: (i) the belief that the *ratio* is *one* rule that must be extracted from the past; it is "buried treasure",[97] ready to be declared for the solution of a future case; (ii) the certainty that it is possible to use *one* test to find it (inversion of the proposition, isolation of the relevant facts or need for the rule); and (iii) the absence of certain theoretical tools in its constructions.[98] For these scholars, as we search for the spirit of the *ratio*, it is a rule to be discovered and declared.

However, the nature of the ratio is not unambiguous, and its journey has not been without conflict; for others the *ratio decidendi* is a matter of construct rather than unearthing.

2.2 Sky Writing: Creating the *Ratio*

Stunt pilots display their skills by drawing words in the air, but the results of their efforts are quick to vanish. Many have argued that the *ratio* is of a similar nature. Created by the court charged with enforcing the precedent, the effect of their briefs last no longer than the writings of the smoke from aeroplanes. The *ratio decidendi* is no more than an imaginary category. This school of thought emerged between the 1920s and 1950s, with US legal realists and their sympathisers leading the charge.[99] They identified (or perhaps created) an elephant in the room which they claimed had long been ignored in the search for the ratio. They sought to highlight the discrepancies in what the court claimed to do and was actually done in utilising precedents in reaching a decision.

In 1928, Oliphant published his emblematic essay *"A Return to Stare Decisis"*.[100] He argued that the doctrine of *stare decisis* should be thought of, not a "vocal behaviour", but a "non-vocal behaviour".[101] Over time, it had become "stare dictis".[102] Jurists focused on what was *said* in the decision, but it was necessary to

---

[96] Cross and Harris (1991), p. 73.

[97] Twining and Miers (2010), p. 306.

[98] Chiassoni (2019), p. 211 (*infra*, item 1.3).

[99] I do not intend to analyse here American legal realism as a whole (on the subject, I recommend Tarello (1962) and Twining (2012). I would like to note, however, that the debate on the *ratio decidendi* and on how to seek legal certainty by the precedent only makes sense to some realists, among whom the most important are Herman Oliphant and Karl Llewellyn (Tarello 1962, pp. 205–220). To others, such as Jerome Frank and Max Radin, the uniformity of judicial decisions would not even be a feasible goal (Tarello 1962, pp. 203–205). Bringing them into the discussion, therefore, escapes the purpose of my text.

[100] Oliphant (1928), pp. 71–76, 107 and 159–162.

[101] Oliphant (1928), p. 161.

[102] Oliphant (1928), p. 72.

recover its old meaning: a focus what was *done*. A return to form would enable an empirical perspective analysis.[103] In assuming that these elements are foreign to the rules that effectively determine a judicial decision,[104] Oliphant advocated the consideration of experiences of the courts[105] and the practical consequences aimed at by the decisions.[106] Thus, jurists would be equipped to predict how the courts would decide a case.[107] What the courts do in response to the facts of the concrete cases presented to them would be the elements that appear in all judicial decisions.[108] These should be analysed with objective tools sought in other social sciences—such as, for example, the statistical method used by economists.[109] Thus, Oliphant redirected the doctrine of *stare decisis* to the analysis of the behaviour of the courts and argued that the *ratio decidendi*—understood as a rule—played a minor role in the decision-making process.[110]

This theory soon appeared in Karl Llewellyn's influential *Introduction* books. In 1930, he published *The Bramble Bush – On Our Law and its Study*; successive editions of which spanned the century, and it remains alive to this day.[111] In the opening four chapters, Llewellyn sought to develop these ideas. After discussing "what law is about",[112] Llewellyn presented the "case system" covering "what lies behind the case",[113] "what to do with the cases",[114] and the "precedent".[115] In a well-known passage,[116] Llewellyn defines the Law as what courts do to resolve cases.[117] The rules—aside from beautiful toys[118]—are only tools capable of helping

[103]Oliphant (1928), pp. 74, 76, and 160–162.

[104]Oliphant (1928), pp. 159–160.

[105]Oliphant (1928), p. 159.

[106]Oliphant (1928), pp. 160–161.

[107]Oliphant (1928), p. 76.

[108]Oliphant (1928), p. 159.

[109]Oliphant (1928), p. 161.

[110]Oliphant (1928), pp. 76 and 107.

[111]Llewellyn (2008).

[112]Llewellyn (2008), pp. 3–18.

[113]Llewellyn (2008), pp. 19–36.

[114]Llewellyn (2008), pp. 37–54.

[115]Llewellyn (2008), pp. 55–71.

[116]Mentioned, for example, by Hart (1983), pp. 124–128.

[117]Llewellyn (2008), p. 5. I decided to make the definition simpler by bundling up all Civil Justice participants in the figure of the courts, but the complete passage is as follows: "What, then, is this law business about? It is about the fact that our Society is honeycombed with disputes. Disputes actual and potential; disputes to be settled and disputes to be prevented; both appealing to law, both making up the business of the law. But obviously those which most violently call for attention are the actual disputes, and to these our first attention must be directed. First, so that there may be peace, for the disputants; for other persons whose ears and toes disputants are disturbing. And secondly, so that the dispute may really be put at rest, which means, so that a solution may be achieved which, at least in the main, is bearable to the parties and not disgusting to the lookers-on. This doing of something about disputes, this doing of it reasonably, is the business of law. And the people who have the doing in charge, whether they be judges or sheriffs or clerks or jailers or lawyers, are officials of the law. What these officials do about disputes is, to my mind, the law itself."

[118]Llewellyn (2008), p. 7.

to perceive patterns of regularity in the courts' behaviour, which—together with society—would be glad to believe that they follow them.[119] Employed in a case, they are merely a psychological crutch, providing assurance as to the continuity of the law. But in the absence of cases, they serve only to hinder.[120]

Although Lewellyn does not cite Oliphant, he echoes his arguments, insisting that we should search for the Law in what the courts *do* and not in what they *say*.[121] He suggests that the rules are incapable of establishing the decision; they act only as "guidelines".[122] Thus, it is necessary to seek predictability indices in the court's behaviour—in their personal preferences, in the way they view the world, in the way they see the consequences of their decisions.[123]

That is not to say the rules are irrelevant, but they are merely the starting point.[124] We consider what is written before moving to what has been done.[125] The material facts of the cases are guides[126] and the rules are simply alibis—the reasons offered by the courts for their decisions.[127] Like outposts, sentinels, chess pawns: the rules are tools for the courts to employ as they decide, not the structure of the decision. They must be known, and the court must know how to utilise them. The facts of the case are not fixed, rather they are *categories*. Therefore, it is necessary to know when the language used in the precedent should be interpreted strictly, narrowly or broadly,[128] but the rules cannot determine this. Consequently, the courts cannot be bound by the rules; they reinterpret the facts, according to their ideology, to achieve the results they seek.[129] The rule is nothing more than figurehead of their true reasons. But, whilst alibis are not always true, comparing cases remains a key method for dealing with the Law; it offers benchmarks for debate and a shared way of working.[130] No case offers the solution of another, but the existence of this shared method at least provides an objective methodology at the disposal of all.[131]

[119]Llewellyn (2008), pp. 6–7.

[120]Llewellyn (2008), p. 4.

[121]Llewellyn (2008), pp. 5, 7, 13–14, 65 and 71.

[122]This essay is the collection of some passages from Llewellyn's classes in Lepzig, Germany, between 1928 and 1929, published there in 1933 (under the title *Präjudizienrecht und Rechtsprechung in Amerika*), with an introduction by Paul Gewirtz. The complete translation came out soon after: Llewellyn (1989).

[123]Tarello (1962), pp. 189, 215, and 220.

[124]Llewellyn (2008), p. 42.

[125]As you may have noticed, I went straight from the first chapter (*"What Law is About"*) to the third (*"The Case System: What to Do with the Cases"*). That is because the second (*"The Case System: What Lies Behind the Case"*) depicts the American Civil Justice and the different functions performed in its floors. Although interesting, it is out of the scope of my text to discuss it here

[126]Llewellyn (2008), pp. 45 and 47.

[127]Llewellyn (2008), pp. 40–42.

[128]Llewellyn (2008), p. 46.

[129]Llewellyn (2008), pp. 6–7.

[130]Llewellyn (2008), pp. 47–50.

[131]Llewellyn (2008), p. 50.

The final piece of Llewellyn's "case system" is the precedent and the predictability it offers as to how a particular court would decide a case. He linked this to the doctrine of *stare decisis*. For Llewellyn, the precedent is employed by courts in two ways—one "strict" and the other one "loose." In being "strict", the courts sever unwanted precedents from the decision with a "scalpel." When they are "loose" they employ welcome precedents and utilise them as "platforms" for their decisions.[132] Therefore, if the precedents were merely rules, these operations would undermine them and, consequently, weaken the doctrine of *stare decisis*.[133] Thus, in order to deal with the precedents, it is necessary to consider not only what is said in the decisions but what was done by the courts. This is how we can explain why some precedents are utilised and others ignored. This perception increases the level of security offered by the system.[134] For Llewellyn, these "leeways" are inherent to the system of precedent.[135] The courts simultaneously work strictly and loosely.[136] It is no wonder, therefore, that he lists no less than sixty-four techniques for working with precedents.[137] The combination of what was said with what was done would result in the value granted by the precedent by the decisional court. Consequently, the court does not discover the *ratio* but creates it.[138]

Julius Stone is not a realist but can be seen as a sympathiser. He entered the debate due to his disagreement with Goodhart's conception of the *ratio decidendi*. This marked a transition—Stone's position is far from the authors who saw the *ratio* as a buried treasure[139] and closer to those who see it as the arch of the bridge.[140] But he shares with the realists, the notion that the *ratio* is something created by the second court. He is an outlier in the debate, far from the established camps, but nonetheless offers a valuable perspective on the nature of the *ratio*.

In 1959, Julius Stone published *"The Ratio of the Ratio Decidendi*[141]". Divided into eight parts, it is possible to organise it into three. In the first, he introduced the subject and prepared the ground.[142] In the second, he criticised Goodhart.[143] In the third, he defended the notion that choice is necessary and inherent to the decision,

---

[132] Llewellyn (2008), pp. 68–69.

[133] Llewellyn (2008), p. 70.

[134] Llewellyn (2008), p. 71.

[135] Llewellyn (1960), pp. 62–120.

[136] Llewellyn (2008), p. 69.

[137] Llewellyn (1960), pp. 77–91. Many years later, with the same goal of demonstrating the flexibility of *stare decisis*, Geoffrey Marshall listed thirty-three things that can be done with a precedent (Marshall 1996, pp. 29–34). In the same vein, he soon after listed some of them as ways to transform the *ratio* into *obiter dictum* ("'*obiter-ing' a precedent*") in Marshall (1997), p. 516.

[138] Llewellyn (2008), p. 71.

[139] *Supra*, item 1.1.

[140] *Infra*, item 1.3.

[141] Stone (1959), pp. 597–620.

[142] Stone (1959), pp. 597–603, items 1 to 4.

[143] Stone (1959), pp. 603–610, items 5 and 6.

thus, the *ratio* is a concept that could act as a mediator of the Common Law's stability and development.[144]

Key to his argument is the distinction between descriptive *ratio* and prescriptive *ratio*.[145] The ratio is not unitary. For Stone, it is necessary to detach the *ratio* as a description of the reasoning that led to the decision from the *ratio* as an elected prescription to determine the solution of a later case.[146] The descriptive *ratio* is devoid of normative force as it only frames the potential prescriptive solutions.[147] The prescriptive *ratio* is the version chosen by the interpreter of those which are made available by the descriptive *ratio*, as embodied in the rule for the solution of the case.[148] This distinction makes it possible to address the *ratio* in two different ways. First, distinguishing descriptive and prescriptive *ratios* could show us, through their relation, the method of court charged with resolving the case to create its rule. The descriptive *ratio* would regulate how the prescriptive *ratio* is created.[149] Alternatively, working only with the prescriptive *ratio* presupposes the existence of a single rule—*ratio*—buried in the text, and a single method to extract it from there.[150]

Hence Stone's distinction demonstrated that there is no single *ratio* and no single method to extract it,[151] the *ratio decidendi* is a category of "indeterminate reference".[152] Its search is "illusory"[153]—like chasing a "ghost".[154] Using *Donoghue v. Stevenson* as an example, Stone argued that there would be as many *rationes*

[144]Stone (1959), pp. 610–620, items 7 and 8.

[145]I couldn't find this distinction in Julius Stone's earlier work, *The Province and Function of Law*. Sydney: PTY, 1946, especially pp. 168 et seq., although the criticism of the "logical" force of the precedent and the "declaratory" character of the decision that enforces it are present there. It's likely that it only appeared in *"The Ratio of the Ratio Decidendi"*.

[146]Stone (1959), pp. 600–601. In other words, this difference could also be read as "text *ratio*" and "rule *ratio*"—keeping in mind Giovanni Tarello's well-known elaboration involving the object of interpretation (the text) and its result (the rule): for example, Tarello (1980), pp. 61 and 63. By the way, Tarello was in Sydney with Stone while studying and writing about American legal realism (Tarello 1962, p. VII).

[147]I am making use of the expression "frame" (*"Rahmen"*) to recall the well-known expression of Kelsen (2000), p. 348, but I must note that Julius Stone did not. I must also point out that, by using this term, Kelsen wanted to show that the text admits several possibilities of interpretation equally correct from the point of view of the normative system (it is for no other reason, moreover, that Chiassoni 2009, p. 357, considers him a "radically realistic" author from the point of view of the theory of interpretation).

[148]Stone (1959), p. 601.

[149]This is the way of working with the *ratio* suggested by Stone (1959), p. 602.

[150]This is how to define and determine the *ratio* that Julius Stone imputed to Arthur Goodhart (Stone 1959, p. 603).

[151]Stone (1959), pp. 603–607.

[152]Stone (1946), p. 186.

[153]Stone (1959), p. 609.

[154]Simpson (1961), p. 168.

decidendi in a case as there are possible combinations of its facts and their various degrees of generalisation.[155]

Donoghue is a prominent Scottish case tried by the House of Lords in 1932. The court determined that the manufacturer *Stevenson* was responsible for a decomposing snail found in the ginger beer *Donoghue* drank at a café in Paisley in 1928.[156] Utilising these facts, Stone formulated several degrees of specificity: (i) regarding the agent of harm (decomposing snail, any snail, any noxious solid foreign body, any noxious element—solid or not, any noxious element?); (ii) the vehicle of harm (opaque bottle of ginger beer, any opaque bottle of beverage, any bottle of beverage, any container of products for human consumption?); (iii) the defendant's identity (manufacturer of goods nationally distributed through retailers, any manufacturer, any reseller, any person who worked on making the object?); (iv) the potential danger from vehicle of harm (object likely to become dangerous by negligence or for some other reason?); (v) the type of injury (pecuniary injury, emotional distress or any other injury?); (vi) the plaintiff's identity (Scottish widow, Scottish woman, woman, any adult or any human being?); (vii) the plaintiff's relation to vehicle of harm (donee of purchaser or retailer who bought directly from the defendant?); (viii) the discoverability of agent of harm (noxious element being not discoverable by inspection of any intermediate party, not so discoverable without destroying the container or not so discoverable by any such party who had the duty to inspect?); (ix) the time (facts occurred in 1932, any time before 1932, any time after 1932 or at any time?).[157] The range potential answers highlight the difficulty of ascertaining the correct combination of facts and their level of generalisation[158] to define a single *ratio decidendi* by a single method—as Goodhart intended.[159] For Stone, the notion that the distinction between descriptive *ratio* and prescriptive *ratio* explains why the search for the *ratio* could never taste like a simple discovery, like a statement of the principle of the case based on certain relevant facts.[160] The court in charge of enforcing the precedent would necessarily have to decide the appropriate combination and the correct level of generalisation of the facts.[161] It is the court responsible for resolving the case that would be in charge

[155] Stone (1946), pp. 187–189; Stone (1959), pp. 603–604. I recall that *Donoghue* was recognised by Arthur Goodhart as a "striking illustration" of his thesis (Stone 1959, p. 120). Stone's criticism is always remembered by legal scholars (e.g. Schauer 2009, pp. 50–51).

[156] Since I am in Edinburgh, I decided to take a short trip to Paisley. The *Wellmeadow Café* has closed, but there is a cool monument in honour of the case (of which I posted a photo on *Instagram*). You can also see it by googling it.

[157] Stone (1959), pp. 603–604.

[158] For Julius Stone, by the way, this is its "crucial difficulty" (Stone 1959, pp. 605–606).

[159] Truth be told, Julius Stone observed that a method such as Goodhart's would only serve to find a *ratio* capable of regulating an identical case in practically all its aspects—which would, however, decrease the potential of the doctrine of *stare decisis* (Stone 1959, p. 604). I will return to this observation later (*infra*, item 2.1).

[160] Stone (1959), p. 606.

[161] Hence, there would be no *ratio* to be declared in the decision—it would, in any event, need to be created by the second court, which is the "essential difference" between Goodhart's and Stone's views on the subject (Stone 1959, p. 607).

of interpreting the descriptive *ratio* and creating the prescriptive *ratio*.[162] Consequently, the court is charged with creating the *ratio*.[163]

Having outlined his reasoning as to why the *ratio* is indeterminate, Stone went on to argue that the main "control centres" for the operation of the precedent would have been taken by the courts' necessity to make "unavoidably choices".[164] Certain terms used by substantive law and their connections would be "categories of illusory reference"[165] (such as, for example, "reasonableness" or "fairness").[166] Different methods for determining the *ratio* could lead to different results.[167] Different reasons used in a trial by a panel of judges could lead to different outcomes.[168] All this would require the court to make choices in determining the *ratio*. Furthermore, the various combination of these choices, would further multiply the possible solutions for the cases.[169] In this context, the *ratio* could only be seen as a choice between possible competing *rationes*. In other words: the prescriptive *ratio* would be the winning version of the descriptive *ratio*. This pliancy of the *ratio* renders possible many different generations to dialogue. It creates a space for coexistence—like a photo album with many, many blank pages—between past, present and future. This flexibility provides both adaptation and stability—allowing smooth changes over time—and enable self-perpetuation and self-rejuvenation for the *Common Law*. This is the *ratio* of the *ratio*.[170]

Before we leave Oliphant, Llewellyn, and Stone, it is worth noting that their ideas—such radical scepticism regarding the ratio, and the assertion that it is created by the court charged with enforcing the precedent—are not confined to their time, nor to the *Common Law* tradition. Michele Taruffo exemplifies this; his works on courts and precedents were instrumental in the development of such ideas. He was—for me, perhaps—the most important jurist who dealt with precedent in the Roman-Canonical tradition in a comparative perspective.[171] His works have been published in several languages and still appear to this day in the majority of notable debates on the subject.

[162] Stone (1959), p. 606.

[163] Stone (1959), pp. 615–618.

[164] Stone (1959), p. 610.

[165] Stone (1959), p. 611.

[166] Stone (1959), p. 612.

[167] Stone (1959), pp. 612–614.

[168] Stone (1959), pp. 614–615.

[169] Stone (1959), p. 615.

[170] Stone (1959), pp. 597–600, and 615–620, vol. XXII.

[171] Such perspective, by the way, is elemental to how to handle the theme (Passanante 2018, pp. 195–197). For a broad view on Michele Taruffo as a comparatist, see Dondi (2015); Pasqualotto (2022).

Taruffo—who participated in the *Bielefelder Kreis*[172] and was especially influenced by Giovanni Tarello[173] when it came to the theory of Law—began to write about courts in the 1980s and precedents in the 1990s.[174] The realistic influence in his work is apparent, not only did he argue that the court charged with enforcing the precedent is responsible for deciding whether it exists or not by creating it.[175] But he also defended, when it comes to the strength of the precedent, that "*non è appropriato dire che il precedente di* common law *è vincolante, nel senso che ne derivi un vero e proprio obbligo del secondo giudice di attenersi al precedente. È noto che anche nel sistema inglese, che pare essere quello in cui il precedente è dotato di maggiore efficacia, i giudici usano numerose e sofisticate tecniche argomentative, tra cui il* distinguishing e *l'*overruling, *al fine di non considerarsi vincolati dal precedente che non intendono seguire. Rimane dunque vero che in quell 'ordinamento il precedente è dotato di notevole forza, in quanto ci si aspetta che in linea di massima il giudice successivo lo segua – come in fatti soltivamente accade –, ma questa forza è sempre* defeasible, *poichè il secondo giudice può disattendere il precedente quando ritenga opportuno farlo al fine di*

172The *Bielefelder Kreis* was a group of theorists led by Neil MacCormick and Robert Summers that published two influential papers throughout the 1990s: *Interpreting Statutes – A Comparative Study*. Dartmouth: Ashgate, 1991 and *Interpreting Precedents – A Comparative Study*. Dartmouth: Ashgate, 1997. Aulis Aarnio, Robert Alexy, Zenon Bankowski, Gunnar Bergholz, Ralf Dreier, Christophe Grzegorczyk, Massimo La Torre, Neil MacCormick, Enrico Pattaro, Aleksander Peczenik, Robert Summers, Michele Taruffo, Michel Troper and Jerzy Wróblewski were part of the first work. Aulis Aarnio, Robert Alexy, Zenon Bankowski, John Barceló, Gunnar Bergholz, Ralf Dreier, Svein Eng, Ernesto Garzón-Valdés, Christophe Grzegorczyk, Francisco Laporta, Massimo La Torre, Neil MacCormick, Geoffrey Marshall, Alfonso Ruiz Miguel, Lech Morawski, Enrico Pattaro, Aleksander Peczenik, Robert Summers, Michele Taruffo, Michel Troper and Marek Zirk-Sadowski were part of the second. Taruffo wrote two texts for *Intepreting Precedents*: *"Precedent in Italy"* (written with Massimo La Torre) and *"Institutional Factors Influencing Precedents"*.

173Taruffo's works are filled with quotations from Tarello. Be that as it may, on several occasions he told me this in person. I particularly remember one time in Pavia when he said to me: Daniel, sometimes when I am in doubt about general themes concerning interpretation, I go straight to Tarello's *L'Interpretazione della Legge*. Because it is now relevant, I remember once again that Tarello studied with Julius Stone (Tarello 1962, p. VII) and that he was a radical skeptic, that is, he assumed that before the interpretation there was no norm (according to the classification carried out by Guastini 2011, pp. 412–415). Another important legal theorist who is noteworhty in the formation of Taruffo was Jerzy Wróblewski—through whom he probably arrived at the *Bielefelder Kreis*. Analyzing his influence, however, is not my interest at the present time.

174In the seventies, in fact, the theme of *ratio decidendi* surrounds Taruffo's interests, as can be seen in Taruffo (1975). It is only in the following decades, however, that his attention specifically is directed to the subjects of the supreme courts—as can be seen in the various essays written throughout the eighties and early nineties collected in Taruffo (1991)—and of the precedents—as can be seen, for example, in the essays Taruffo (1994) and Taruffo (2007). Neither ever left Taruffo's agenda, so much so that some essays on the subjects also appear in Taruffo (2020) (e.g., *"Un Vertice Giudiziario Astratto"* and *"Note Sparse sul Precedente Giudiziale"*, both from 2018).

175Taruffo (2007).

formulare una soluzione più giusta del caso che deve decidere".[176] It is impossible to make it clearer.[177]

Oliphant, Llewellyn and Stone—and many others, such as Taruffo—significantly relativised the value of what was previously decided. They offer a particular depiction of the *ratio decidendi,* emphasising the role of the court in charge of enforcing the *ratio*, even to the point of creation. Through their eyes, the *ratio* can be perceived as nothing more than smoke drawn in the air. Its force lasts only a moment; created by the determination of the court in charge of resolving the case, it is destined to quickly disintegrate into the clouds. What, however, can we take from all this? How can these theories and critiques help us define and determine the *ratio decidendi*? Now, we simply need to cross a bridge to gain the required perspective.

2.3 The Arch of the Bridge: Rebuilding the *Ratio*

Invisible Cities, from 1972, is perhaps one of my favourite novels by Italo Calvino. An amazing book: in one of its extraordinary passages, Marco Polo states that Venezia is always inside him. Calvino sets up the following dialogue:

> "Marco Polo describes a bridge, stone by stone.
> 'But which is the stone that supports the bridge?' Kublai Kahn asks.
> 'The bridge is not supported by one stone or another,' Marco answers, 'but by the line of the arch that they form.'
> Kublai Kahn remains silent, reflecting. Then he adds:
> 'Why do you speak to me of the stones? It is only the arch that matters to me'. Polo answers: 'Without stones there is no arch[178]".

My impression is that, when he wrote this, he was thinking about the *ratio decidendi*. In leaving the proposition that there a single *ratio* and a single method to find it and embracing the idea that the decision offers a framework for competing versions of the *ratio*, our search is no longer haunted by its spirit but sustained by the rationality of the path that leads to its rebuilding. This idea of the ratio as stone supporting the bridge is a relatively recent development in its debate. The line of this arch had not yet been formed at the times when the ratio was viewed as buried treasure or simply a drawing in the air. Richard Wasserstrom, Jerzy Wróblewski, and Neil MacCormick are three scholars that helped to clear this path.

---

[176] Taruffo (2007), p. 716.

[177] In *Precedentes* I have examined this passage (Mitidiero 2023). Later I will return to this subject (*infra*, item 2.3).

[178] Calvino (2010).

In 1961, Wasserstrom published *The Judicial Decision – Toward a Theory of Legal Justification.* A seminal piece which brings the epistemological distinction between "context of discovery" and "context of justification"[179] to the field of Law. He distinguished "context of decision" from "context of justification", showing that reasons unrelated to the law can indeed influence decision-making but cannot be used as its justification.[180] Thus, in response to the realists, he refocused the debate on the interpretation of the Law to what was *said* in the decision. What really mattered were the reasons capable of justifying the decision, which can only belong to the Law. A decade later, Wróblewski published "Legal Decision and its Justification".[181] He followed Wasserstrom's line of reasoning to distinguish between the internal and external justification of a decision. The first demonstrates the courts' logical reasoning (how one uses, for example, deduction, induction and abduction to reach their conclusions), while the second concerns the selection of the material utilised in the decision (how the court carries out the argumentation necessary to resolve the case).[182] Hence, the foundational stones were laid.

These definitions gained global acceptance and influenced later debates in both legal theory[183] and in civil procedure.[184] Based on these ideas, Neil MacCormick presented his definition of the *ratio decidendi* in 1978 in his *Legal Theory and Legal Reasoning.*[185] This was then refined in his 1987 essay "*Why Cases Have Rationes*

---

[179] In epistemology, the distinction first appears with Carnap (1974), its elaboration being useful to the later developments of Popper (1935) and Reichenbach (1961) (all according to Ronaldo Kochem's detailed research, Kochem 2021, pp. 60–66).

[180] Wasserstrom (1961).

[181] Wróblewski (1971). This distinction is one of the foundations of Wróblewski's thinking, especially in his 1988 *Sadowe Stosowanie Prawa*, whose English version was prepared by Wróblewski in Edinburgh in 1989 and revised by Neil MacCormick and Zenon Bankowski (Wróblewski 1992, pp. 209–262).

[182] In *Precedentes*, I wrote that "on the one hand, a decision presents internal justification whenever the provision arises logically from the statement of reasons and that it contemplates all the grounds argued by the parties. In the internal justification, therefore, we are interested in the logical correction and completeness of the statement of reasons for the decision. Hence, internal justification is a formal justification that responds to the need for non-contradiction in legal discourse. It is the field in which logic acts in the interpretative process, in which the judge reasons deductively to resolve the issues. On the other hand, a decision has external justification whenever the assumptions adopted in the decision are adequate. The external justification, therefore, concerns the adequacy of the choices of the premises used in the internal justification. Along those lines, it constitutes a material justification that responds to the need to adopt sufficient reasons for decision-making, involving the examination of both rules and facts, insofar as there is an absolute implication between the two. It is the field in which argumentation acts in the interpretative process, in which the judge individualises, values and decides in a non-deductive way. As the field of legal argumentation, the legal rule, rules on interpretation, argumentative preferential rules and doctrinal constructions used in the decision are taken into account in the external justification. In other words, the material that is available to the interpreter to carry out the interpretative process is within the scope of external justification" (Mitidiero 2023).

[183] Alexy (1978), p. 273; Aarnio (1987), pp. 119–120; Chiassoni (2007), pp. 14–15. According to Atienza (1991), these ideas formed the basis of the standard theory of argumentation.

[184] For example, Taruffo (1975).

[185] MacCormick (1978), p. 215.

and What These Are",[186] a definition he reaffirmed in 2005 in *Rhetoric and the Rule of Law*.[187] The line of this arch was complete.

On the very first page of his essay, MacCormick seeks to distance himself from the rule-based approach perpetuated by Cross and aligns himself with Stone's intuition. He states that the reasons capable of justifying decisions are what set precedents and links the *ratio* to the activity performed by the second court to produce it. The justification—of path and outcome—was the ace in the hole. Without a method, there would be no precedent. As the bridge depends on the arch, the theory of precedent hinges upon a theory of justification.[188] Without the fitting of its stones, the line cannot hold. This was a methodological leap.[189] Precedent requires an activity capable of rationally leading to a result—emphasising the need to both deductively base the decision on a legal rule[190] and to submit it to tests of consistency, coherence and consequences.[191] Furthermore, MacCormick recognised Stone's arguments as to the difficulties of the different degrees of generalisation with which the facts can be analysed, He made clear that this does not prevent the context of the cases from helping to define them.[192] The briefs formulated in the decisions would have precisely the role of better determining the *rationes*, even if new argumentative rounds were necessary in other trials.[193]

Having shown that justification would be able to provide a model for arguing and deciding in court, that is, for interpreting and enforcing the law, and also for helping define the appropriate degree of generalisation of the facts,[194] MacCormick subsequently presents his definition of *ratio decidendi*. The *ratio* would be a "ruling" that is expressly or implicitly used by the court to decide a matter of law sufficiently necessary to justify the decision.[195]

However, he notes that this combination of justification and *ratio* would not be the only way to rebuild it, but is the method has the power to carry it out as rationally as possible.[196] In placing the link between rules and facts at the heart the justification process, MacCormick defended the need to adopt the identification of the *ratio*'s

---

[186] MacCormick (1987), pp. 170–171.

[187] MacCormick (2005), p. 153.

[188] MacCormick (1987), pp. 155 and 169. For a further development of the relation between precedent, justification and argumentation, see Michelon (2023), pp. 117–129.

[189] Hence why it seems unfair to put MacCormick along with Goodhart and Cross, as was done in Twining and Miers (2010), p. 306. For MacCormick, the treasure does not exist without a map—that is, the precedent necessarily depends on a theory of justification capable of leading to the place where it is buried (*retro*, item 1.1).

[190] MacCormick (1987), pp. 159–160.

[191] MacCormick (1987), pp. 161–162.

[192] MacCormick (1987), pp. 166–169 and 182.

[193] MacCormick (1987), p. 182—as, by the way, Goodhart himself did not fail to observe in response to Stone in Goodhart (1959), p. 124.

[194] MacCormick, (1987), p. 169. In the same vein, Eisenberg (1988), p. 55; Duxbury (2008), p. 87.

[195] MacCormick (1987), p. 170.

[196] MacCormick (1987), p. 172.

relevant facts as a guide for determining it, making the "Goodhart method" the "important corollary" of his theory.[197] But simultaneously demonstrated that definition of *ratio* elaborated by Cross in relation to the rules was too broad, as not all normative material necessary for the solution of the case would be a part of it. To emphasise this point, he highlighted that a statute used by the court is not part of the *ratio*, rather only the interpretation of it carried out and considered correct in the specific case.[198] That is why, in his opinion, it is more appropriate to talk about "sufficiency"[199]—and not necessity—of a certain rule for the solution of a matter of law. The purpose of the *ratio* would be to provide a way for the solution of a later issue, thus allowing the universalisation of the Law.[200]

This was no small feat.

The link between *ratio* and justification stipulates a clear methodology of determination but allows flexibility for the recognition of the various issues that are submitted to it and the different ways to face them. It provides—in a nutshell—an objective structure,[201] demystifying the path to its definition.[202] It combines a good map, a good strategy and a pot of gold at the end of the bridge. Consequently, unifying the search for the spirit of the *ratio* and its fleeting construction in smoke. Now that these various conceptions of the *ratio* are understood, we can move on to Brazilian Law. Between us, what is the *ratio*? How can it be determined? When is an issue identical, similar, or distinct? How should these categories be handled in a case?

I have a few theories.

References

Aarnio A (1987) The rational as reasonable — a treatise on legal justification. Kluwer, Dordrecht

Abramowicz M, Stearns M (2005) Defining Dicta. Stanford Law Rev 57(4):953–1036

Alexander L (1989) Constrained by precedent. South Calif Law Rev 63(1):1–63

Alexander L (2023) Precedent: the what, the why, and the how. In: Endicott T, Kristjánsson HD, Lewis S (eds) Philosophical foundations of precedent. Oxford University Press, Oxford

Alexy R (1978) Theorie der juristischen Argumentation. Suhrkamp, Frankfurt im Main

Allen CK (1939) Law in the making, 3rd edn. Oxford University Press, Oxford

---

[197] MacCormick (1987), p. 181.

[198] MacCormick (1987), p. 179. This interpretation limitation adopted by the court would even function as an element of protection of the legal order in the face of possible limitations in the debate of a specific case (MacCormick 1987, p. 170).

[199] MacCormick (1987), pp. 179–180, which attributed to Brian Simpson, however, the primacy in solving the problem based on the criterion of "sufficiency". Indeed, Simpson's criticisms of the "necessity" test appear in Simpson (1961), pp. 163–168.

[200] MacCormick (1987), p. 162; MacCormick (2005), p. 143.

[201] Chiassoni (2019), p. 211.

[202] Raz (2009), pp. 184 and 188–189.

Atienza M (1991) Las Razones del Derecho — Teorías de la Argumentación Jurídica. Centro de Estudios Constitucionales, Madrid

Atiyah PS, Summers R (1987) Form and substance in Anglo-American law. Oxford University Press, Oxford

Austin J (1873) In: Campbell R (ed) Lectures on jurisprudence, vol 2. Linn, Jersey

Baker J (2002) An introduction to English legal history, 4th edn. Oxford University Press, Oxford

Berman H (2003) Law and revolution. Harvard University Press, Cambridge. v 2

Blackstone W (1979) Commentaries on the Laws of England (1765-1769). The University of Chicago Press, Chicago. v 1

Brand P (2006) Reasoned judgments in the English Medieval Common Law — 1270 to 1307. In Bryson W H, Dauchy S (eds) Ratio Decidendi — guiding principles of judicial decisions. Duncker & Humblot, Berlin. v 1

Calvino I (2010) Invisible cities (trans: Weaver W). Vintage Books, London

Câmara AF (2018) Levando os Padrões Decisórios a Sério. Atlas, São Paulo

Carnap R (1974) Der logische Aufbau der Welt, 4th edn. Felix Meiner, Hamburg

Chiassoni P (2007) Tecnica dell'Interpretazione Giuridica. Il Mulino, Bologna

Chiassoni P (2009) L'Indirizzo Analitico nella Filosofia del Diritto. I. Da Bentham a Kelsen. Giappichelli, Torino

Chiassoni P (2019) Interpretation without truth — a realistic enquiry. Springer, Cham

Cramer R (2016) Precedentes Judiciais — Teoria e Dinâmica. Forense, Rio de Janeiro

Cross (1961) Precedent in English Law. Oxford University Press, Oxford

Cross R (1977) The House of Lords and the rules of precedent. In: Hacker PM, Raz J (eds) Law, morality and society — essays in honour of H. L. A. Hart. Oxford University Press, Oxford

Cross R, Harris J (1991) Precedent in English Law, 4th edn. Oxford University Press, Oxford

Dawson J (1986) Oracles of the law. William Hein, New York

Didier Júnior F, Fernandez L (2022) O Conselho Nacional de Justiça e o Direito Processual — Administração Judiciária, Boas Práticas e Competência Normativa. JusPodivm, Salvador

Dondi A (2015) Taruffo Comparatista — Uno Sguardo Originale ai Problemi del Processo Civile. Rivista Trimestrale di Diritto e Procedura Civile 69(2):485–518

Duxbury N (2008) The nature and authority of precedent. Cambridge University Press, Cambridge

Duxbury N (2021) The Intricacies of Dicta and Dissent. Cambridge University Press, Cambridge

Eisenberg M (1988) The nature of the Common Law. Harvard University Press, Cambridge

Evans J (1987) Change in the doctrine of precedent during the nineteenth century. In: Goldstein L (ed) Precedent in law. Oxford University Press, Oxford

Freda D (2012) "Una Dispotica Creazione" — Il Precedente Vincolante nella Cultura Giuridica Inglese dell'Ottocento. Giappichelli, Torino

Friedman L (2005) A history of American law, 3rd edn. Touchstone, New York

Fulbeck W (1829) Direction or preparative to the study of the law — wherein is shewed what things ought to be observed and used of them that are addicted to the study of the law, 2nd edn. Clark, London

Garner B (ed) (2016) The law of judicial precedent. Thomson Reuters, St. Paul

Goodhart A (1937a) Three cases on possession. In: Essays in jurisprudence and the Common Law, 2nd edn. Cambridge University Press, Cambridge

Goodhart A (1937b) Determining the Ratio Decidendi of a Case. In: Essays in jurisprudence and the Common Law. Cambridge University Press, Cambridge

Goodhart A (1959) The Ratio Decidendi of a Case. Mod Law Rev 22(2):117–124

Guastini R (2011) Interpretare e Argomentare. Giuffrè, Milano

Hale M (1971) The history of the Common Law of England. Chicago University Press, Chicago

Hart H (1983) American jurisprudence through English eyes: the nightmare and the noble dream. In: Essays in jurisprudence and philosophy. Oxford University Press, Oxford

Hogue A (1986) Origins of the Common Law. Liberty Fund, Indianapolis

Kelsen H (2000) Reine Rechtslehre. Österreich, Wien

Kochem R (2021) Fundamentando Decisões — Uma Doutrina Lógico-Argumentativa. Thoth, Londrina
Langbein J, Lerner R, Smith B (2009) History of the Common Law — the development of Anglo-American legal institutions. Aspen, New York
Lewis TE (1930a) The history of judicial precedent — I. Law Q Rev 46:207–224
Lewis TE (1930b) The history of judicial precedent — II. Law Q Rev 46:341–360
Lewis TE (1931) The history of judicial precedent — III. Law Q Rev 47:411–427
Lewis TE (1932) The history of judicial precedent — IV. Law Q Rev 48:230–247
Llewellyn K (1960) The Common Law Tradition — deciding appeals. Little, Brown and Company, Boston, p 1960
Llewellyn K (1989) The case law system in America. Chicago University Press, Chicago, p 1989
Llewellyn K (2008) The Bramble Bush — the classic lectures on the law and law school. Oxford University Press, Oxford
Maccormick N (1978) Legal reasoning and legal theory. Oxford University Press, Oxford
Maccormick N (1987) Why cases have Rationes and what these are. In: Goldstein L (ed) Precedent in law. Oxford University Press, Oxford
Maccormick N (2005) Rhetoric and the rule of law. Oxford University Press, Oxford
Maccormick N, Summers R (eds) (1991) Interpreting statutes — a comparative study. Ashgate, Dartmouth
Maccormick N, Summers R (eds) (1997) Interpreting precedents — a comparative study. Ashgate, Dartmouth
Marinoni LG (2022) Precedentes Obrigatórios, 7th edn. RT, São Paulo
Marshall G (1996) Trentatre Cose che si Possono Fare con i Precedenti. Un Dizionario di Common Law (trans: Rota F). Ragion Pratica 6
Marshall G (1997) What is binding in a precedent. In: Maccormick N, Summers R (eds) Interpreting precedents — a comparative study. Ashgate, Dartmouth
Mello PCP (2008) Precedentes. Renovar, Rio de Janeiro
Micheli GA (1938) Contributo allo Studio della Formazione Giudiziale del Diritto — "Case Law" e "Stare Decisis". Treves, Pavia
Michelon C (2023) The uses of precedent and legal argument. In: Endicott T, Kristjánsson HD, Lewis S (eds) Philosophical foundations of precedent. Oxford University Press, Oxford
Mitidiero D (2022a) Cortes Superiores e Cortes Supremas — do Controle à Interpretação, da Jurisprudência ao Precedente, 4th edn. RT, São Paulo
Mitidiero D (2022b) Processo Constitucional — do Controle ao Processo, dos Modelos ao Sistema. RT, São Paulo
Mitidiero D (2023) Precedentes — da Persuasão à Vinculação, 5th edn. RT, São Paulo
Mitidiero D (2024) Processo Civil, 2nd edn. RT, São Paulo
Montrose JL (1957a) The Ratio Decidendi and the House of Lords. Mod Law Rev 20(2):124–130
Montrose JL (1957b) The Ratio Decidendi of a Case. Mod Law Rev 20(6):587–595
Oliphant H (1928) A Return to Stare Decisis. Am Bar Assoc J 14
Pasqualotto V (2022) Processo Civil Comparado — do Direito Comparado à Comparação no Processo Civil. RT, São Paulo
Passanante L (2018) Il Precedente Impossibile — Contributo allo Studio del Diritto Giurisprudenziale nel Processo Civile. Giappichelli, Torino
Popper K (1935) Logik der Forschung. Springer, Wien
Postema G (2002) Classical Common Law Jurisprudence (Part I). Oxford Univ Commonwealth Law J 2
Ram J (1871) The science of legal judgment — a treatise designed to show the materials whereof, and the process by which, the Courts of Westminster Hall construct their judgments and adapted to practical and general use in discussion, and determination of questions of law, 2nd edn. Baker, New York
Raz J (2009) Law and value in adjudication. In: The authority of law, 2nd edn. Oxford University Press, Oxford

Reichenbach H (1961) Experience and prediction. Phoenix Books, Chicago
Salmond J (1913) Jurisprudence, 4th edn. Stevens, London
Schauer F (2009) Thinking like a lawyer. Harvard University Press, Cambridge
Simpson AWB (1958) The Ratio Decidendi of a Case. Mod Law Rev 21(2):155–160
Simpson AWB (1959) The Ratio Decidendi of a Case. Mod Law Rev 22(5):453–457
Simpson AWB (1961) The Ratio Decidendi of a Case and the doctrine of binding precedent. In: Guest AG (ed) Oxford essays in jurisprudence. Oxford University Press, Oxford
Stone J (1946) The province and function of law. PTY, Sidney
Stone J (1959) The Ratio of the Ratio Decidendi. Mod Law Rev 22(6):597–620
Tarello G (1962) Il Realismo Giuridico Americano. Giuffrè, Milano
Tarello G (1980) L'Interpretazione della Legge. Giuffrè, Milano
Taruffo M (1975) La Motivazione della Sentenza Civile. Cedam, Padova
Taruffo M (1991) Il Vertice Ambiguo — Saggi sulla Cassazione Civile. Il Mulino, Bologna
Taruffo M (1994) Dimensioni del Precedente Giudiziario. Rivista Trimestrale di Diritto e Procedura Civile 48(2):411–430
Taruffo M (2007) Precedente e Giurisprudenza. Rivista Trimestrale di Diritto e Procedura Civile 61(3):709–725
Taruffo M (2020) Verso la Decisione Giusta. Giappichelli, Torino
Twining W (2012) Karl Llewellyn and the Realist Movement. Cambridge University Press, Cambridge
Twining W, Miers D (2010) How to do things with rules, 5th edn. Cambridge University Press, Cambridge
Viana A, Nunes D (2018) Precedentes — A Mutação no Ônus Argumentativo. Forense, Rio de Janeiro
Wambaugh E (1894) The study of cases — a course of instruction in reading and stating reported cases, composing head-notes and briefs, criticising and comparing authorities, and compiling digests, 2nd edn. Little, Brown and Company, Boston
Wasserstrom R (1961) The judicial decision — toward a theory of legal justification. Stanford University Press, Stanford
Wróblewski J (1971) Legal decision and its justification. Logique et Analyse 14
Wróblewski J (1992) The judicial application of law (trans: Wróblewski J). Kluwer, Dordrecht

Chapter 3
Among Us

I could fill a dozen books with the various critiques of the theories of *ratio* discussed in the previous chapter. Time precludes this endeavour, however, even if it did not, I am inclined to take a more optimistic perspective—how can we draw from these constructions: the *ratio* as the spirit of cases, a drawing in the air, and the arch of a bridge? How can Brazilian Law benefit from these many pages of Common Law tradition?

Just a few seminal notes can render a piece of music an instant classic. A lesson that can be well-employed in our endeavours here.

I define *ratio decidendi* as a rule formulated from the decision[1] of a case[2] by a Supreme Court in which necessary[3] and sufficient reasons[4] operate on material facts[5] to determine, in whole or in part, the solution of an identical or similar issue. As many factors influence this formulation,[6] it is necessary to take the text of the decision as a framework capable of providing, in the face of its competing descriptions, a normative prescription[7] by means of its logical-argumentative rebuilding.[8] Everything that does not form the *ratio* constitutes an *obiter dictum*.[9]

---

[1] I am here considering that what makes precedents are not the very words of the decision, but its spirit—as Lord Mansfield observed in 1762 in *Fisher v. Prince* (Allen 1939, p. 207).

[2] Ram (1871), p. 102; Wambaugh (1894), p. 29.

[3] Cross and Harris (1991), p. 72.

[4] Simpson (1961), pp. 163–168; MacCormick (1987), pp. 179–180.

[5] Goodhart (1937b), pp. 2–9, 22 and 25.

[6] Llewellyn (2008), pp. 5, 7, 13–14, 65 and 71.

[7] I am using here the distinction drawn by Julius Stone between descriptive *ratio* and prescriptive *ratio* (Stone 1959, pp. 600–601) to stress the difference between text *ratio* and rule *ratio*.

[8] MacCormick (1987), pp. 155 and 169.

[9] Not being part of the *ratio*, everything that is *obiter dictum* is not binding (Duxbury 2008, pp. 67–68 and 90). Fleeting comments, observations on unnecessary rules for the solution of the issue and so on constitute *obiter dictum*. As drawing its limits is also an interpretative matter, its

D. Mitidiero, *Ratio Decidendi and Obiter Dictum*,
https://doi.org/10.1007/978-3-031-93152-9_3

Let's go.

In the opening chapter I stressed that the decision and *ratio decidendi* are distinct. They lie at different discursive levels;[10] a common observation in my work.[11] This double discourse facilitates the understanding of civil procedure as an instrument for the protection of rights. Furthermore, in addition to being on different steps of the ladder, decision and *ratio* are different because not every decision generates a precedent. The *ratio* is an elaboration carried out by the interpreter from a decision whose grounds were accepted by unanimity or majority of the panel of judges.[12] Consensus regarding only the legal device is irrelevant. Without at least the majority embracing its grounds, no decision supports the formulation of the *ratio*. Additionally, a particular decision can flow from the *ratio* elaborated from another decision.[13] If a decision cites a precedent arising from another, without making any new specification and without any particularity being extracted from the case, the *ratio* remains with *leading case*;[14] it does not belong to a decision that simply follows it.

The *ratio* derives from the solution of a court case. Two implications flow from this. First, what matters for its configuration is what was said expressly or implicitly in court at the moment of the decision.[15] Observations made outside the trial do not matter.[16] Second, the issue faced must have been well identified and considered from all relevant angles.[17] To derive from a court case means that the *ratio* was—at least[18]—the object of effective debate between the parties and the court.[19] Hence,

---

image is being constructed *pari passu* with the *ratio's*, being collected from its edges. For a broad view on this subject, Duxbury (2021), pp. 3–123.

[10] *Retro*, item 1.1.

[11] For a monography on this theme, Mitidiero (2023); Mitidiero (2022b). In their *Courses* and *Manuals*, Marinoni et al. (2023); Marinoni et al. (2022); Mitidiero (2024).

[12] Marinoni (2022a), p. 154; Ferraz (2017), p. 260.

[13] Zaneti Júnior (2017), p. 333.

[14] *Leading case* is the first case—the first decision—in which the interpretation of a certain matter of law is based, being followed by other decisions in a constant and frequent manner. In other words, it is the case that is followed by the others (Garner 2016, p. 173).

[15] Ram (1871), pp. 97–102; Wambaugh (1894), p. 29.

[16] Ram (1871), p. 102: the *ratio* stems from an issue *"cited on the bench"*. For example: as *ratio*, the considerations made by Lord Hoffmann in Hoffmann (2012), pp. 257–271, vol. XXXIX, do not matter although he participated in the trial of *Fairchild v. Glenhaven Funeral Services Ltd.*, decided by the *House of Lords* in 2002.

[17] Wambaugh (1894), p. 29: the *ratio* stems from the decision of the "very case" that is before it, which, therefore, must be in the "mind of the court". Deciding the "very case" presupposes precisely identifying the issue that must be faced (art. 1.037, item I, CPC). Having it in "mind" means analysing all the relevant grounds related to its solution (art. 1.038, § 3°, CPC). In the same vein, emphasising the adversary proceeding and the grounds in the conformation of the *ratio*, Marinoni (2022a), p. 154; Câmara (2018), pp. 177 et seq.

[18] Ideally, the debate may also include the manifestation of persons, authorities or entities with an interest in the dispute (*amicus curiae*) (art. 1.038, item I, CPC) and the holding of public hearings (art. 1.038, item II, CPC).

[19] According to arts. 9, 10, 11, 489, § 1, item IV, 1.022, item II, 1.037, item I, and 1.038, § 3, CPC.

it is anchored at the heart of the right to due process. When docked outside the court, there is a violation of the right to adversary proceedings[20] and the duty to substantiate[21] the formation of the *ratio*, harming the due process and judicial accountability.[22]

The different floors of Civil Justice perform different functions; it must be recognised that only the Supreme Courts are charged with providing unity in the law through precedents.[23] The *ratio decidendi* must, therefore, be sought in the reasons employed by this court. It is a rule formed by reasons entangled in facts.[24] It is a rule grounded on facts that constitute reasons—*fact-reasons*. More specifically: it is a rule rebuilt upon the reasons embraced—by unanimity or majority of votes—of one of its panels.[25] Only the reasons shared, at least by the majority of the votes of the panel of judges, are part of the *ratio decidendi*. Only through these reasons can the characterisation of the precedent be determined. Hence, the architecture of the *ratio* is legal reasons cemented in material facts. Even the most sceptical authors

---

[20] According to arts. 5, item LV, CRFB, and 9, 10, 11, 489, § 1, item IV, 1.022, item II, 1.037, item I, and 1.038, § 2, CPC.

[21] According to arts. 9, 10, 11, 489, § 1, item IV, 1.022, item II, 1.037, item I, and 1.038, § 3, CPC.

[22] Without adversary proceeding and reasoning, there is no due process (art. 5, item LIV, CRFB). Without adversary proceeding, reasoning and due process, there is no way to assess most of the indexes capable of pointing to the degree of judicial accountability (such as reasoning, responsiveness and transparency). On the subject, with the appropriate bibliographic indications, Mitidiero (2019).

[23] Justifying the connection between Supreme Courts and precedents in Brazilian Law—as well as the different solutions that can be adopted in different systems—is out of my scope at this time. For a debate on the subject, with the appropriate bibliographical indications, Mitidiero (2022a); Marinoni (2019). I note, however, that the same methodology to identify and determine the *ratio* can be used for the same purposes before the decisions of the Courts of Justice that lend themselves to the standardisation of caselaw. The method for identifying and determining the reasons does not vary—what changes is the *status* that precedent and uniform caselaw have in the Brazilian legal system (Mitidiero 2023, pp. 98–105).

[24] Even authors such as Goodhart, who emphasised the material facts as the core of the *ratio*, never failed to see it as a legal rule (Goodhart 1937b, pp. 10, 22 and 25). In Brazilian legal literature, Marinoni (2022a), p. 158; Arruda Alvim (2012), p. 44; Zaneti Júnior (2017), pp. 328–329.

[25] There are means to make the identification of the *ratio* in the decisions of the Supreme Courts easier. Marinoni (2023a), pp. 33 et seq., draws attention to the fact that a precedent system depends not only on an adequate identification of the issue that must be interpreted (art. 1.037, item I, CPC), but also of an adequate trial system in the Supreme Courts. For the composition of this picture, it is appropriate to distinguish between collegiate decisions (in which there are shared grounds) and plural decisions (in which there are no shared grounds), between majority grounds (same grounds and same conclusions) and concurrent grounds (different grounds and same conclusions) and between divergent vote (in which there is no concern as opposed to *ratio decidendi*) and dissenting vote (in which there is concern as opposed to *ratio decidendi*) as useful definitions. Ideally, a precedent system should rely on collegiate (rather than plural) decisions, on unanimous or majority (rather than concurring) grounds, and on the contrariety expressed in terms of dissenting votes (rather than simple divergent votes). All this facilitates the rebuilding of the *ratio*.

agree that fact and Law make up two distinct levels of a decision and that this distinction—albeit relative[26]—matters for the characterisation of the precedent and can provide the data for the design of its blueprint.[27]

The reasons that support the *ratio* are legally protected, necessary, and sufficient. Legally protected reasons are those that have the *pedigree* of law and determine the adoption of a given behaviour.[28] These are reasons endowed with authority.[29] Necessary reasons are those without which it is impossible to reach the resolution.[30] Sufficient reasons are those which allow the court to obtain the resolution of the analysed issue.[31]

The interpretation given by a Supreme Court to a given provision is part of the *ratio decidendi*, if it is necessary and sufficient for the solution of the issue put to judgment.[32] The adscription of meaning to a given provision in the face of a given issue is never a simple announcement of what is written in the law or its mere reflection.[33] For the solution of an issue, there is at least a granting of meaning to the text and definition of its scope given the facts—and without a judicial decision, there is neither an election of meaning nor a determination of the facts.[34] That is why,

[26]The relationship between fact and Law is complex, and the literature on it extensive (on the subject, Knijnik 2004; Lanes 2014). An inventory of the theme is out of the scope of the present work. However, it must be borne in mind that there is *an ontological inseparability* between fact and Law, although there is a *functional separability*. There is an ontological inseparability because every allegation of fact already enters the procedure from a certain normative framework (that is to say, the rule functions as a "scheme of interpretation" of the facts—*"Norm als Deutungsschema"*, Kelsen 2000, p. 3). However, it is possible to dissociate fact and Law in the procedure—after establishing the cause in all its factual-legal contours—for certain functions (for example, for individualisation of the object of proof and comparison between cases). That is why one can, within these limits, affirm the possibility of functional separability of the cause.

[27]For a representative view on this matter, Llewellyn (2008), p. 61.

[28]The construction of the idea that the *ratio* is composed of "legally protected reasons" is by Duxbury (2008), p. 105, who elaborated it based on Raz (1999).

[29]Reasons endowed with legal authority are reasons that require the adoption of a certain conduct regardless of its merits (Michelon 2007, pp. 111–114).

[30]Cross and Harris (1991), p. 72. The idea that necessary reasons—those capable of leading to judgment—make up the *ratio* predominates among *Common Law scholars* (e.g., Abramowicz and Stearns 2005, p. 1065; Garner 2016, p. 46) as in Brazilian legal literature (for instance, Marinoni 2022a, pp. 183–185; Motta 2015, pp. 192–198; Cramer 2016, p. 106).

[31]Simpson (1961), pp. 163–168; MacCormick (1987), pp. 179–180. As observed by MacCormick (1987), p. 170, only sufficient reasons are protected, because otherwise there is a risk that any reasons argued by the parties, but not examined or not adequately considered, would also be considered as part of the *ratio decidendi*.

[32]Cross and Harris (1991), p. 72; MacCormick (1987), p. 179; Duxbury (2008), p. 78. Note: it is the interpretation given to the provision (that is, the rule rebuilt from the provision in the specific case) that integrates the *ratio*—and not the provision abstractly considered.

[33]Against it, noting that in certain cases the interpretation of the provision does not integrate the *ratio*, Schauer (2009), p. 52; Marinoni (2022a), pp. 154–155; Zaneti Júnior (2017), p. 333.

[34]Barber (2023), p. 51.

normally, the interpretation given by the Supreme Court to a given provision integrates the *ratio*.

A decision can resolve an issue by means of express or implied reasons.[35] Sometimes, certain reasons are presupposed in others or are irreconcilable with each other. In these cases, the implied reason can be considered part of the *ratio*, but the party has the burden, and the judge has the duty to justify why one necessarily had to piggyback on the other or why they cannot coexist.[36]

Allow me to clarify with an example.

Sometimes, adopting a certain interpretative postulate and implicitly refusing another can compose the *ratio*.[37] When considering a writ of mandamus filed with the President of the Federal Senate as a coercive authority, the Federal Supreme Court had to give a "systematic, teleological and integrative" interpretation to the expression "board of the Federal Senate" to include the figure of its President.[38] In doing so, the court implicitly rejected the grammatical interpretative postulate as a reason for deciding; to do otherwise ran the risk of not recognising its own competence.

One of the most important features of the *ratio decidendi* is that it is grounded in facts. More specifically, in material facts.[39] Rules serve to demonstrate the materiality of the facts.[40] Material facts are those on which the rules that determine the solution of a matter of law operate.[41] Whilst developing a method to determine the *ratio* may sound fossilised today,[42] it is nonetheless true that linking the *ratio* with the material facts was one of the main and most successful attempts to guide the comparison between two or more cases.[43] What guides the justification of the decision is the determination of the materiality of the facts by the rules.[44] Justification is a tool for the logical-argumentative rebuilding of the *ratio*.[45] There is no

---

[35] Wambaugh (1894), p. 26; Cross and Harris (1991), p. 72; MacCormick (1987), p. 170; Abramowicz and Stearns (2005), pp. 1070–1072; Garner (2016), p. 46.

[36] Wambaugh (1894), p. 26.

[37] Abramowicz and Stearns (2005), p. 1071.

[38] *Zoghbi v. Presidente do Senado Federal* (STF, Pleno, MS n. 28.538/DF, Rel. Min. Marco Aurélio, j. 23.04.2014, DJe 04.08.2014).

[39] Goodhart (1937b), pp. 2–9, 22 e 25; Cross and Harris (1991), p. 43; MacCormick (1987), pp. 180–181; Duxbury (2008), pp. 80–83. In Brazilian legal literature, Cruz e Tucci (2004), p. 175; Mello (2008), p. 120; Marinoni (2022a), p. 162; Arruda Alvim (2012), p. 48; Ferraz (2017), pp. 260–262; Theodoro Júnior and Andrade (2021), p. 99.

[40] Goodhart (1937b), p. 18; Sunstein (2023), p. 229.

[41] Goodhart (1937b), pp. 2–9, 22 e 25; Cross and Harris (1991), p. 43; MacCormick (1987), pp. 180–181; Duxbury (2008), pp. 80–83.

[42] Duxbury (2008), p. 83.

[43] Cross and Harris (1991), p. 43; MacCormick (1987), pp. 180–181; Duxbury (2008), pp. 80–83; Abramowicz and Stearns (2005), p. 1055.

[44] MacCormick (1987), pp. 155 and 169; Schauer (2009), p. 53.

[45] MacCormick (1987), pp. 155 and 169; da Rosa de Bustamante (2012), pp. 278–279.

single correct way to formulate it.[46] The text is a lazy machine,[47] thus, one must interpret it. The *ratio* is not affixed with a label;[48] it is necessary to highlight it in the justification.

What does it mean? Three things.

The first is that the *ratio* must be formulated based on the justification of the decision and possibly the justification of other decisions that developed it.[49] This is how the rule in which embodies the *ratio decidendi* is derived. The second is that the decomposition of justification—both in its logical line and in its argumentative line[50]—serves to demonstrate "what" was considered by the court and "how".[51] This is an activity that requires skill, usually achieved with practical experience.[52] The third is that the description of the possible meanings of the material used in the justification forms a framework that will allow the definition of the *ratio*, that is, the formulation of its normative prescription.[53] Various interpretive methods are welcome.[54] The court that has the duty to decide the current case looks back—retrospectively[55]—to rebuild the meaning of the *ratio*. In interpreting it, it does

---

[46] This was acknowledged in 1959 by Arthur Goodhart himself (Goodhart 1959, p. 124), especially in the face of criticism from Stone (1959), pp. 597–620. In the same vein, Hart (2012), p. 134.

[47] Eco (2013), p. 34.

[48] Cardozo (1991), p. 30 (he states, in fact, that the *obiter dictum* does not come labelled, but the same reasoning obviously applies to the *ratio*, as observed by Duxbury 2008, p. 69).

[49] Cross and Harris (1991), p. 45; Dworkin (1986), p. 228 (hence the famous metaphor of the precedent as "chain novel"); Marinoni (2022a), pp. 174–176 and 205.

[50] On the identification of the internal (logical) and external (argumentative) justification of the decision, *retro*, item 1.3.

[51] Domit (2018), pp. 144–148.

[52] Lamond (2023), p. 27.

[53] Llewellyn (2008), pp. 5, 7, 13–14, 65 and 71; Stone (1959), pp. 600–601. As I have already noted in *Precedentes*, "the potential equivocity of the texts, however, is not something that can be eliminated simply by the linguistic refinement in their writing. In fact, equivocity is not exactly an objective flaw of the text, but a result of different interests and conceptions about the justice of interpreters and the multiplicity of dogmatic conceptions and interpretative methods used by them that interfere with the activity of individualization, valuation and choice of meanings. The interpretation varies according to the position taken by the interpreter in society or in the face of a certain conflict (different interests), with its ethical-political inclinations (conceptions of justice), with the legal concepts it relies on (dogmatic conceptions) and with the interpretative arguments chosen (interpretative methods)—and it is precisely for this reason that the life of Law, concretised in its interpretation and application, does not depend only on logic, but is—first and foremost—experience ('the life of the law has not been logic: it has been experience')" (Mitidiero 2023, p. 60). These vicissitudes make the texts—whether legislative or judicial—always subject to different interpretations, demanding a decision for one of the competing meanings by those who are in charge of interpreting and applying it (in the same vein, Miranda 2022, p. 285). That is why it can be said that the profile of those who are in charge of interpreting the *ratio* ends up determining its effective scope (Barber 2023, p. 53).

[54] Concentration on the essential elements, abstraction of accidents, generalisation, and the several interpretative postulates are examples of interpretative operations aimed at the logical-argumentative rebuilding of the *ratio*. To imagine that the interpretation of the *ratio* is resolved with a single formula is a "vain hope"—as Arthur Goodhart himself admitted in 1959 (Goodhart 1959, p. 124).

[55] Cramer (2016), p. 113.

not declare it, nor does it create it—it rebuilds[56] it, using only the material that is already there; the construction site is situated in the previous justification.

Two particularities, however, stand out in the interpretation of the *ratio* when compared with that of the legislation.[57] The first is that it is an interpretation surrounded by facts. The facts of the case—its material facts—provide the context in which the rules operate and determine their outcome, allowing a certain degree of discretion in the application of the precedent given the variability of the facts.[58] The second is that certain normative meanings are no longer available to the interpreter. When interpreting legislation, all meanings that fit within the framework are listed on the menu. When interpreting the justification, some meanings have already been discarded, and one was attached to the text by the Supreme Courts in the face of a particular factual context.[59] To observe the precedent, the interpreter cannot ignore these interpretative decisions.[60]

Normally, the *ratio* is rebuilt by the judges and courts charged with interpreting and enforcing the precedent.[61] This is the English tradition, recalled, for example, by Viscount Dunedin at the *House of Lords* in 1928 when he tried the *Great Western Ry case. Co. v. Owners of S. S. Mostyn*, in stating that it was not the court's duty to indicate the *ratio* to the others.[62] Although in some cases[63] and in some theoretical elaborations a certain relaxation[64] may be justified, giving a greater explanation of

[56] Mitidiero (2022a), pp. 21, 27, 40, 65, 84, 87, 88; Mitidiero (2023), pp. 68, 87 and 92. In the same vein, Sunstein (2023), p. 232.

[57] Were it based on a definition of precedent as a decision, there would still be a third: although the legislation does not use words in vain, the decision has many that do not matter for the characterisation of the *ratio*. However, since I am here assuming that decision and precedent are not synonymous and that precedent is synonymous with *ratio*, this distinction does not apply: in both legislation and precedent—in *ratio*—there are no words in vain.

[58] Goodhart (1937b), p. 24; Raz (2009), pp. 188–189.

[59] Mitidiero (2023), p. 101.

[60] In the STF caselaw, *Portela Santana v. União* (STF, Plenário, RE n. 655.265/RS, Rel. Min. Luiz Fux, Rel. para Acórdão Min. Edson Fachin, j. 13.04.2016, DJe 04.08.2016); in the caselaw of STJ, *Pettená Filho v. Tribunal de Justiça de São Paulo* (STJ, HC n. 274.806/SP, Rel. Min. Rogério Schietti, j. 14.02.2014, DJe 18.02.2014). In Brazilian legal literature, Marinoni (2022a), p. 79; Zaneti Júnior (2017), pp. 328–329; Mitidiero (2023), p. 101.

[61] Arruda Alvim (2012), p. 44.

[62] Goodhart (1937a), p. 75.

[63] As in the *R. v. Moloney* case, tried in 1985 by the *House of Lords*, and cited by MacCormick (1987), p. 178. In a similar vein, Passanante (2018), pp. 254 et seq., the tendency of the Italian *Corte di Cassazione* to arrogate to itself the power to indicate which—among its decisions—it considers to have precedential force.

[64] Eisenberg (1988), pp. 54–55, which defines the *ratio decidendi* including the "announcement approach", that is, its announcement or proclamation by the court that decided the case from which the precedent originated.

the *ratio* by the court in charge of forming the precedent, the rule is that of its retrospective rebuilding.

In Brazilian Law, however, there is a peculiarity:[65] the thesis tends to divert the attention that, strictly speaking, should be given to the *ratio*.[66] It is true that the thesis cannot be disregarded; it represents an effort of court to formulate the *ratio*. It is an act of kindness which serves to improve communication—within the court, with other courts, and with all participants of the justice system.[67] But equally, it cannot be overvalued. Even when a Supreme Court formulates a thesis to frame the *ratio*, the legal interpretation may be incongruent with it. It may not mirror it the ratio,[68] as it is a statement without facts, elaborated without the boundaries offered by its context. It is always necessary, in other words, to read the thesis in the light of the *ratio*.[69]

The *ratio* serves to resolve, in whole or in part, a matter of law[70]—identical or similar.[71] It is quite true that one has already considered that the great virtue of Common Law was that the issue was first decided, and then the *ratio* was formulated.[72] I suspect, however, that this well-known lesson gained prominence due to its simplicity rather than as an effective description of Common Law operations. It is intuitive that the solution of an issue is the consequence of at least an outline of a general rule that can be universalised.[73] Identical and similar issues anchor—attract—the precedents. It is to resolve these issues that the *ratio* is applied.[74]

---

[65] Domit (2018), p. 155; Monnerat (2019), p. 409.

[66] A trend that has already spread even to the field of CNJ recommendations (Recommendation no. 134, of 2022, of Cnj, for example, arts. 4, 5, 11, 13, 14, 19 and 48), whose importance suggests its consideration as *soft law* (Didier Júnior and Fernandez 2022, pp. 70–75).

[67] The *thesis* and the *themes* that index them are, therefore, also ways of organising the work of the Supreme Courts, recording it—so to speak—*ad perpetuam rei memoriam* (Marchiori 2022, p. 54).

[68] Garner (2016), p. 59; Mitidiero (2023), p. 104; Lessa (2022), p. 153.

[69] Mitidiero (2023), p. 104. Analogically, art. 926, § 2, CPC.

[70] Cruz e Tucci (2012), p. 123; Marinoni (2022a), p. 154.

[71] As my central objective in *Precedentes* was only to substantiate the need for mandatory linking to the precedent, I paid attention only to similar issues (issues with *"relevant similarities* or *essential identity*") as a means of exemplifying the use of the *ratio* to resolve a case (Mitidiero 2023, pp. 116–117). Since my central objective now is to define the *ratio* and show how it operates to resolve different issues that appear in court, it seems indispensable for the sake of clarity to separate the two categories: identical issues and similar issues. Also on distinguishing identical issues and similar issues, Schauer and Spellman (2023), pp. 242–251.

[72] Holmes Jr. (1931), p. 725: *"it is the merit of the common law that it decides the case first and determines the principle afterwards"*.

[73] Sunstein (2023), p. 230.

[74] It is true that this is the rule: a court decision uses the *ratio* to resolve a case. However, it must be borne in mind that it is possible to take advantage of a case or combine the *rationes* of several cases in order not to resolve a particular matter of law, but to develop law in general. In these situations, the *ratio* is used as a space for certain rules to find a common expression. This occurs when the courts, especially the Supreme Courts, reason using the "inference to the best legal explanation" of a given problem (on this subject, Michelon 2023, pp. 126–128). I'm not concerned right now about this kind of use of the *ratio*. While interesting, exploring it would divert me from my purpose at this point.

When, however, is an issue identical, similar, or distinct? How do we identify and deal with each of them?

3.1 When Is an Issue Identical, Similar, or Distinct?

Identical issues are issues in which, having abstracted one or all of the people involved, the value, time and place of the facts, exhibit a normative congruence among all their essential elements, that is, their legally relevant elements. The *ratio* formed on an identical issue already judged serves as a precedent for another pending analysis by means of subsumption. The identical issue is an issue already decided—it constitutes "settled law".[75] As no issue is exactly identical to the other,[76] the matter of legal identity turns out to be a matter of abstraction of accidental elements and congruence among essential elements. It is a matter of *essential identity*.

Similar issues are issues in which, having abstracted their accidental elements, there is normative congruence at a certain level of generalisation among their essential elements. The *ratio* formed on the similar issue already judged serves as a precedent for another that is pending analysis, once having defined the level of generalisation in which they are in tune by means of analogy. The similar issue is not one already decided. It is a new issue, however close to the one already resolved; it constitutes a "case of first impression".[77] The matter of legal similarity becomes, therefore, a matter of abstraction of accidental elements and congruence among essential elements at a certain level of generalisation. It is a matter of *relevant similarity*.

Distinct issues are issues in which there is no normative congruence exhibited at any level of generality, or that present normative congruence at a certain level of generality, but is characterised by the existence of a fact not previously considered. The *ratio* formed on the distinct issue already judged does not serve as a precedent for another that is pending analysis, or it does in a restricted way. The matter of legal distinction becomes a matter of difference among accidental elements and essential elements, including at any level of generalisation, or of congruence among essential elements, including at a certain level of generality, characterised by the existence of a fact not considered in the *ratio* of an identical or similar issue.

If the aim is to promote legal certainty, freedom and equality in the resolution of identical issues, several procedural techniques are available. Non-mutual collateral

[75] Michelon (2023), pp. 122 and 126.

[76] Wambaugh (1894), p. 14; Benditt (1987), p. 90; Schauer (2009), p. 45; Garay (2013), p. 74.

[77] Michelon (2023), pp. 121 and 126.

estoppel,[78] class actions,[79] incidents of *collectivization of issues* (*Musterverfahren* and group litigation order),[80] and precedents (*stare decisis*)[81] are all potential tools.[82] Thus, whilst identical issues can be resolved by means of precedents, they respond well to other tools that offer greater precision to measure congruence. Identical issues can be addressed both in "rigid decision-making environments"[83] and through a simpler—"mystical"[84] or "naive"[85]—view of precedents. The *ratio* is just one method of resolving identical issues.

However, to resolve similar issues, alternative means are unavailable. It is not possible to use tools that require greater precision in measuring congruence. Characterising similarity requires gathering two or more elements at a certain level of generalisation, it would be an almost inexcusable naivety to imagine that a method designed to deal with identical issues could handle issues that require, by definition, a decision that can calibrate the appropriate level of generality that justifies dealing with them the same way. When faced with identical issues, there is no room for debating the degree of generalisation. Hence the reason why the *rationes decidendi* aimed at resolving similar issues need more space—they need a room of their own, designed for justifying the categorisation that needs to be undertaken by the

[78] Arts. 503 and 506, CPC. For a broad view on this subject, with appropriate bibliographic indications, Marinoni (2022b); da Silva (2019); do Passo Cabral (2019).

[79] Arts. 16, Lei n. 7.347, de 1985, 81, parágrafo único, inciso III, e 103, inciso III, CDC, according to the interpretation given by the Supreme Federal Court in the case Caixa Econômica Federal v. Instituto Brasileiro de Defesa do Consumidor (STF, Pleno, RE n. 1.101.937/SP, Rel. Min. Alexandre de Moraes, j. 08.04.2021, DJe 14.06.2021). For a broad view on this subject, with appropriate bibliographic indications, Arenhart and Osna (2022); Didier Júnior and Zaneti Júnior (2019); Zavascki (2017); Gidi (2007); Vitorelli (2016).

[80] Arts. 976 to 987 (incident of the resolution of multiple claims on the same point of law) and 1036 to 1042 (multiple appeals). For a broad view on this subject, with appropriate bibliographic indications, Arenhart (2013); Marinoni (2016); Temer (2020); Cavalcanti (2016); de Camargo Mancuso (2016); do Passo Cabral (2007), n. 147; Arenhart and Pessoa (2019), n. 10; Pasqualotto (2022).

[81] Arts. 926 and 927, CPC. For a broad view on this subject, with appropriate bibliographic indications, Marinoni (2022a); Zaneti Júnior (2017); de Macedo (2019); Cramer (2016); Câmara (2018); Viana and Nunes (2018); Theodoro Júnior and Andrade (2021). Also, Mitidiero (2023).

[82] Although it is very common to jointly address res judicata (especially collateral estoppel) with *stare decisis* in Common Law (e.g., Wells 1878, preface, explained it due to its systematic meaning), its connection is practically ignored in Brazilian legal literature—the exception that confirms the rule is Luiz Guilherme Marinoni who, after having faced the theme of *Precedentes* in 2010 and the *Incidente de Resolução de Demandas Repetitivas* in 2016, decided to dedicate himself to the *Coisa Julgada sobre Questão* in 2018, thus drawing a more airy panorama of the techniques capable of solving identical issues. Without adequately linking these institutes or even recognising their partially coincident fields, it is difficult for Brazilian Civil Justice to be able to throw overboard all the weight that threatens to sink it in the whirlpool of multiple issues.

[83] Arruda Alvim (2012), pp. 17 and 57.

[84] Raz (2009), p. 188.

[85] Marinoni (2023b), pp. 40 et seq.

interpreter in order to enforce the precedent.[86] That is why precedents, despite being just one of the available methods in the face of identical issues, are the only tools capable of promoting legal certainty, freedom and equality, when confronted with the need to resolve similar issues.

Solving both identical and similar issues depends on comparison. This is the basic game of precedents.[87]

3.2 Comparison: The Game of Matching Cases

Dealing with precedents requires a concrete instruction manual. Book theories are insufficient; we require cases that are enacted in court. It is easier to compare issues and determine identity, similarities, or differences in the context of a living case. It is via practical comparison that one can infer the need to enforce or dismiss the precedent by subsumption, analogy or distinction.

Let's start with identical issues.

In 1930, Llewellyn noted that there was a huge group of cases that are predestined to be out of court work. He characterised these cases as those whose results anyone could foresee. Their *ratio* would be easy to interpret.[88] These were cases that were pre-decided: everyday cases.[89] Yet, despite this, these types of cases remain frequent in our courts and tribunals, doing enormous damage to judicial maps, judicial statistics and the lives of the parties. To create adequate mechanisms to resolve them and a culture capable of dismissing them, one must first know how to identify them. I propose the following definition: *one issue is identical to the other when the relevant factual-legal propositions pertaining to positions and things are the same, abstracted, as a rule, from the people, time, place and value involved in the situation from which they originated.* This combines the congruence of *essential* elements (the factual-legal propositions—that is, the necessary and sufficient reasons—relevant to positions and things of a given situation) and the abstraction of *accidental* elements (the people, time, place and value involved).[90]

---

[86] I imagine that this is what Teresa Arruda Alvim meant by the expression "loose decision-making environments" (Arruda Alvim 2012, pp. 18 and 58).

[87] Llewellyn (2008), p. 47.

[88] This observation is recurrent in the literature about precedents. Although it does not always expressly establish these cases as those related to identical issues, legal scholars usually refer to the existence of cases in which it is very simple to interpret the *ratio* and resolve the issue, their connection being an intuitive one: Hart (2012), p. 134; Schauer (2009), pp. 52–53.

[89] Llewellyn (2008). pp. 58–59.

[90] I'm essentially reproducing the lessons of Wambaugh (essential and accidental elements) and those of Goodhart (legally relevant facts) to identify the legal issue that must be resolved by *ratio* (Wambaugh 1894, pp. 14–17; Goodhart 1937b, pp. 10 and 25). My definition also comes close to that formulated by Alvim regarding issues with "integral identity": there is "integral identity of situations" when "the facts and the legal issue, *stricto sensu*, are absolutely the same", "not necessarily the underlying factual framework fully considered: but, among the facts, those considered relevant by the Law for the incidence (or not) of the consequence at stake", being identical to

Before moving on to the necessary steps for resolving identical issues and to the sample test bench, I want to remind you of one thing. Even Julius Stone—Goodhart's most notorious and remembered critic—agreed that the approach based on *legally relevant facts* works to resolve *identical issues*.[91] Stone, writing in 1959 in Australia, argued that the *ratio* would have a very restricted scope if it were doomed to only deal with identical cases.[92] But this was his only criticism of Goodhart on the matter of identical issues. His other, more severe, critiques concerned Goodhart's ideas on the resolution of similar issues—a matter that I will discuss in due course. But, having made this observation, I ask you: is solving identical issues a major concern for us? Would the reach of the *ratio* be an insignificant "vanishing point",[93] given the number of identical issues in Brazilian courts? In terms of identical issues, can you compare 1959 Australia with contemporary Brazil?

Whether one issue is identical to the other is a matter of interpretation. Identical issues are not labelled as such. This equation of legal identity requires their interpreter to qualify the issues. Hence, one says that identifying the *ratio decidendi* for the solution of an issue constitutes a "mutual coeffort of two or more courts".[94] Individualising the elements that identify the issues is a matter entrusted to the valuation and decision of the interpreter in charge of enforcing the *ratio* to resolve the case.[95] It is a sophisticated and adept activity.[96] The logical-argumentative reconstruction for the solution of identical issues involves interpretation to measure the congruence of the essential elements and abstraction of the accidental ones.

Thus, when the legislation states that "judges and courts will observe" the precedents (the *rationes decidendi*) in cases where they have no basis to make distinctions or power—and good reasons[97]—to overrule those precedents.[98] It seeks to set forth a duty to interpret the precedents by comparing their essential elements and, if they are congruent, also the duty to enforce them. *Stare decisis et quieta non movere*.[99] Identical issues presuppose "settled law"; the recipe for resolution is well-known. Judges and courts must justify the decision of the case by adopting

"the traits elected by the legislator as essential to the hypothesis of incidence of the consequence" (Arruda Alvim 2012, p. 57).

[91] Stone (1959), p. 604.

[92] Stone (1959), p. 604.

[93] Stone (1959), p. 604.

[94] Siltala (2000), p. 65.

[95] Guastini (2011), p. 263.

[96] Mitidiero (2023), pp. 101–102.

[97] Michelon (2023), p. 118. The bibliography on overruling, even in Brazilian Law, is already considerable, but I cannot fail to mention at least three here: Ávila (2009); Peixoto (2015); Arruda Alvim (2019). Also, Mitidiero (2021).

[98] Arts. 489, § 1, items V and VI, and 927, *caput*, CPC.

[99] To recall the classic closing of the argument in favour of Lord Mansfield's *stare decisis* in *Rex v. Inhabitants of Underbarrow and Bradleyfield*, tried in 1766, in which the King's Bench ended up following a precedent begrudgingly: "for several reasons... we should not depart from the adjudged cases; but chiefly from the inconvenience of altering and overturning settled determinations. It is best, *stare decisis*" (Oldham 2006, p. 140).

the *ratio* in the major premise and the relevant facts in the minor premise, so that they can reach a solution for the case.[100] Once the argument has been made around the correct premises, the good old syllogism ensures the best dish presentation.

Identical issues can be exemplified in many cases. Such as whether public universities in Brazil can charge fees for enrolment,[101] if candidates with higher education in the specific area approved in a civil service examination for a vocational high school or complete education with a technical course are entitled to be appointed[102] and if, unless expressly provided for in the contract, health insurance plans are obliged to pay for *in vitro*[103] fertilisation. These are just a few.

For instance, once it's decided that public universities in Brazil cannot charge fees for enrolment, it does not it matter if it's the Federal University of Goiás or the Federal University of Rio Grande do Sul that wish to charge fee. If the applicant to enrol is João or Maria. If the fee was charged on March 14, 2014, or April 29, 2018. If it was in Goiânia or Porto Alegre. Or if the amount charged was R$150.00 or R $250.00? What matters is whether those who have passed the public university entrance exam have the right to enrol regardless of whether they pay a fee. This is the important issue; it stems from the legal relevance of the fact,[104] the legal positions[105] and the thing that is intended to be ensured.[106]

This script could be applied to each of the above examples. In abstracting the parties, the time, the place and the value involved, I've directed the focus to the comparison of the material facts, those that give rise to an issue around which legal positions are articulated in relation to a thing. It's from this encounter—this *match*—that the need to enforce the *ratio* for the solution of the case arises.

The time has come to consider the greater challenges presented by similar issues.

These offer an even greater degree of complexity;[107] they are the elephants in the realm of issues concerning the application of *ratio*. The countless pages written on

---

[100] Michelon (2023), p. 119; Schauer and Spellman (2023), pp. 242–244.

[101] *Universidade Federal de Goiás v. Alves Lopes* (STF, Pleno, RE n. 500.171/GO, Rel. Min. Ricardo Lewandowski, j. 13.08.2008, DJe 24.10.2008).

[102] *Instituto Federal de Educação, Ciência e Tecnologia do Ceará v. Azevedo* (STJ, 1ª Seção, REsp n. 1.888.049/CE, Rel. Min. Og Fernandes, j. 22.09.2021, DJe 29.09.2021).

[103] *Unimed de Cascavel v. Malikoski* (STJ, 2ª Seção, REsp n. 1.822.240/SP, Rel. Min. Paulo de Tarso Sanseverino, j. 13.10.2021, DJe 27.10.2021).

[104] Legally considered facts: approval in the entrance exam and requirement of a registration fee in the light of art. 206, item IV, CRFB.

[105] Legal positions of those who obtained approval: right to enrol and right to attend the course. Legal positions of the University: duty to enrol and duty to enable attendance in the course. Of course, I'm describing the positions of the parties taking into account the *outcome* of the lawsuit. If I were doing so *throughout* the lawsuit, the *uncertainty* inherent in the allegations in court would prevent such a description, a terminology more appropriate to the *expectations* of the parties in relation to the lawsuit would be recommended. It's impossible not to recall at this point the various invocations of James Goldschmidt by Alvaro de Oliveira and Ovídio Baptista da Silva—the procedure as a machine capable of transforming rights and duties into expectations.

[106] Thing intended to be ensured: the right to higher education at official educational institutions.

[107] Schauer and Spellman (2023), p. 243.

Donoghue, for example, bring forth the multitude of debates that revolve how we characterise similarity.[108] It is no coincidence that this embodies the most attacked flank of Goodhart's proposal. I suggest defining similar issues as follows: *one issue is similar to the other when the relevant factual-legal propositions pertaining to positions and things are congruent at a certain level of generalisation, abstracted, as a rule, from the people, place, time and value involved in the situation from which they originated.* This definition combines the congruence of *essential* elements at a given level of *generalisation* (the factual-legal propositions—that is, the necessary and sufficient reasons—concerning positions and things in a given situation) and the abstraction of *accidental* elements (people, time, place and value involved).[109]

Whether one issue is similar to another is also a matter of interpretation. Similar issues are not labelled as such. The equation of legal similarity requires their interpreter to qualify the issues, thus promoting a dialogue between the *ratio* of an issue already decided with that—similar—still pending solution. Individualising the elements that identify the issues is a matter entrusted to the valuation and decision of the interpreter in charge of enforcing the *ratio* to resolve the case.[110] It's an even more intricate activity than the comparison of issues to establish identity. The logical-argumentative reconstruction for the solution of similar issues involves not only the abstraction of accidental elements but, also the measurement of the congruence of essential elements at a given level of generalisation.

The similar issue is undecided, although it is close to the other, already resolved issue. Thus, its terrain isn't that of the "settled law"; it is a "case of first impression". Before the duty to decide the case according to the *ratio* of the similar issue arises, it's necessary to place the undecided issue under a category capable of justifying its handling within the domains of the already resolved issue. It's necessary to justify, in other words, the similarity—the analogy between the issues.[111] As the similarity isn't established in advance[112] either, it is necessary to demonstrate this in the reasoning.

---

[108]Stone (1959), pp. 603–604, vol. XXII; Schauer (2009), pp. 50–51. For a defence of Goodhart against Stone, Duxbury (2008), pp. 86–87.

[109]I'm essentially reproducing the lessons of Wambaugh (essential and accidental elements) and those of Goodhart (material facts) to identify the legal issue that must be resolved by *ratio* (Wambaugh 1894, pp. 14–17; Goodhart 1937b, pp. 10 and 25). I have added, however, the note of "congruence at a certain level of generalisation" inspired by the "categorization" of facts for dealing with similar issues suggested by Schauer (1987), p. 577, vol. XXXIX; Schauer (2009), pp. 46–54 (adopted among us by Marinoni 2022a, pp. 178–179) and that of the "framing" of particular "sub-issues" in a "general issue" capable of ensuring the similarity proposed by Michelon (2023), p. 124 (before, Michelon and D'Almeida 2017; also, D'Almeida 2023, pp. 133–135). In my view, this framing of "particular sub-issues" into a "general issue" constitutes a good strategy for identifying the *purpose* of comparison—without which, incidentally, it's difficult to sustain the rationality on deciding the similarity (Sherwin 2023, pp. 160–161).

[110]Guastini (2011), p. 263.

[111]Michelon (2023), pp. 123–126. For a broad view on this subject, Michelon and D'Almeida (2017), vol. XXXI; Lessa (2022), pp. 176–212.

[112]Sunstein (2023), p. 229.

This justification may involve more or fewer steps. Imagine the issue is situated on a bifurcated staircase—for example, right in front of the Victory of Samothrace at the *Louvre*. In one case, the reasons may push the interpreter only to the stairs on the right. However, other cases see a tug of war between reasons ensue; the decision-maker is simultaneously pulled to the right and left stairs. In the first case, the path is shorter; the reasons are heavily weighted. Once the analogy is justified, the *ratio* of the issue already decided to the one still pending solution is enforced. The "case of first impression" becomes "settled law" by virtue of similarity. In the second case, it is necessary to appraise the reasons which steps will guide you up the stairs.[113] It is slightly longer path, but with the same outcome: the case is resolved by an existing *ratio*. The *ratio* is extended to offer the solution of the similar issue.[114]

Let us revisit our previous examples.

In considering Article 206, Item IV of the CRFB, the Brazilian Supreme Court determined that it is unconstitutional to demand a fee for public university enrolment.[115] Given this, is it permissible to set a fee for the issuance of a diploma? These issues are not identical: a fee for enrolment is distinct from a fee for diploma issuance. However, they are clearly related payments. In practise, the same legal positions and the protection the same thing are at stake. The material facts are inextricably intertwined: the former pertains to the entrance door and the latter, to the exit door. Leaving the concrete level of controversies and climbing a few rungs on the ladder of generalisation, both are fees that economically condition the enjoyment of higher education.[116] For this reason, the Brazilian Supreme Court understood that both issues are similar, enforcing the *ratio* of *Goiás* to the solution of *Rondônia*.[117] This is the basis of the need to *treat like cases alike*.[118]

One of the most prominent tugs of war in the field of analogy is *Adams v. New Jersey Steamboat Company*.[119] Tried by the *New York Court of Appeals* in 1896,

---

[113]Michelon (2023), pp. 125–126.

[114]Other steps may require justification for applying the analogy. For example, as Grant Lamond recalls in Lamond (2014), analogies can be close (sought within the same branch of law) or distant (belonging to different branches). The greater the proximity, the safer the analogy and the less intense the duty to justify its relevance. In Brazilian legal literature, Mendonça (2018); Lessa (2022), pp. 209–212.

[115]*Universidade Federal de Goiás v. Alves Lopes* (STF, Pleno, RE n. 500.171/GO, Rel. Min. Ricardo Lewandowski, j. 13.08.2008, DJe 24.10.2008).

[116]It should be noted that I left the most concrete level—that of fees for enrolment and for the issuance of the diploma—and went only up to the *sufficient* level of generalisation. Moving up steps beyond this may imply abandoning the necessary "referability" to the material facts that welcome the *ratio* (Domit 2018, p. 163).

[117]*Fundação Universidade Federal de Rondônia v. Sousa Leitão* (STF, 1ª Turma, AgRg no RE n. 597.872/RO, Rel. Min. Marco Aurélio, j. 03.06.2014, DJe 26.08.2014).

[118]On the way in which coherence acts in argumentation, Ávila (2014), pp. 166 et seq. Michelon (2011); Pessoa (2014). For a broad debate, Amaya (2015).

[119]Schauer (2009), pp. 98–99; Michelon (2023), p. 125.

this is a case in which Adams had his money stolen from inside his passenger cabin on the Steamboat owned by the New Jersey Steamboat Company. The issue was if the company could be held responsible for Adams's loss. A possible similarity could be found in *Carpenter*, tried in 1891,[120] in which it was understood that it was impossible to hold a company that owns trains responsible for thefts that occurred in their sleeping cars. Another similarity, however, could be traced to *Hulett*, decided in 1865,[121] in which it was decided that the innkeepers were responsible for the luggage left by their guests in their rooms. The first thing that should be noted is that the three issues: exclusive cabins on boats, rooms at inns and sleeping cars on trains are similar, but not identical things. Boats and trains are means of transport, while rooms and cabins have exclusive access. In weighing the similarities, the Court ruled that New Jersey was liable, highlighting that Adams's reliance on private space was the overriding reason. The existence of a private space was the common category that drove *Carpenter* away and ensured the enforcement of *Hulett* to *Adams*. As the issues are only next-door neighbours, *Carpenter* did not have its strength weakened or its reach restricted in general—rather it was simply not applicable to the resolution of *Adams*.[122] Conversely *Hulett's* ratio was strengthened by the decision; it was extended to encompass *Adams* and, having then led to its characterisation as a precedent, the duty arose to make the decision according to the respective *ratio*.

Consequently, two elements differentiate the use of *ratio* for solving similar issues from solving identical issues. First, the *ratio* is used for the decision of an issue not yet decided. Second, the similarity capable of justifying its extension must be sought in a categorisation of its essential elements. Extracting them from the accidental, one is tasked with finding the essential elements on the horizon of generalisations. It is from this combination that stems the duty to apply the *ratio* of an issue already decided to another pending solution.[123]

In sum, the identical issues belong to the realm of "settled law" and require, for their solution, a reconstruction of the *ratio* through a logical-argumentative operation that can be eventually well represented by a syllogism. Whereas the issues similar to those of the "cases of first impression" require for their solution a reconstruction of the *ratio* through a logical-argumentative operation focused on analogy.[124] We can now move to establish how a case can be differentiated from another.

[120] *Carpenter v. New York N.Y., N. H. H. R. R.*, 1891, tried by the *New York Court of Appeals*.

[121] *Hulett v. Shift*, 1865, tried by the *New York Supreme Court*.

[122] Michelon (2023), pp. 125–126.

[123] Apart from the analogy, other arguments can be applied to the *ratio* to provoke its expansion to cases not yet decided, but similar, such as, for example, *a fortiori* and *a contrario sensu* argument (Michelon 2023, p. 117). Exploring them at this time, however, is out of the scope of this work.

[124] This is, in short, Claudio Michelon's idea, Michelon (2023), pp. 117–129, previously presented in Michelon and D'Almeida (2017). In Brazilian legal literature, also following Michelon's approach, Lessa (2022), p. 171.

3.3 Distinguishing

In some circumstances, the comparison of issues may lead to the conclusion that the *ratio* does not apply. The rule in which the *ratio* is embodied is not applicable because, when interpreting the issue, no relevant identity or similarity was reached or because a relevant fact not previously considered arose. In these cases, there is a distinct issue; this requires distinguishing to rule out the application of the precedent.[125]

I suggest defining distinct issues as follows: one issue is distinct from the other when the relevant factual-legal propositions pertaining to positions and things in a given situation are different at any level of generality or are congruent, including any level of generality *but marked by the existence of a relevant fact not previously*

[125] There is another proper technique to deal with the *ratio*—overruling. As it assumes precisely the existence of an identical or similar issue already resolved ("settled law"), there is no need to address it here. I would like only to highlight two points so as not to leave loose ends on the matter. The first: a precedent can be overruled fully ("overruling") or partially ("overturning"), in the latter case being rewritten ("overriding") or transformed ("transformation"). As I have already noted in *Superação*, "total overruling constitutes the judicial response to the evident misunderstanding in its solution or to the wear and tear of its normative coherence or social congruence. When the precedent is evidently mistaken or lacks coherence or congruence, the basic principles that support the rule of *stare decisis*—legal certainty, freedom and equality—no longer authorise their replicability, and must be overruled, otherwise the process of continuous development of the Law will be stopped. This conjugation is taken by scholars as the basic rule for overruling precedents. Partial alteration occurs upon transformation or rewriting of the precedent. For the development of the law, it may not be opportune or necessary to totally overrule the precedent. There is transformation when the court, without formally denying the precedent, that is, without admitting wear and tear or misunderstanding of the old solution, partially reconfigures it, taking into account factual and legal aspects not considered relevant in the previous decision. In theory, the transformation serves to partially alter the precedent by producing a result compatible with it. There is rewriting when the court redefines the scope of the precedent, which is usually rewritten in order to restrict its scope. Based on the rewriting, something that was not considered in the previous decision is weighed and then its scope is compressed" (Mitidiero 2021, p. 56). The second: the only court that can overrule the *ratio* is the one that formed it. As I have already written in *Precedentes*, "the Courts of Justice and the judges of the first degree connected to it cannot fail to enforce a precedent only because they do not agree with the solution formulated therein, that is, with its content. To imagine that the Courts of Justice and the Federal Regional Courts may depart from the precedents of the Federal Supreme Court and the Superior Court of Justice by not agreeing with the briefs and solutions formulated therein is a misconception that stems from a lack of understanding of the nature of the Federal Supreme Court and the Superior Court of Justice as Supreme Courts – of interpretation rather than control, of precedents rather than caselaw. A Court of Justice that drifts away from a Supreme Court precedent that must be enforced is not diverging from such a court. It is, in fact, disobeying the interpretation of the laws meant by the Supreme Court. The possibility of divergence presupposes courts that occupy the same degree in the judicial hierarchy. To imagine that a Court of Justice can contradict or fail to enforce a precedent of a Supreme Court by disagreeing with its content is equivalent to assuming that there is no order and organisation in the structure of the Judiciary and that all judicial courts perform the same function within the justice distribution system – which, of course, constitutes a blatant misunderstanding" (for a broad view of this subject, Mitidiero 2023, pp. 120–123).

considered. This definition combines both the distinction of *essential* elements, including at any level of generalisation (the relevant factual-legal propositions concerning positions and things in a given situation), marked or not by the existence of a material fact not considered, as that of *accidental* elements (people, time, place and value involved).

Verifying the existence of identical, similar and distinct issues is a customary practise of the court. All courts—of any instance—must assess identity, similarity or distinction and act in accordance with what the Law prescribes.[126] When concluding that there is a distinct issue, the court is not weakening a precedent or attesting to the absence of its obligation—on the contrary,[127] it affirms the authority of the precedent.[128] In making a distinction, the court is simply concluding that the precedent does not apply.[129] Whether one issue is distinct from another is also a matter of interpretation. Distinct issues are not labelled as such. Assessing the distinction requires their interpreter to qualify the issues, promoting a dialogue between the *ratio* of an issue already decided with that still pending solution. The individualisation of the elements that distinguish the issues is a matter entrusted to the valuation and decision of the interpreter charged with resolving the case.[130]

The distinction sometimes moves in tranquil waters—it may be apparent that two issues are distinct. Hence, it is quick to discern that the precedent does not apply. Sometimes, however, it is less obvious. The *ratio* may initially seem applicable, but upon deeper analysis a distinction can be emerge; the presence of an additional element that should be considered. The distinction may feel gentle (*tame view*), or restless (*changing view*).[131]

---

[126] Arts. 489, § 1, item VI, and 927, § 1, CPC.

[127] The possibility of distinguishing is sometimes invoked as proof that the precedent is not binding (e.g. Taruffo 2007, p. 716, *retro*, item 1.2). In *Precedentes*, however, I note that "it must be borne in mind, on the one hand, that distinguishing and overruling are techniques that precisely *assume* the binding force of the precedent. The distinction serves precisely to show that there is no possible analogy between the cases, so that the case is out of the scope of the precedent. Overruling is the total superseding of the precedent and constitutes a power given only to the bodies that were in charge of its formulation through a complex argumentative burden, which involves demonstrating the wear and tear of the precedent with regard to its social congruence and systemic consistency. Distinction and overruling, therefore, are techniques that, far from invalidating the link to the precedent, assume it. On the other hand, in a logical-argumentative perspective of interpretation, defeasibility is far from being a characteristic only of judicial precedent. As noted by scholars, the fact that rules can be constantly overruled is a characteristic of the Law as a whole, so that such an argument also does not serve to invalidate the binding force of the precedent" (Mitidiero 2023, p. 95).

[128] Duxbury (2008), p. 115.

[129] Duxbury (2008), p. 115; Jobim (2014), p. 416, n. 237; Jobim and Oliveira Jr. (2022).

[130] Guastini (2011), p. 263.

[131] I was inspired by Raz (2009), pp. 185–186, and by Marinoni (2022a), p. 229. I note, however, that this difference is pointed out, at least by Joseph Raz, to emphasise that the distinguishing technique that really matters is the one at service of the development of the Law—it is the "changing distinguishing" (Raz 2009, p. 186). The "tame distinguishing" would, in fact, only cover up the difficulties of working with the *ratio decidendi*—an essentially flexible definition, in his opinion,

In view of the *ratio decidendi*, only after interpreting it and interpreting the pending issues alleged by the parties may the court conclude that there is no identity or any relevant similarity between the issues, thus the precedent does not apply. The court has the duty to distinguish, that is, to push away the enforcement of the *ratio* from the resolution of the case.[132] It may occur, however, that there is a relevant identity or similarity between the issues, but there is also a fact not considered in the previous *ratio*. In this scenario, the *ratio* of the identical or similar issue is *preserved*, which creates the new *ratio* by limiting the previous *ratio* for the solution of the distinct issue.[133]

Let us return to our examples.

When deciding on the impossibility of charging for registration fees and for issuance of diplomas in public universities, the STF was analysing the right to access higher education in the face of the rule that imposes its gratuity. This was the issue examined in *Goiás* in 2008[134] and in *Rondônia* in 2014.[135] In *Goiás*, Minister Ricardo Lewandowski stated that Art. 208, CRFB, "signals to the State the obligation to maintain an institutional structure that allows ordinary citizens, regardless of their financial conditions, access to higher education, at its various levels, from undergraduate to graduate, taught in official establishments, with the only limitation being their intellectual competence".[136]

---

given the need to generalise the "material facts" (Raz 2009, p. 185). When Raz drew up this criticism, however, his concern was especially directed to the solution of similar issues. Differentiating the terrain of identical issues from that of similar ones, however, makes the two views of distinguishing have their place under the sun—it was for this reason, by the way, that I made an attempt to trace it at this point too (in *Precedentes*, because I was concerned with another matter, I limited myself to working on distinction as non-incidence, according to Mitidiero 2023, p. 117). For an inventory of distinguishing in Brazilian legal scholarship, Lessa (2022), pp. 213–218.

[132] Arts. 489, § 1, item VI, and 927, § 1, CPC. This definition of distinction—which among *common lawyers* is usually treated as a simple hypothesis of *"inapplicable law"* (e.g. Duxbury 2008, pp. 114–115; Garner 2016, pp. 97–104)—seems essential to me in view of Brazilian law to mark a proper tool for the difference between the issues, especially to show how the non-application of a precedent must be justified (arts. 485, § 1, items V and VI, and 927, § 1, CPC), may be invoked to substantiate a complaint for the protection of precedent portrayed in a binding precedent (art. 988, item III, CPC) and termination action (art. 966, item V and § 5, CPC) (*infra*, item 3.3). This is the "conceptual and functional gain" of *distinguishing* as non-application in Brazilian law (contra, Lessa 2022, pp. 218–219).

[133] Goodhart (1937b), p. 24; Raz (2009), p. 186; Marinoni (2022a), pp. 229–234; Lessa (2022), pp. 218–221. Strictly speaking, in this scenario, the issues are also similar—the difference is that, with the analogy, the similarity finds shelter with the extension of the *ratio* (retro, item 2.2), while with the distinction the similarity is resolved by its reduction. The distinction in this hypothesis can be defined more as a result than as an activity.

[134] *Universidade Federal de Goiás v. Alves Lopes* (STF, Pleno, RE n. 500.171/GO, Rel. Min. Ricardo Lewandowski, j. 13.08.2008, DJe 24.10.2008).

[135] *Fundação Universidade Federal de Rondônia v. Sousa Leitão* (STF, 1ª Turma, AgRg no RE n. 597.872/RO, Rel. Min. Marco Aurélio, j. 03.06.2014, DJe 26.08.2014).

[136] *Universidade Federal de Goiás v. Alves Lopes* (STF, Pleno, RE n. 500.171/GO, Rel. Min. Ricardo Lewandowski, j. 13.08.2008, DJe 24.10.2008, voto do Relator, p. 1.023).

However, in 2017, the Brazilian Supreme Court decided that it does not violate the principle of free education in public universities to charge tuition in specialisation courses.[137] What enabled this solution? According to Minister Edson Fachin, in *Goiás* and in *Rondônia*, the Brazilian Supreme Court was not analysing the specific issue related to the possibility of demanding payment due to the offer of specialisation courses but was only dealing with the offer of undergraduate, master's and doctoral courses.[138] This fact—the concentration of the debate around the collection of tuition fees for specialisation courses—not previously considered led to the limitation of *Goiás* in *Santos*. Although the natural indeterminacy of the *Goiás* text could lead to the apparent framing of *Santos* in its domains, the *highlight* of a fact not previously considered justified its limitation and the solution given.

Likewise, after assimilating accountants' and lawyers' firms,[139] the Brazilian Supreme Court faced the following issue: what if the accountants' firms are not characterised by the personal provision of services by its partners, assuming a complex corporate structure, markedly corporate and multinational? Does the same *ratio* apply? Taking these facts not previously considered into account, the Brazilian Supreme Court distinguished accountant firms with these characteristics, such as *Price, Waterhouse & Coopers*, deciding that, in this case, the *ratio* does not apply.[140]

Whether the distinction arises due to a lack of overall similarity or the presence of a new material fact, the *ratio decidendi* does not apply in either such case. This act of comparison leads to the non-incidence or limitation of the *ratio* for the distinct issue, formulating another for its solution. For *ratio decidendi*, the land ends, and the sea begins on the sands of different issues. Once the *ratio* has been formed and the identical, similar and distinct issues have been flagged, our next step in our journey is to hit the road and explore the role of the *ratio* in the enaction of a lawsuit. How do we plead the *ratio* as a plaintiff and as a defendant? How do we plead it when challenging decisions? How do we decide based on the *ratio*?

This route lies ahead. A couple of pages more, and you'll catch a glimpse, amid the avenues of the lawsuit, of the different floors of Civil Justice.

---

137 *Universidade Federal de Goiás v. Macedo dos Santos* (STF, Pleno, RE n. 597.854/GO, Rel. Min. Edson Fachin, j. 26.04.2017, DJe 21.09.2017).

138 *Universidade Federal de Goiás v. Macedo dos Santos* (STF, Pleno, RE n. 597.854/GO, Rel. Min. Edson Fachin, j. 26.04.2017, DJe 21.09.2017, voto do Relator, p. 12).

139 Based on *OAB/RS v. Porto Alegre* (STF, Pleno, RE n. 940.769/RS, Rel. Min. Edson Fachin, j. 24.04.2019, DJe 12.09.2019), it was decided in *Porto Alegre v. Conselho Regional de Contabilidade do Rio Grande do Sul* (STF, Rcl n. 54.888/RS, Rel. Min. Nunes Marques, j.01.09.2022, DJe 13.09.2022) that accounting firms must have the same treatment as law firms for the purposes of taxation through ISSQN.

140 For example, in *PriceWaterhouseCoopers v. São Paulo* (STF, 2ª Turma, AgRg no RE n. 1.365.583/SP, Rel. Min. Gilmar Mendes, j. 23.05.2022, DJe 26.05.2022).

References

Abramowicz M, Stearns M (2005) Defining Dicta. Stanford Law Rev 57(4):953–1036

Allen CK (1939) Law in the making, 3rd edn. Oxford University Press, Oxford

Amaya A (2015) The tapestry of reason — an inquiry into the nature of coherence and its role in legal argument. Hart, Oxford

Arenhart SC (2013) A Tutela Coletiva de Interesses Individuais — Para Além da Proteção dos Interesses Individuais Homogêneos. RT, São Paulo

Arenhart SC, Osna G (2022) Curso de Processo Civil Coletivo, 4th edn. RT, São Paulo

Arenhart SC, Pessoa P (2019) Precedentes e Casos Repetitivos — Por que não se Pode Confundir Precedentes com as Técnicas do CPC para Solução da Litigância de Massa? Revista de Processo Comparado 5(10):17–53

Arruda Alvim T (2012) Precedentes e Evolução do Direito. In: Arruda Alvim T (ed) Direito Jurisprudencial. RT, São Paulo

Arruda Alvim T (2019) Modulação na Alteração da Jurisprudência Firme ou de Precedentes Vinculantes. RT, São Paulo

Ávila AP (2009) A Modulação de Efeitos Temporais pelo STF no Controle de Constitucionalidade. Livraria do Advogado, Porto Alegre

Ávila H (2014) Teoria dos Princípios, 15th edn. Malheiros, São Paulo

Barber N (2023) Why precedent work. In: Endicott T, Kristjánsson HD, Lewis S (eds) Philosophical foundations of precedent. Oxford University Press, Oxford

Benditt T (1987) The rule of precedent. In: Goldstein L (ed) Precedent in law. Oxford University Press, Oxford

Câmara AF (2018) Levando os Padrões Decisórios a Sério. Atlas, São Paulo

Cardozo B (1991) The nature of judicial process. Yale University Press, New Haven

Cavalcanti M de A (2016) Incidente de Resolução de Demandas Repetitivas. Revista dos Tribunais, São Paulo

Cramer R (2016) Precedentes Judiciais — Teoria e Dinâmica. Forense, Rio de Janeiro

Cross R, Harris J (1991) Precedent in English Law, 4th edn. Oxford University Press, Oxford

Cruz e Tucci JR (2004) Precedente Judicial como Fonte de Direito. RT, São Paulo

Cruz e Tucci JR (2012) Parâmetros de Eficácia e Critérios de Interpretação do Precedente Judicial. In: Arruda Alvim T (ed) Direito Jurisprudencial. Revista dos Tribunais, São Paulo

D'Almeida LD (2023) The 'Expiscation' of Legal Principles. In Endicott T, Kristjánsson HD, Lewis S (eds) Philosophical Foundations of Precedent. Oxford University Press, Oxford

da Rosa de Bustamante T (2012) Teoria do Precedente Judicial — A Justificação e a Aplicação de Regras Jurisprudenciais. Noeses, São Paulo

da Silva RA (2019) A Nova Dimensão da Coisa Julgada. RT, São Paulo

de Camargo Mancuso R (2016) Incidente de Resolução de Demandas Repetitivas. Revista dos Tribunais, São Paulo

de Macedo LB (2019) Precedentes Judiciais e Direito Processual Civil, 3rd edn. JusPodivm, Salvador

Didier Júnior F, Fernandez L (2022) O Conselho Nacional de Justiça e o Direito Processual — Administração Judiciária, Boas Práticas e Competência Normativa. JusPodivm, Salvador

Didier Júnior F, Zaneti Júnior H (2019) Curso de Direito Processual Civil, vol 4, 13th edn. JusPodivm, Salvador

do Passo Cabral A (2007) O Novo Procedimento Modelo (*Musterverfahren*) Alemão: uma Alternativa às Ações Coletivas. Revista de Processo 32(247):123–146

do Passo Cabral A (2019) Coisa Julgada e Preclusões Dinâmicas, 3rd edn. JusPodivm, Salvador

Domit O (2018) Interpretando Decisões e Precedentes — Proposta de uma Abordagem Antiformalista Moderada sobre a Interpretação das Decisões Judiciais Aplicada à Metodologia dos Precedentes. Doctoral thesis, UFRGS

Duxbury N (2008) The nature and authority of precedent. Cambridge University Press, Cambridge

Duxbury N (2021) The intricacies of dicta and dissent. Cambridge University Press, Cambridge

Dworkin R (1986) Law's Empire. Harvard University Press, Cambridge
Eco U (2013) Confissões de um Jovem Romancista (trans: Pen M). Cosac Naify, São Paulo
Eisenberg M (1988) The nature of the Common Law. Harvard University Press, Cambridge
Ferraz T (2017) O Precedente na Jurisdição Constitucional. Saraiva, São Paulo
Garay A (2013) La Doctrina del Precedente en la Corte Suprema. Abeledo Perrot, Buenos Aires
Garner B (ed) (2016) The law of judicial precedent. Thomson Reuters, St. Paul
Gidi A (2007) A *Class Action* como Instrumento de Tutela Coletiva dos Direitos. RT, São Paulo
Goodhart A (1937a) Three cases on possession. In: Essays in jurisprudence and the Common Law, 2nd edn. Cambridge University Press, Cambridge
Goodhart A (1937b) Determining the Ratio Decidendi of a Case. In: Essays in jurisprudence and the Common Law. Cambridge University Press, Cambridge
Goodhart A (1959) The Ratio Decidendi of a case. Mod Law Rev 22(2):117–124
Guastini R (2011) Interpretare e Argomentare. Giuffrè, Milano
Hart H (2012) The concept of law, 3rd edn. Oxford University Press, Oxford
Hoffmann L (2012) Fairchild in retrospect. The Advocates' Q 39
Holmes OW Jr (1931) Codes and arrangements of law. Harv Law Rev 44:725–737
Jobim M (2014) A Técnica da *Distinguishing* a Partir da Análise do Julgamento do Caso *Escola v. Coca-Cola Bottling Co*. Revista de Processo 39(237):408–412
Jobim M, Oliveira Júnior Z (2022) Súmula, Jurisprudência e Precedente — da Distinção à Superação, 3rd edn. Livraria do Advogado, Porto Alegre
Kelsen H (2000) Reine Rechtslehre. Österreich, Wien
Knijnik D (2004) O Recurso Especial e a Revisão da Questão de Fato pelo Superior Tribunal de Justiça. Forense, Rio de Janeiro
Lamond G (2014) Analogical Reasoning in Common Law. Oxford Journal of Legal Studies 34
Lamond G (2023) The doctrine of precedent and the rule of recognition. In: Endicott T, Kristjánsson HD, Lewis S (eds) Philosophical foundations of precedent. Oxford University Press, Oxford
Lanes J (2014) Fato e Direito no Processo Civil Cooperativo. Revista dos Tribunais, São Paulo
Lessa G (2022) Precedentes Judiciais e Raciocínio Jurídico — Aplicação, Analogia e Distinção. RT, São Paulo
Llewellyn K (2008) The Bramble Bush — the classic lectures on the law and law school. Oxford University Press, Oxford
Maccormick N (1987) Why cases have Rationes and what these are. In: Goldstein L (ed) Precedent in law. Oxford University Press, Oxford
Marchiori M (2022) A Atuação do Poder Judiciário na Formação de Precedentes Definitivos — Experiências e Desafios. JusPodivm, Salvador
Marinoni LG (2016) Incidente de Resolução de Demandas Repetitivas. Revista dos Tribunais, São Paulo
Marinoni LG (2019) O STJ enquanto Corte de Precedentes, 4th edn. RT, São Paulo
Marinoni LG (2022a) Precedentes Obrigatórios, 7th edn. RT, São Paulo
Marinoni LG (2022b) Coisa Julgada sobre Questão, 3rd edn. RT, São Paulo
Marinoni LG (2023a) Julgamento nas Cortes Supremas, 3rd edn. RT, São Paulo
Marinoni LG (2023b) O Filtro da Relevância — do Precedente Ingênuo ao Precedente Relevante. RT, São Paulo
Marinoni LG, Arenhardt SC, Mitidiero D (2022) Manual do Processo Civil, 6th edn. RT, São Paulo
Marinoni LG, Arenhart SC, Mitidiero D (2023) Curso de Processo Civil, vol 2, 9th edn. RT, São Paulo
Mello PCP (2008) Precedentes. Renovar, Rio de Janeiro
Mendonça RB (2018) Raciocínio Analógico no Direito. Master's thesis, UFRGS
Michelon C (2007) Being apart from reasons — the role of reasons in public and private moral decision-making. Springer, Dordrecht
Michelon C (2011) Princípios e Coerência na Argumentação Jurídica. In: Macedo Júnior RP, Barbieri CHC (eds) Direito e Interpretação — Racionalidades e Instituições. Saraiva, São Paulo

Michelon C (2023) The uses of precedent and legal argument. In: Endicott T, Kristjánsson HD, Lewis S (eds) Philosophical foundations of precedent. Oxford University Press, Oxford

Michelon C, D'Almeida LD (2017) The structure of arguments by analogy in law. Argumentation 31. Springer, Dordrecht

Miranda VV (2022) Precedentes Judiciais — Construção e Aplicação da *Ratio Decidendi*. Revista dos Tribunais, São Paulo

Mitidiero D (ed) (2019) *Accountability* e Transparência da Justiça Civil — Uma Perspectiva Comparada. RT, São Paulo

Mitidiero D (2021) Superação para Frente e Modulação de Efeitos — Precedente e Controle de Constitucionalidade no Direito Brasileiro. RT, São Paulo

Mitidiero D (2022a) Cortes Superiores e Cortes Supremas — do Controle à Interpretação, da Jurisprudência ao Precedente, 4th edn. RT, São Paulo

Mitidiero D (2022b) Reclamação — entre a Autoridade da Decisão e a Eficácia do Precedente, 2nd edn. RT, São Paulo

Mitidiero D (2023) Precedentes — da Persuasão à Vinculação, 5th edn. RT, São Paulo

Mitidiero D (2024) Processo Civil, 2nd edn. RT, São Paulo

Monnerat F (2019) Súmulas e Precedentes Qualificados — Técnicas de Formação e Aplicação. Saraiva, São Paulo

Motta O (2015) Justificação da Decisão Judicial — a Elaboração da Motivação e a Formação do Precedente. RT, São Paulo

Oldham J (2006) Lord Mansfield, Stare Decisis, and the Ratio Decidendi 1756 to 1788. In: Bryson WH, Dauchy S (eds) Ratio Decidendi — guiding principles of judicial decisions, vol 1. Duncker & Humblot, Berlin

Pasqualotto V (2022) Processo Civil Comparado — do Direito Comparado à Comparação no Processo Civil. RT, São Paulo

Passanante L (2018) Il Precedente Impossibile — Contributo allo Studio del Diritto Giurisprudenziale nel Processo Civile. Giappichelli, Torino

Peixoto R (2015) Superação do Precedente e Segurança Jurídica. JusPodivm, Salvador

Pessoa P (2014) Legitimidade dos Precedentes — Universabilidade das Decisões do STJ. Revista dos Tribunais, São Paulo

Ram J (1871) The science of legal judgment — a treatise designed to show the materials whereof, and the process by which, the Courts of Westminster Hall construct their judgments and adapted to practical and general use in discussion, and determination of questions of law, 2nd edn. Baker, New York

Raz J (1999) Practical reason and norms, 2nd edn. Oxford University Press, Oxford

Raz J (2009) Law and value in adjudication. In: The authority of law, 2nd edn. Oxford University Press, Oxford

Schauer F (1987) Precedent. Stanford Law Rev 39(3):571–605

Schauer F (2009) Thinking like a lawyer. Harvard University Press, Cambridge

Schauer F, Spellman B (2023) Precedent and similarity. In: Endicott T, Kristjánsson HD, Lewis S (eds) Philosophical foundations of precedent. Oxford University Press, Oxford

Sherwin E (2023) Do precedents constrain reasoning? In: Endicott T, Kristjánsson HD, Lewis S (eds) Philosophical foundations of precedent. Oxford University Press, Oxford

Siltala R (2000) A theory of precedent. Hart Publishing, Oxford

Simpson AWB (1961) The Ratio Decidendi of a case and the doctrine of binding precedent. In: Guest AG (ed) Oxford essays in jurisprudence. Oxford University Press, Oxford

Stone J (1959) The Ratio of the Ratio Decidendi. Mod Law Rev 22(6):597–620

Sunstein C (2023) Analogical reasoning and precedent. In: Endicott T, Kristjánsson HD, Lewis S (eds) Philosophical foundations of precedent. Oxford University Press, Oxford

Taruffo M (2007) Precedente e Giurisprudenza. Rivista Trimestrale di Diritto e Procedura Civile 61(3):709–725

Temer S (2020) Incidente de Resolução de Demandas Repetitivas, 4th edn. JusPodium, Salvador

Theodoro Júnior H, Andrade É (2021) Precedentes no Processo Brasileiro. Forense, Rio de Janeiro

Viana A, Nunes D (2018) Precedentes — A Mutação no Ônus Argumentativo. Forense, Rio de Janeiro
Vitorelli E (2016) Devido Processo Legal Coletivo. RT, São Paulo
Wambaugh E (1894) The study of cases — a course of instruction in reading and stating reported cases, composing head-notes and briefs, criticising and comparing authorities, and compiling digests, 2nd edn. Little, Brown and Company, Boston
Wells JC (1878) A treatise on the doctrine of Res Adjudicata and Stare Decisis. Mills, Iowa
Zaneti Júnior H (2017) O Valor Vinculante dos Precedentes — Teoria dos Precedentes Normativos Formalmente Vinculantes, 3rd edn. JusPodivm, Salvador
Zavascki T (2017) Processo Coletivo — Tutela de Direitos Coletivos e Tutela Coletiva de Direitos, 6th edn. RT, São Paulo

Chapter 4
On the Road

The civil procedure aims to protect rights.[1] This purpose goes in a twofold direction—to decide the present case fairly and to give Law unity.[2] As in Borges's well-known tale, these two paths diverge and gradually develop their own rules. Each set out different ways of enabling a fair decision for the parties involved and guiding people in general through precedents. These procedures render a double discourse, speaking both to the concerned parties and, in the pretext of the case, to the legal system as well.[3] These two ends sometimes run in parallel: when deciding a concrete case, there are reasons that, reconstructed logically and argumentatively, give rise to precedents. Sometimes, they interpenetrate; concrete cases depend on the solution of identical or similar issues to those already decided. Here, the *ratio decidendi* is the subject of debate throughout the process.

Whether a precedent capable of resolving the issue debated in court is recognised, determines which route is taken to ensure the protection of rights. The "circuits"[4]

---

[1] As I wrote in my *Processo Civil*, "the link between civil procedure and the protection of rights comes from Italian law – the 1942 *Codice Civile* has its last book dedicated to *'tutela dei diritti'*. Although the expression has German inspiration (*Rechtsschutz*) – which reflects, in the relations between law and procedure, a general aspect of the Italian culture of the time – its legislative use was original and innovative, and legal scholars developed it widely. In Brazil, Marinoni started a tradition with a series of books – *Novas Linhas*, *Tutela Inibitória*, *Tutela Específica* and *Técnica Processual e Tutela dos Direitos*. After reading *Precedentes Obrigatórios*, however, I realised that it was necessary to add another dimension to the protection of rights – the general one. I have tried to do so in some essays and in my *Cortes e Precedentes*. In 2015, this idea served as a guide for the *Curso*, the *Manual* and the *Comentários* which I wrote with Marinoni and Sérgio" (Mitidiero 2024, pp. 30–31).

[2] Arts. 489, § 1, items V and VI, 926 and 927, CPC.

[3] This idea is gaining increasing acceptance: Marinoni et al. (2023); Mitidiero (2024); Didier Júnior et al. (2016). See also, Zaneti Júnior (2017); Motta (2015); Abreu (2015); Oliveira (2015); Robles (2021); Lessa (2022); Osna (2023).

[4] Oliveira (2018), p. 34.

D. Mitidiero, *Ratio Decidendi and Obiter Dictum*,
https://doi.org/10.1007/978-3-031-93152-9_4

taken—may be different.[5] This procedure may undergo, in other words, adaptations depending on the existence or absence of an applicable *ratio* for the solution of the case.

The recognition of a *ratio* may impact the right to the protection of evidence,[6] the duty to deny the claim on a preliminary basis,[7] the right to full provisional execution without security bond,[8] the duty of the rapporteur to try the appeals monocratically,[9] the right to *reclamação*,[10] the right to allow the extraordinary appeal and the special appeal[11] and the right to neutralise[12] or revoke the *res judicata*.[13] Obviously, whether the *ratio* exists or not—the need to set it, develop it, or overcome it—are all matters that require interpretation. Being a lazy machine, the text of court decisions depends upon the parties and on the court to do this job. Therefore, establishing an adequate dialogue between the parties' burden of allegation and the judicial duty to interpret the *ratio* is an essential procedural element of rights protection. For this reason, I suggest analysing how this can occur in the most important corners of the common procedure and the different floors of the Civil Justice in which its participants dispute the *ratio*, before considering what options are left when the parties reach the end of the road.

4.1 Alleging the *Ratio* and Deciding the Case

The classic characterisation of this procedure is an act of three people—a plaintiff who files an action, a respondent who defends him or herself, and a judge who tries it.[14] A process that originated in Bologna, it penetrated the Ordinances, before

[5] For an account of procedural lines and routes, Mitidiero (2024); Marinoni et al. (2023).

[6] Art. 311, item II, CPC. For a monograph on this, see Dotti (2020).

[7] Art. 332, CPC.

[8] Art. 521, item IV, CPC.

[9] Arts. 932, items IV and V, 1.011, item I, and 1.019, *caput*, CPC.

[10] Art. 988, item III, first part, CPC (on the impossibility of *reclamação* for the protection of the precedent outside the hypotheses of precedent portrayed in a binding precedent, *infra*, item 3.2).

[11] Art. 1.030, items I and III, CPC.

[12] Arts. 525, §§ 12 and 14, and 535, §§ 5 and 7, CPC.

[13] Art. 966, item V, and § 5, CPC (on the unconstitutionality of arts. 525, § 15 and 535, § 8, CPC, *infra*, item 3.3).

[14] Definition attributed to Bulgarus (1115–1166), *Summa de Judiciis* (1141), according to Picardi (1987), p. 102, vol. XXXVI. Around this idea, moreover, Alvaro de Oliveira suggested his definition of "procedural formalism" as "the delimitation of the powers, faculties and duties of procedural subjects, coordination of their activity, ordering of the procedure and organisation of the procedure, with a view to achieving their primary purposes" (Alvaro de Olveira 2010, p. 28).

arriving in Brazil.[15] Here, one can perceive the traits that formed its modern conception: a succession of acts that autonomously involve certain people in a contradictory dialogue.[16]

The deprivation of this basic dynamic is one of the shocking things about Kafka's *Der Prozess*; the absence of debate subverts the procedural aims. The right to due process of Law[17]—marked by the right of action,[18] the right of defence,[19] the right to be heard[20] and the duty of reasoning[21] exist to ensure the protection of rights. This is the traditional response given defenders of the *Rule of Law* since the transformation of the Magna Carta by Edward Coke into the basic piece of *Common Law*.[22] As such, the procedure must discipline the dialogue that unfolds as it travels along its road—for our purposes, this concerns the debate of the *ratio* by the parties and the court. It is the burden of specific allegation[23] and the duty of analytical reasoning[24] that seeks to meet this need.

A burden is an imperative of conduct desired by the legal system; the absence of performance does not generate an unlawful act, but a simple refusal to obtain the

---

[15] The idea that the procedure—the "*iudicium*"—"*est actum trium personarum*" was accepted in the Afonsine Ordinances (1446) (Book III, Title XX, § 1) and repeated both in the Manuelines (1521) (Book III, Title XV, title) and in the Philippines (1603) (Book III, Title XX, title). On the historical meaning of the expressions "*iudicium*" and "*processus*", with the appropriate bibliographical indications, Mitidiero (2019), pp. 43–44, 50–104.

[16] As I have already noted in my *Processo Civil*, "the procedure is an adversarial process aimed at providing adequate, effective and timely judicial protection for rights. Put in these terms, it is formed with the identification of the concepts of procedure and procedural acts in the eighteenth century, with the separation between Law and procedure in the nineteenth century and its polarization by the adversarial proceeding in the twentieth century. In 1748, Daniel Nettelbladt states that the procedure (the '*ordo*') consists of procedural acts ('*singuli actus*'). In 1767, he observes that the 'procedure itself' can be seen not only as a sequence of 'four phases' (postulatory, probative, decisional and enforceable), but also as a 'theory of procedural acts' (demand, summons, defence and so on). In 1868, Oskar von Bülow characterises the procedure as a procedural legal relationship ('Processrechtsverhältniss') in order to demonstrate its autonomy from the substantive legal relationship discussed therein. Having its own assumptions of existence and validity (procedural assumptions—'*Processvoraussetzungen*'), procedure and Law are not to be confused. In 1957, Elio Fazzalari, invoking the lessons of Aldo Sandulli and Feliciano Benvenuti, characterises and popularises the definition of the procedure as an adversarial process" (Mitidiero 2024, p. 100). I note that, to rebuild the birth certificate of the procedure in the eighteenth century, I used especially Nörr (1976), pp. 22, 32 and 43, and Denti (1999), p. 14. In the same vein, Robles (2022), n. 325.

[17] Art. 5, item LIV, CRFB.

[18] Art. 5°, item XXXV, CRFB.

[19] Art. 5, item LV, CRFB.

[20] Art. 5°, item LV, CRFB.

[21] Art. 93, item IX, CRFB.

[22] Who for the first time in history pointed to Magna Carta as the "*fountaine*" of the *Common Law* was Coke (1823), L2, C4, S108, 81a. For a contextualization, Corwin (2008), pp. 28–29.

[23] Arts. 319, item III, 336, 489, § 1, a *contrario sensu,* 966, § 5, and 1,022, item II, a *contrario sensu*, CPC.

[24] Arts. 489, § 1°, e 1.022, item II, CPC.

result foreseen in its exercise. As it does not generate an unlawful act, one cannot be compelled to exercise it, nor sanctioned for the absence of its service. The placing of a burden merely signals that a particular behaviour is expected. It is akin to a nudge—an incentive to adopt a conduct.[25] On the other hand, duty is an imperative of conduct required by the legal order. The violation or threat of violation generates an unlawful act susceptible to prevention or sanction. Consequently, one can demand the fulfilment of a duty by its recipient. A duty is a sign of the legal order that a particular behaviour is required. It is a tug—a constraint to adopt a command.[26]

The parties are burdened to allege the *ratio* in a specific way[27] and the court has the duty to face it in an analytical manner. The burden of specific allegation is reflected by the duty of analytical reasoning. In addition to being a work community, civil procedure is an argumentative work community.[28] In all postulations, the parties have the burden of specifying their reasons by connecting rules with their case, rendering vague terms concrete, illustrating the goals pursued by the principles and the solutions given by the postulates in situations of antinomy, and clarifying the due distinctions between the precedents and any need to overruling.[29] Just as the court is prohibited from carrying out a general trial, earmarked by a decision which is vague and disconnected from the specific case, so too are the parties when postulating in court.[30] As the procedure is symmetric in its dialogue and asymmetric in its decision, it is also necessary to recognise a division of argumentative work between the court and the parties in the civil procedure.

So, what does it mean to say that the parties have the burden of dealing with the *ratio* in a specific way in the action and in the defence?

The *ratio decidendi* aims to resolve both identical and similar issues. The notions of identity and similarity are its markers. The complainant alleges legally relevant facts to characterise its cause of action.[31] Likewise, the respondents must allege the

---

[25] With the appropriate bibliographical indications, Marinoni et al. (2023); Mitidiero (2024). For a monography on this theme, Gavazzi (1970); Azzoni (1991); Gometz (2008). Many debates on the burden occur within the scope of works on the burden of proof, its most famous example. On this subject, Paula Ramos (2018); Carpes (2017); Mitidiero (2020), n. 306.

[26] With the appropriate bibliographical indications, Marinoni et al. (2023); Mitidiero (2024).

[27] Controverting the existence of an effective burden of allegation, allocating it in the figure of duty, Aubert (2020). Its understanding within the category of burden, however, is traditional among Brazilian legal scholars: for a representative view on this matter, Dinamarco (2003), pp. 204–206.

[28] With the appropriate bibliographic indications, Mitidiero (2019); Didier Júnior (2010).

[29] Arts. 319, item III, 336, 489, § 1, a *contrario sensu*, 966, § 5, and 1.022, item II, a *contrario sensu*, CPC.

[30] Marinoni et al. (2023), pp. 433–434; Didier Júnior et al. (2016), p. 459. In *Bosquirolli v. IPERGS* (2ª Turma, AgInt no AREsp n. 853.152/RS, Rela. Mina. Assusete Magalhães, j. 13.12.2016, DJe 19.12.2016), the STJ decided that "there should have been, by the appellant, the demonstration of the possibility of distinction or overruling, in relation to the precedents established in the challenged decision (whether binding or persuasive), by confronting its determining grounds, arguments that should have been brought by the appellant. Interpretation of art. 489, § 1, of CPC/2015, which, *mutatis mutandis*, also translates into an obligation for the parties".

[31] Art. 319, item III, CPC.

entire defence matter, stating its reasons of fact and law.[32] *Rationes decidendi* are commonly claimed by both parties—who postulate either their application or non-application, extension, reduction or overruling. Although integrated by relevant facts, the *ratio* constitutes a legal rule so that the division of labour carried out by the legislator focuses on the facts, and the burden of proof[33] does not exempt the interested parties from the burden of alleging it. Those who wish to see it debated, interpreted and enforced have the burden of allegation of the *ratio decidendi.*

In formulating their case, each party may offer a set of claims that may be debated by the opposing party and must be examined by the court. These submissions—formed by the allegations of legally relevant facts—may be identical or similar to others already decided. Characterising them in a specific way means demonstrating how they conform (or not) to the *ratio decidendi* of the previous case.[34] It all begins, therefore, with the very signalling of identity, similarity or distinction by the party.

How does one do this?

First, by demonstrating that there is a precedent. It is necessary to identify a decision—or more—of a Supreme Court and particularise its essential elements, abstract the accidental ones and elaborate, based on its reasons, the *ratio*. When the issue at hand is identical, then this is sufficient. But, in the case of a similar issue, it is necessary to also justify the generalisation carried out—the party must legitimise their chosen category to gather the essential elements, and the level of generalisation proposed.

Identifying a decision to elaborate its *ratio* does not only mean indicating its synopsis, pointing out summulas, theses or even the name of a case or the number it received in a Supreme Court. Simply collating a range of decision synopsis does not support the identification of the *ratio*. In fact, this will thwart the objective. Therefore, it is necessary to resist such endeavours. It is a vastly outdated practice to stack cases in an attempot to reinforce the authority of a precedent. As early as 1673, the Chief Justice of Common Pleas, Sir John Vaughan, in *Bole v. Horton* noted, however, that citing "millions of precedents" is meaningless.[35] Hiding the *ratio*—consciously or unconsciously—among several synopses can only hinder the debate, stickling the individualisation of the issue, its proper confrontation and the adequate resolution. In other words: it does not collaborate with the right to due process—from the right to be heard to the duty of reasoning

[32] Art. 336, CPC.

[33] Art. 373, CPC.

[34] In the traditional dogmatics of civil procedure, the issue is a controversial point (Carnelutti 1936, p. 353). However, since my goal here is simply to particularise identical or similar points or issues for the purpose of organising the *ratio* debate in procedure, I take the liberty of using them as synonyms to facilitate communication.

[35] Allen (1939), p. 199 (which quoted the excerpt mentioned from *Vaughan's Reports*, p. 419). I note that the expression "precedents" is used in this passage as a synonym for "decisions" because it was precisely with Fulbeck and Vaughan that the distinction between decision and precedent (*ratio decidendi*) began to be drawn in the seventeenth century (*retro*, item 1.1).

Instead, it is necessary to provide context. It is true that, ideally, the synopsis should contain the summary of the facts and reasons that led to the decision, which could suggest the sufficiency of its claim for characterising the *ratio*. Like other syntheses, however, it does not exempt the particularisation of the case from which it originates: precedents, theses and synopsis only make sense in the light of the legally relevant facts—the "factual circumstances of the precedents"[36]—that serve to delimit their respective scope.

Thus, the second step is to outline the legally relevant facts of the *ratio decidendi* and relate them to the identical or similar issue already decided. The ability to delineate the identical or similar issue on which the postulation rests is essential for a rapid capitulation of the *thema decidendum*. As markers of the *ratio*, identity and similarity serve to indicate the result that must be achieved through the activity of comparison between the essential elements and abstraction of the accidental elements that make up the legally relevant facts.

To claim the *ratio*, the party has the burden of distilling into its essential and accidental elements.[37] These essential elements reveal the core of the case and serve to characterise the *ratio*; they are the facts that are integral in furnishing the precedent.

If the allegation is one of identity, then the party has the burden of demonstrating that the propositions are identical in relation to the facts considered in the light of the law, the legal positions of the parties and the things intended.[38] This is the formula of the material facts.[39] Moreover, the party must demonstrate that the people, time, place and value involved do not exert any influence to dictate a solution other than the one already given. These aspects are immaterial[40] and do not compose the *ratio*.

The relationship between the burden of allegation identical and similar issues characterised as that between *al sugo* and *bolognese* pasta. When dealing with a similar claim, the process requires an additional ingredient.[41] The party must still demonstrate the materiality of some facts and the immateriality of others, but they must also justify the generalisation that allows the assimilation of cases in a given category and the level of abstraction employed. The degree of generalisation determines the existence of similarity between the issues, allowing the application of the ratio—the "settled law"—to an issue not yet addressed. It is this generalisation that determines the extent of the *ratio* for the solution of the similar issue.

The party may be interested, however, in distinguishing one issue from another already decided, pointing to the need for its non-application or reduction of the scope

[36] Art. 926, § 2, CPC.

[37] *Retro*, item 2.2.

[38] *Retro*, item 2.2.

[39] I use the expression "relevant facts" (inspired by Goodhart's "*material facts*") for the sake of brevity: read, in fact, legally relevant facts.

[40] Same observation. I use the expression "irrelevant facts" for the sake of brevity: read, in fact, legally irrelevant facts.

[41] *Retro*, item 2.2.

of the *ratio* by introducing a material fact previously not considered.[42] The burden of denying the *ratio* is exercised in demonstrating that the essential elements of the issue decided and the issue under examination are neither identical nor similar. The factual-legal propositions, legal positions and things at stake do not embrace each other either on the ground or at any level of generalisation. In asserting that the *ratio* does not apply, the party proposes the distinction of the issues due to the lack of identity or similarity. The burden of reducing the scope of the *ratio* is carried out by demonstrating that, although the essential elements of the issue decided and the issue under examination are identical or similar, there is a material fact not previously considered and this is capable of determining a different result.

Alternatively, the party may argue for the need to overrule a certain precedent. In this case, the first assumption of the debate is in the allegation of an identical issue, whose solution given by the *ratio* needs to be reviewed. Again, the party has the burden of characterising the identity of the issues: it has to show that the propositions are identical in relation to the facts considered in the light of the Law, the legal positions of the parties and the things intended. Once this is established, the party must demonstrate good reasons to overrule the precedent.[43]

Finally, the result of the activity of comparison—the existence or not of identity, similarity or distinction between the issues—dictates the relevance of the *ratio*. A positive result suggests the duty of its enforcement,[44] whereas a negative outcome obliges one to push it away or restrict its reach.[45]

---

[42] *Retro*, item 2.3.

[43] As I have already said (*retro*, item 2.3), dealing with the overruling of the precedent falls outside the scope of this book. Yet, two or three words regarding the reasons that may justify it may be helpful. In *Superação,* I wrote: "overruling the precedent demands the demonstration of material and procedural requirements. From a material point of view, a precedent can be overruled when it is evidently mistaken or eroded in its normative coherence or social congruence. In this case, the principles of legal certainty, freedom, and equality no longer support its application. Overruling the precedent constitutes a traumatic event in the life of Law – hence the need to be seen as a 'last resort'. This explains, by the way, the constant allusion in our law regarding the need to consider the 'principles of legal certainty, protection of trust and equality' for the revocation of the precedent: seen as the last resort, only its evident mistake or its irreconcilable wear and tear authorises it. When in doubt, the precedent remains. In order to be overruled, it is necessary that the misunderstanding or wear and tear be able to overrule the reasons for safety, freedom and equality that fight for its maintenance. To overrule it, the mistake must be evident and the wear and tear, irreconcilable. If the interpretation is out of the frame, there is a clear mistake in the previous one, and it is possible to think about overruling it. The simple opportunity for its refinement, however, does not constitute a sufficient reason for its overruling. If coherence wears out, weakening the degree of their relations of reciprocal dependence and affinity, or if social congruence wears out, losing the ability to respond to social facts, it is also possible to think of overruling the precedent. The simple weakening of its bases does not authorise its overruling. From a procedural point of view, a precedent can only be overruled by the Supreme Court that formed it through effective adversarial proceedings and adequate and specific reasoning. Otherwise, there is a violation of due process" (Mitidiero 2021, pp. 57–58).

[44] Arts. 485, § 1, items V and VI, 926 and 927, CPC.

[45] Arts. 485, § 1, items V and VI, 927, § 1, CPC.

Once this claim has been asserted by the party, the court has the duty to face it analytically.[46] What does it mean? It means that it must be considered in a concrete, structured and complete way.[47]

[46] As is known, after the postulation is closed, the common procedure moves on to its organisation and evidentiary instruction before reaching the decision. Since I am, at this moment, concerned only with the debate about the *ratio*, I bought a ticket for a non-stop flight from filing to decision.

[47] My goal here is not to deal with the duty to state reasons for decisions in general, but only when the *ratio* is concerned. On duty in general, however, I wrote in *Processo Civil* the following: "to sentence, the judge must first decide. The judgment consists of several decisions regarding the meaning of the facts, evidence and law. It's clear, however, that it matters little how judges actually arrived at those decisions. The heart has its reasons which reason knows not. Trying to trace the judges' different arguments does not make much sense in legal terms, since the objective is to demonstrate only how their decision is linked to the law. What matters are the judicial reasons – the way in which decisions are justified. On the game board of ideas, you can see the passage from decision to reasons moving three squares forward. In 1961, Richard Wasserstrom suggested distinguishing between the context of discovery and the context of justification for judicial decisions. It's the beginning of the story. In 1971, Jerzy Wróblewski piggybacked on such distinction and suggested the distinction between internal and external justification, demonstrating that the propositions of fact and the legal statements formulated by the judge in the decision must be justified from the logical (internal justification) and argumentative (external justification) points of view. In 1975, Michele Taruffo concluded by suggesting the adoption of these concepts to draw the profile of the reasoning of decisions, scrutinising their minimum content. This led to a framework for grounding capable of accounting for the interpretation and application of law in judicial decisions based on logical-argumentative theories of Law. From this point onwards, assessing the decision's fidelity to the law and its rationality is linked to the *method* by which the legal reasons employed to justify the different interpretative decisions that the judge has to take to solve a case are worked out – that is, they still depend on the reasoning. It is from the reasons justifying the decision that it is possible to control it in an intersubjective manner. Not by chance, Chiassoni starts the *Tecnica dell 'Interpretazione Giuridica* addressing precisely the reasoning: interpreting and enforcing the law wear the same skin as reasoning. In a very Almodóvar way. It requires as its *minimum scheme*: i) the enunciation of the choices developed by the judicial body to, i.i) individualization of the applicable rules, i.ii) verification of the allegations of fact, i.iii) legal qualification of the factual support, i.iv) legal consequences arising from the legal qualification of the fact, ii) the establishment of the context of the links of implication and coherence between the enunciations, and iii) the justification of the enunciations based on criteria that show the respective rationality. The right to be heard and the reasoning, engines of due process, serve as beacons for the legitimate exercise of power. Brazilian Law, however, is not content with the minimum scheme. It requires concrete, structured and complete reasoning. What does it mean? Concrete: the case has to be tried. It is not enough: i) indication, reproduction or paraphrase of provisions, *without explaining their relationship with the case*, ii) invocation of vague terms, *without explaining the concrete reason for their incidence*, iii) use of grounds that would lend themselves to justify any other decision, and iv) enforcement or not of precedents, without demonstrating the *ratio*, subsumption, distinction or overrule. Structured: interpretation and application must be based on clearly identified facts, evidence and standards. Complete: there must be an effective dialogue between the reasons alleged by the parties and those used in the decision. This dialogue, of course, does not need to encompass all the allegations of the parties, but has to necessarily contemplate all those that are capable of, by themselves, invalidating the conclusion adopted. The metre of reasoning ceases to be only the judge's own reasoning and also becomes the activity of the parties. In other words: passage from the criterion of sufficient decision to that of complete justification. Brazilian Law does not specifically refer to the need for analytical reasoning in relation to facts and evidence, but this duty is inherent in the minimum scheme of the duty to substantiate. Judges will assess the evidence regardless of who

First, the court has a duty to concretely establish the claim. Both the issue decided, and the issue under examination must be delineated, at least in relation to its essential elements. This requirement ensures that the *ratio* is referred to in the specific case.[48] Second, the court has a duty to operate it in a structured manner. The logical-argumentative reconstruction carried out by the court for interpretation and application of the *ratio* must be exhibited step by step, as clearly as possible.[49] This justification—along with the universalisation inherent to the precedent—ensures the rationality of the decision. Third, the court has a duty to face it fully. The arguments made by the parties around the *ratio* need to be considered in the decision—at least those capable of invalidating the conclusion the court adopts of its interpretation and application.[50] This dialogue ensures the responsiveness of the decision in relation to the expectations legitimately deposited by the parties regarding the *ratio*'s vocation to resolve or not the issue brought to court.

This need for dialogue around the *ratio decidendi* does not exclusively affect the definitive decision of the identical, similar or distinct issue. Decisions facing applications for interim relief,[51] for example, must follow the same roadmap. Consequently, the *ratio* must be faced precisely, clearly and completely.[52] For the court to enact the incorrect enforcement (or not) of the *ratio* configures *error in iudicando*; this concerns the merits of the case. Whereas the court's failure to address the *ratio* appropriately is an *error in proceeding*; this violates the right to due process, specifically the duty of analytical reasoning of decisions.[53] The party too may fail to perform its specific claim burden of the *ratio*. In the spirit of collaboration, the judge may direct the parties to do so, reminding them to outline precisely what the *ratio* of the issue decided is and how it connects or not with the issue under examination.[54] A generic dialogue represents the failure of good practices expected by the legal system from those who participate in Civil Justice.

Additionally, the court may take different legal view of the facts debated between the parties. The court has the duty to enforce the legal order considering the allegations of the parties,[55] thus it is necessary to reconcile the principle of demand

produced it – the evidence is produced for the procedure and cannot be considered as evidence of the party – and must indicate in the reasoning the reasons why they interpreted each of them in a given sense or another. It is not enough just to indicate the evidence that comforts your view of the facts – it is necessary to say why the other evidence does not have the same strength" (Mitidiero 2024, pp. 214–216).

[48] Art. 489, § 1, items V and VI, CPC.

[49] Art. 489, *caput*, §§ 1 and 2, CPC.

[50] Art. 489, § 1, item IV, CPC.

[51] With the appropriate bibliographic indications, Mitidiero (2022a).

[52] Arts. 298 and 489, § 1, CPC.

[53] Mitidiero (2023), p. 117.

[54] This is a duty to disclose (*"Aufklärungspflicht"*), usually accompanied by a judicial duty to give hints and feedback (*"Hinweispflicht"*), inherent to the principle of collaboration, arts. 6 and 321, CPC—with the appropriate bibliographic indications, Mitidiero (2019).

[55] Arts. 2, 8 and 141, CPC.

with the duty to properly enforce the precedents arising from the *Iura Novit Curia* maxim, its requirements and limits.[56] But the application of the *Iura Novit Curia* brochure is only authorised in cases with no variation in the facts alleged by the parties in court. As such, invoking the *ratio decidendi* judgment not yet debated by the parties is subordinated to the maintenance of the same material facts. If the court cites an older or more recent case but whose *ratio* is the same as that debated between the parties, there is no variation from the precedent. Second, invoking the *ratio* not yet discussed for the solution of the case is conditioned to the previous right to be heard, under penalty of unfair surprise in the enforcement or not of the precedent.[57]

In sum, this is the basic dialogue that can and should occur around the *ratio decidendi*. Specific allegations, analytical responses, a fair decision of the specific case. Of course, not everyone can be satisfied. It is for this reason that the legal system established stairs between the different floors of Civil Justice.

4.2 Challenging and Trying the Objection

My paternal grandmother used to like making pumpkin jam. In my childhood, my mother would add pumpkin to the ground beef skillet. My wife enjoys pumpkin soup. Maybe someone can write a book one day—*How to Do Things with Pumpkins* (perhaps in the style of Austin or Twining and Miers). The decisions of the court are not unlike pumpkins: you can do many things with them. Perhaps not cook with them, but they can be challenge in a variety of ways.

Throughout the proceeding, a decision may be challenged in an appeal. If a decision violates a precedent—a *ratio decidendi*—portrayed in a binding summula, it can also be challenged by a *"reclamação"*. Despite a decision becoming *res judicata*, if it violates the *ratio*, it can be challenged by a motion for relief from judgment or neutralised by other means.[58]

I'll start with the appeals.

The most important classification of appeals relates to the different functions that each of the courts performs in Civil Justice. Appeals function as stairs, allowing the parties to access different levels. Interlocutory appeals and appeals for final judgment concern the fair decision of the case, a function assigned to the Courts of Justice.[59] Special appeals and extraordinary appeals seek to ensure the unity of law, a

[56] For a broad view on this subject, with the appropriate bibliographic indications, Domit (2018).

[57] Art. 10, CPC. In the STJ, *INSS v. Santos* (STJ, 2ª Turma, REsp n. 1.676.027/PR, Rel. Min. Herman Benjamin, j. 26.09.2017, DJe 11.10.2017).

[58] *Infra*, item 3.3.

[59] I mention the Courts of Justice (TJ) and the Federal Regional Courts (TRF), but the Regional Labour Courts (TRT) also fit the same logic.

function conferred on the Supreme Courts.[60] Internal interlocutory appeals and motions for clarification, are functionally linked to the appeals from which they originate, thus they are common to all floors.[61]

In lodging an appeal, the party has the burden of specifically challenging the decision they wish to appeal. This is a requirement of appeal admissibility.[62] The party may not simply repeat the claims they have already made in court. Although, if appropriate, it is possible to make use of them. Rather, it is necessary submit an

---

[60] I mention the Federal Supreme Court (STF) and the Superior Court of Justice (STJ), but the Superior Labour Court (TST) also fits the same logic.

[61] The division of Civil Justice into judges and Courts of Justice on the one hand and Supreme Courts on the other is quite common according to legal scholars: apart from my books—Mitidiero (2022b); Mitidiero (2024)—, those of the duo (Marinoni and Mitidiero 2021)—, and those of the trio (Marinoni et al. 2023; Marinoni et al. 2022); I also remember, for example, those of Marinoni (2019), Zaneti Júnior (2017), Alvim and Dantas (2018), Robles (2021), and Osna (2023).

[62] In *Processo Civil,* I tried to explain the distinction between deciding on admissibility and deciding on merits of the appeals as follows: "when I order pizza at home, the box comes with a seal. It says: do not accept if this seal is broken or something like that. The first analysis I make, therefore, concerns the possibility of accepting or not accepting the pizza (fortunately, I never had to send any pizza back). The second, concerns the possibility of liking or disliking its flavour when eating it. The distinction between admissibility and merits corresponds to the distinction between accepting and eating the pizza. In order to be able to analyse whether the appeal should be granted or denied, I first have to know whether it should be known or not. If it can be accepted, acknowledged, admitted, then I can analyse whether its claims are founded or not, making it possible to grant it or deny it, accept it or reject it. This distinction was consolidated by Brazilian legal scholar Barbosa Moreira – first with the publication of *O Juízo de Admissibilidade* in 1968 and then with *Comentários* in 1974. It is listed as a historical heritage. 'Every postulatory act,' writes Barbosa Moreira, 'is subject to examination from two distinct perspectives: a first measure aims to verify whether the conditions imposed by law for the authority to consider the substance of the request have been met; a subsequent measure seeks to scrutinize its grounds, to grant it, if well-founded, or to reject it, otherwise. (…) The term 'judgment of admissibility' is used to refer to the stage in which the presence or absence of such requirements is declared; 'judgment on the merits' refers to the stage in which the existence or nonexistence of grounds for the request is determined, drawing the appropriate consequences therefrom'. (…). The admissibility of the appeal depends on intrinsic and extrinsic requirements. The former concerns the existence of the right to appeal, while the latter affects the way of exercising it. The intrinsic requirements of admissibility are: i) applicability; ii) appeal interest; iii) legitimacy to appeal; iv) absence of extinguishing facts. An applicable appeal is the appropriate appeal for the objection to the challenged decision. One has an appeal interest if they can achieve a more favourable situation than that established by the appealed decision. The interested third party and the Public Prosecutor's Office have the legitimacy to appeal to the party. The facts that extinguish the right to appeal are the waiver of the appeal and the acceptance of the decision. (…). The extrinsic admissibility requirements are: i) timeliness, ii) formal regularity, iii) appeal bond, and iv) absence of a deterrent fact. A timely appeal is one that is filed before the final deadline. A regular appeal is one that is written in the manner indicated in the law. A bonded appeal is one that is accompanied by proof of the advance payment of the financial expenses necessary for its proceeding. The facts that deter the exercise of the right to appeal are discontinuance and the nonpayment of procedural fines imposed on the appellant. (…). Once the appeal is acknowledged, the merits must be addressed. The claims concerning the objection and the requests made – for alteration, annulment or improvement of the decision – must be analysed. Only the decision arising therefrom replaces the appealed decision" (Mitidiero 2024, pp. 257–263).

effective dialogue with the grounds of the decision they wish to appeal in order to demonstrate the error of its conclusions. Aside from this idiosyncrasy, the burden of challenging the decision obeys the same rules as the burden of specific claim. Depending on their interest, the party must demonstrate the identity, similarity or distinction of the issue and illustrate why the *ratio decidendi* does or does not apply.[63]

A failure to submit a specific objection to the decision may see the appeal not being entertained.[64] When appealing to the Courts of Justice, such non-performance entails the duty of the rapporteur to enable the amendment of the appeal.[65] It is treated as a curable defect, given the need to honour the examination of merits to the detriment of formal solutions[66] and the party has the opportunity to remedy this. However, before the Supreme Courts, the solution cannot be the same. As the extraordinary appeal and the special appeal are not erected in *jus litigatoris*, but in *jus constitutionis*, the possibility of enabling the amendment depends on whether the appeal is able to promote the unity of law, that is, to convey an issue with general repercussion or relevance. Only in such circumstances is there a right to amendment.

In the face of the disposition, the *ratio* plays two roles: a primary and a secondary one. Such roles regulate what the ratio can offer to the decision—either in relation to deciding on admissibility or in relation to deciding on merits. The role of the *ratio* differs depending on whether the appeal is aimed at the fair decision or at the unity of law.

In appeals related to the fairness of the decision, the *ratio*'s primary function is to serve as a basis for granting or denying the objection. It is, therefore, linked to determining the merits. The fact that a precedent on the matter exists or not, that it has been properly enforced or not, or that it has to be overruled by the court that originally set it or not, are all scenarios that touch upon the need to grant or deny the appeal. They do not prevent its admissibility. In Brazilian Law, access to the Courts of Justice by appeal or interlocutory appeal is not conditioned on an authorisation to appeal (on a "leave to appeal", as occurs, for example, at the English courts[67]) or on the particular importance of the issue under appeal (as occurs, for example, with the German *Berufung*, which can only be known in cases where the issue under appeal has a fundamental meaning—"*grundsätzliche Bedeutung*"[68]). Upon establishing the scenario for the admissibility of the appeal,[69] there is the right to file it and, once the

---

[63] For the description of identical, similar and distinct issues, *retro* items 2.2 and 2.3. For the burden of allegation in the action and defence, *retro* item 3.1.

[64] Art. 932, item III, *in fine*, CPC.

[65] Arts. 6 and 932, sole paragraph, CPC. On the link between the principle of collaboration and the duty to enable to cure the defection (duty of prevention), with the appropriate bibliographic indications, Mitidiero (2019), pp. 69–70 and 174–177. For a broad view on the subject, do Passo Cabral (2007); Scarparo (2013).

[66] Didier Júnior (2015), pp. 136–137.

[67] Andrews (2013), pp. 425–431.

[68] Jauernig and Hess (2011), pp. 281–282 and 291–292.

[69] For the appeal from final judgment, art. 1,009, CPC; for the interlocutory appeal, art. 1,015, CPC.

other admissibility requirements have been met, the right to its knowledge and judgment. These are appeals based on *jus litigatoris*, which aim to control the challenged decisions in all their factual and legal aspects.[70]

In the appeals relating to the unity of law, the *ratio*'s primary function differs somewhat. In addition to operating in the sphere of merits as a basis for granting or denying the objection, the *ratio* also operates on the sphere of admissibility.[71] Given that the precedent is an instrument to promote of the unity of law, the *ratio* plays a role of filtering the access to the Supreme Courts. *Prima* facie it indicates the legal importance of the challenged issue—and, therefore, is one of the requirements for establishing general repercussion in the extraordinary appeal or relevance in the special appeal.[72]

When the extraordinary appeal or special appeal deals with an issue identical to the other already resolved ("settled law"), the Court of Justice president or vice-president shall "deny the hearing" of the appeal if the objection is contrary to the *ratio decidendi* established in the STF or STJ.[73] If the *ratio*, however, supports the objection, it must "send" the procedure to a panel of judges that exercise the right to revoke it.[74] If the panel of judges understands that it is not the case to revoke, they "refer" the appeal to the Supreme Court responsible for its disposition.[75]

When the extraordinary appeal or special appeal deals with issues not yet addressed ("cases of first impression"), either because they are similar to another or because it is distinct (in whole or in part, due to the existence of a material fact not previously considered), the Court of Justice president or vice-president determines its admissibility, ascertaining the claim of violation of the Constitution or of the federal law.[76] If found, they must admit the appeal to the Supreme Courts.[77] If there are many identical appeals, it is possible to select one or a few[78] and suspend the others.[79] What gives access to the stairs to the Supreme Courts is the claim that there is no *ratio decidendi* to resolve the issue. The need to give unity to the law through

---

[70] Mitidiero (2024), pp. 239–246.

[71] For the extraordinary appeal, art. 102, item III, CRFB; for the special appeal, art. 105, item III, CRFB. For a broad view on the link between the *ratio* claim and the hypotheses of appropriateness of these appeals, Marinoni and Mitidiero (2021), pp. 154–163.

[72] For a link between the filters of "general repercussion" and "relevance" with the function of the Supreme Courts of giving unity to the law through precedents, with the appropriate bibliographical indications, Marinoni and Mitidiero (2012); Marinoni (2023). For a comparative law perspective, Giannini (2016).

[73] Art. 1,030, item I, subitems "a", *in fine*, and "b", CPC.

[74] Art. 1,030, item II, CPC.

[75] Art. 1,030, item V, subitem "c", CPC.

[76] Art. 1,030, item V, CPC.

[77] Art. 1,030, item V, CPC.

[78] Art. 1,030, item IV, CPC. If it is unduly suspended, an interlocutory appeal will be applicable (art. 1,030, § 2, CPC).

[79] Art. 1,030, item III, CPC.

precedents is what entitles the Federal Supreme Court or the Superior Court of Justice to their roles.

Thus, the function of the Court of Justice president or vice-president in the analysis of the extraordinary appeal or the special appeal differs depending on whether they are faced with a case of "settled law" or a "cases of first impression". This is due to the existence or absence of a properly established *ratio* for the solution of a given issue.

There is, however, a further differentiation in the cases assigned to the category of "settled law". When confronted with an issue identical to the one already decided, the Court of Justice president or vice-president makes a decision that goes beyond deciding on admissibility. It is not limited to "denying the hearing" or "sending" it to the panel of judges to exercise the judgment to revoke. In enacting these decisions, the Court of Justice is telling the party—it is deciding—that they are not right in what they are claiming (since the panel of judges decide according to the *ratio*) or that they are right in what they are claiming (since the panel of judges decided contrary to the *ratio* and, for this reason, needs to revoke). When the Court of Justice decides to revoke, and the panel of judges does not revoke, the president or vice-president refers the appeal to the STF or STJ so that the appeal can be examined.[80] However, when the president or vice-president decides on the party's appeal, declaring it in accordance with the *ratio* of the Supreme Courts,[81] the applicable appeal is the internal appeal to the same Court of Justice.[82] The asymmetry of the solution is evident.[83] In the first case, the jurisdiction of the Supreme Courts to analyse the appeals is preserved. But in the second, the appeals do not reach the Supreme Courts and the Court of Justice is the final say. As such, the only way to show that the *ratio* has been violated—for example, because the "settled law" was mistakenly enforced, contrary to what was estimated by the Court of Justice—is by filing a motion for relief from judgment.[84]

Why has the Code enacted a twofold break in the symmetry of the solution? Firstly between cases in which there is "settled law" and "cases of first impression" and, secondly, among cases in which the claim of violation of the *ratio* is in consonance or not with the "settled law", according to the Court of Justice president or vice-president's decision?

---

[80] Art. 1,030, item V, CPC.

[81] Art. 1,030, item I, subitems "a", *in fine*, and "b", CPC.

[82] Art. 1,030, § 2, CPC.

[83] It was to avoid such asymmetry—and the unconstitutionality arising from it—that Marinoni, Sérgio and I suggested that once the panel of judges indicated by the internal regulations of the Court of Justice has tried the interlocutory appeal (art. 1,030, § 2, CPC), it would be possible to file an interlocutory appeal in an extraordinary appeal or an interlocutory appeal in a special appeal (art. 1.042, CPC) (among other books, Marinoni et al. 2023, pp. 1183–1184). This solution, however, was rejected by the STJ in *Itaú v. Romano* (STJ, 4ª Turma, AgRg na MC n. 23.595/RJ, Rel. Min. Raul Araújo, j. 04.08.2016, DJe 12.08.2016).

[84] Art. 966, item V and § 5, CPC) (*infra*, item 3.3).

First, because it claimed—correctly—that there is no *ratio decidendi* for the solution of an identical issue as a cause capable of establishing the *prima facie* legal significance of the issue discussed in the appeal. In other words, it made use of the absence of "settled law" as an indication of the need to give law unity by means of setting a precedent on the issue. Suppose the issue has not yet been considered by the Supreme Courts, making up a "case of first impression". In that case, it fulfils the first requirement of the binomial relevance and transcendence that authorises the cognisance—from the angle of general repercussion and relevance—of the extraordinary appeal and the special appeal. Hence the breaking of symmetry is justified.

Second, because it assumes—incorrectly—the homogeneity of two scenarios: one in which there is no general repercussion of the constitutional issue or relevance of the federal issue[85] and another in which, once the issue had been decided by the Supreme Courts, the *ratio* was presumably respected by the Court of Justice.[86] Since the lack of general repercussion or relevance means that there is no right to appeal to the Supreme Courts, the legislator assumed—correctly, by the way—that, once the precedent was set, its interpretation and application would be the task of the Courts of Justice, which should be faithful to it.[87] The legislator presumed the conformity to the precedent.

The problem is that these situations differ.

The lack of general repercussion or relevance relates to the appeal admissibility. This, after having been defined by the Supreme Courts, can be enacted by the Courts of Justice.[88] But the "hearing denial" due to the conformity to the *ratio* constitutes a refusal to grant the appeal hidden beneath a guise of non-cognisance. The legal presumption of deciding, according to the Courts of Justice, is incapable of transferring the power to decide on the merits of the extraordinary appeal or the special appeal; this constitutionally belongs to the STF and the STJ, to the Courts of Justice president or vice-president. This presumption does not authorise the legislator of ordinary law to fabricate a fiction.[89]

Hence, it necessary to decouple the assumption of the non-existence of general repercussion and relevance to the law from the existence of the *ratio* for identical issues. In the first case, the Court of Justice—after declaring the absence of general repercussion or relevance by the Supreme Courts—may not legitimately cognise an appeal since it is a matter regarding the admissibility decision.[90] At the same time, the Court of Justice cannot definitively assess the conformity or not to the *ratio* in

---

[85] Art. 1,030, item I, subitem "a", CPC, analogously applicable to the relevance of the federal issue.

[86] Art. 1,030, item I, subitem "a", *in fine*, and subitem "b", CPC.

[87] Arts. 926 and 927, CPC.

[88] Art. 1,030, item I, subitem "a", CPC, analogously applicable to the relevance of the federal issue.

[89] Presumption is a rule that indicates something that usually occurs, exempting it from proof and attributing legal consequences based on it. The presumed fact may or may not be true (Wróblewski 1992, p. 166). Fiction is a rule that attributes legal consequences to false facts (Gascón Abellán 2004, p. 148).

[90] Art. 1,030, item I, subitem "a", CPC, analogously applicable to the relevance of the federal issue.

relation to the extraordinary appeal and the special appeal since it is a matter concerning the decision on merits, a domain designated by the Constitution for the Supreme Courts.

For the Court of Justice president or vice-president to be able to decide on conformity to the precedent in cases in which there is already a *ratio* formed, a constitutional reform would be necessary.[91] One would have to provide a fiction in the Constitution: that the issue already decided by the STF or the STJ with precedential force has no general repercussion or relevance. Thus, the Constitution would be fictitiously equivalent to both hypotheses, allowing the Courts of Justice president or vice-president not to hear extraordinary appeals or special appeals due to the absence of general repercussion or relevance in the face of the existence of a precedent on an identical issue. The appeal would be an internal interlocutory appeal to the same Court of Justice.[92] If the party remained dissatisfied, they could file a motion for relief from judgment.[93]

Until then, however, both the regime created by the illegitimate legal fiction of equivalence between the absence of general repercussion or relevance and the existence of a precedent supported by the legal presumption of conformity to the precedent by the Courts of Justice constitute an unjustified break of symmetry within the realm of identical issues—of "settled law". That is to say: such a regime puts at the end of the line the internal interlocutory appeal for decisions in accordance with the *ratio* (according to the decision of the Court of Justice president or vice-president)[94] and the interlocutory appeal in an extraordinary appeal or interlocutory appeal in a special appeal for decisions that violate it (according to the Court of Justice president or vice-president).[95] For now, the solution is to also send to the Supreme Courts the appeals dealing with identical issues that the Courts of Justice president or vice-president understood to be in accordance with the *ratio*, admitting the filing of an interlocutory appeal in an extraordinary appeal or interlocutory appeal in a special appeal after the filing of the interlocutory appeal, which increases the Supreme Courts presidents' jurisdiction to examine these appeals.[96] With this

---

[91] One would have to provide a fiction in the Constitution: that the issue already decided by the STF or the STJ with precedential force has no general repercussion or relevance. Thus, the Constitution would be fictitiously equivalent to both hypotheses, allowing the Courts of Justice president or vice-president not to hear extraordinary appeals or special appeals due to the absence of general repercussion or relevance in the face of the existence of a precedent on an identical issue. The appeal would be an internal interlocutory appeal to the same Court of Justice. If the party remained dissatisfied, they could file a motion relief from judgement.

[92] Art. 1,030, § 2, CPC.

[93] Art. 966, item V and § 5, CPC.

[94] Art. 1,030, item I and § 2, CPC.

[95] Arts. 1,030, items II and V, subitem "c", § 1, and 1,042, CPC.

[96] Marinoni et al. (2023), pp. 1183–1184. This solution, however, was rejected by the STJ in *Itaú v. Romano* (STJ, 4ª Turma, AgRg na MC n. 23.595/RJ, Rel. Min. Raul Araújo, j. 04.08.2016, DJe 12.08.2016).

adjustment, the *ratio* will be able to coherently signal *prima facie* the legal significance of the challenged issue for all who litigate identical issues.

In addition to this primary role, the *ratio* has a secondary one in such cases. This function, however, is the same on all floors: to shorten the route, to accelerate the decision. The existence of a *ratio* applicable to the issue—identical or similar—allows the rapporteur of the case to decide in a monocratic way.[97] The *ratio* enables the appeal to be denied[98] or granted after having considered in the adversary proceeding.[99] This decision is an internal interlocutory appeal for the panel of judges.[100]

We can now move to the *"reclamação"*.

I recently discussed the *"reclamação"* to argue that the 2015 Code took a road prohibited by the Constitution. In *Reclamação*, I affirmed that a *"reclamação"* is a claim aimed at protecting the provision of a decision, not the *ratio decidendi*. It is not intended to enforce compliance with the precedent. To do so would transform the Supreme Courts into courts of case trial control, denaturing their function of giving law unity. Moreover, it would be useless to have closed the door to the extraordinary appeal and to the special appeal through appeal filters and have opened the window to *"reclamações"*: the STF and the STJ would remain unduly buried in a sea of pages. However, to ensure we are not blind to cases of fundamental importance in which the *ratio* is violated and in which the right, if not protected, runs the risk of disappearing in the face of exceptional urgency, I suggested the applicability of *"reclamação"* for the protection of the precedent should only operate as an escape valve from the system. Although I recognise the legitimate concerns of the legislator, I argue that in rendering the *"reclamação"* a standard response to the violation of the *ratio*, it has deviated from its constitutional mission

In general, a *"reclamação"* only endeavours to protect the *ratio decidendi* when portrayed in a binding summula.[101] These are the circumstances in which the Constitution permits its employment. In this case, the *"reclamação"* seeks to enforce the precedent underpinning a binding summula which was either not enforced or improperly enforced.[102] The party has the burden of specifically claiming the *ratio*, identifying the issue and the need for its application or distinction—which here means non-application. Concurrently, the court has the duty to address the claim analytically.[103]

---

[97] Mitidiero (2023), pp. 107–108.

[98] Art. 932, item IV, CPC.

[99] Art. 932, item V, CPC.

[100] Art. 1,021, CPC.

[101] Arts. 103-A, CRFB, and 988, item III, CPC.

[102] Art. 988, § 4, CPC.

[103] *Retro*, item 3.1.

Beyond appeals and *"reclamação"*, the *ratio* can also spark a debate between the parties to neutralise or deconstitute the *res judicata*. The final and unappealable decision—which occurs when all avenues of appeal have been exhausted[104] and serves as a red light for *"reclamação"*[105]– is often the end of the road. But not always.

4.3 Vacating or Neutralising the *Res Judicata*

Despite the apparent finality of the decision, the journey of the *ratio* may continue in the motion for relief from judgment or the objection, in the motion to stay execution, in its own action or upon communication from the government in an administrative proceeding. These are different situations, with different effects, in which the *ratio decidendi* can be alleged to change the legal situation of the parties.

The objection[106] and the motions to stay execution[107] can enforce the *ratio decidendi* against the *res judicata* set to its detriment, but they are limited to neutralising its effects for the future.[108] In some regards, these are powerful tools, but less so in others. Likewise, alongside its own action[109] and the communication of the public authority in administrative proceedings,[110] the motion to stay execution can also neutralise the effects of the *res judicata*. But this also subject to temporal limitations; it considers a precedent subsequent to the establishment of the *res judicata* as sufficient cause to neutralise its effects *ex nunc*—without also erasing everything that, due to the *res judicata*, had been consolidated or guaranteed for the party before the precedent altered the state of law.[111] We are primarily concerned with the motion for relief from judgment. This aims to overturn the *res judicata* established when a precedent has been violated—which obviously already existed by the time it was established.[112] Its effects are *ex tunc*; it retroacts to erase the *res judicata* and reestablish the *statu quo ante*.

---

[104] Art. 502, CPC.

[105] Art. 988, § 5, item I, CPC.

[106] Art. 525, §§ 12 and 14, CPC.

[107] Art. 535, §§ 5 and 7, CPC.

[108] Marinoni and Mitidiero (2023), pp. 60–61.

[109] Art. 505, item I, CPC.

[110] Art. 505, item I, CPC, interpreted by STF in *União v. TBM* (STF, Pleno, RE n. 949.297/CE, Rel. Min. Edson Fachin, Rel. para o Acórdão Min. Roberto Barroso, j. 08.02.2023) e *União v. Braskem* (STF, Pleno, RE n. 955.227/BA, Rel. Min. Roberto Barroso, j. 08.02.2023).

[111] Marinoni and Mitidiero (2023), pp. 60–61. In the same vein, Marinoni et al. (2023); Didier Júnior and Cunha (2016), pp. 497–498. For a monography on this subject, Zavascki (2017), pp. 97 et seq.; Marinoni (2016); do Passo Cabral (2019); Oliveira (2015).

[112] Art. 966, item V and § 5, CPC.

The final and unappealable decision on merits may be rescinded when it manifestly violates a legal rule.[113] As the precedent is a rule,[114] a motion for relief from judgment for its violation may be filed. Both the decision that fails to enforce the *ratio decidendi* and the one that enforces it without considering a distinction between the issues[115] violate the precedent.

This violation must be manifest. Hence the party has the burden of demonstrating it regardless of evidentiary production. The motion for relief from judgment is not a tool suited to discussing the proof of the allegations of facts. Otherwise, it would be an appeal from final judgment with an extended deadline.[116] The party must start from the facts established by the *res judicata* to demonstrate the precedent has been violated. It matters little whether this has been debated in the rescinded decision. Pre-questioning or expressly treating the rule deemed violated in the rescinded decision is not required.[117] Rather, it is required that the party establish the precedent that is considered violated. This is the pivotal element of filing a motion for relief from judgment based on a manifest violation of a legal rule.

In claiming the manifest violation of the *ratio decidendi*, the party has the burden of demonstrating the identity or similarity between the issues—comparing its essential material elements and leaving aside the accidental ones. Here, this includes resorting to analogy—and the diversity of solutions adopted for both, demonstrating the violation of the maxim of treat like cases alike. The motion for relief from judgment is based on the failure to enforce the *ratio* when it is due.[118] If the motion for relief from judgment aims to point out the existence of a distinction, the party has the burden of demonstrating it by comparing all relevant elements that characterise the issues or of carrying it out based on the existence of a material fact not previously considered.[119] In each case, the party has the burden of pointing out the need for a solution other than that granted by the precedent that they claim to have been mistakenly enforced.

Once the violation of a precedent is claimed, either due to the absence of its application or its misapplication, the issue has to be decided through analytical reasoning.[120] If this violation is recognised, the rescinding court is established, paving the way for the rescissory proceeding.[121] Only one more hurdle must be

[113] Art. 966, item V, CPC.

[114] For a broad view on this subject, with the appropriate bibliographic indications, Marinoni (2022); Mitidiero (2023).

[115] Art. 966, item § 5°, CPC.

[116] Marinoni and Mitidiero (2023), pp. 184–189; Robles (2021).

[117] Cramer (2016), pp. 198–202.

[118] Art. 966, item V, CPC.

[119] Art. 966, §§ 5° and 6°, CPC.

[120] Art. 489, § 1, items V and VI, CPC (*retro*, item 3.1).

[121] Rescinding court is the one focused on the termination of *res judicata* and is bound by the hypotheses of art. 966, CPC. Once the termination request is granted, the rescissory proceeding, that is, the opportunity for the retrial of the case, if applicable, is filed (for a broad view on the subject, with the appropriate bibliographical indications, Marinoni and Mitidiero 2023, pp. 354–357).

surpassed: the violation must be current. It is axiomatic that a decision protected by the *res judicata* cannot violate a precedent that did not exist at the time it is rendered. One can only violate a precedent that exists at the time the decision is rendered. Besides that, there is retroactivity of the law, which is forbidden by the principle of legal certainty.[122] Nevertheless, the 2015 Code risked this logical juggling by admitting actions for relief from judgment based on subsequent precedent.[123] In doing so, it incurred unconstitutionality by way of violating the principle of legal certainty.[124]

By nature, the law is indeterminate;[125] it must be borne in mind that the Courts of Justice may have different positions on an identical issue until a precedent is established in a Supreme Court. In this case, the already consolidated situations—all decisions upon which the *res judicata* was established—up to the precedent establishment are governed by the *res judicata*. The established precedent will be valid for the *res judicata* and for future cases. It cannot apply to cases which are already finalised. The case decision has *ex tunc* effect, but the precedent only has *ex nunc* effect. To safeguard the *res judicata* established when the precedent itself was being established, the summula n. 343 from STF shall be applied, being insusceptible to a motion for relief from judgment.[126]

Thus, when a precedent is being established, there may be multiple synchronous judicial interpretations in the Courts of Justice on how a certain issue should be resolved. It may even occur that, at the same time, different solutions coexist within the Supreme Courts, without any of the bodies responsible for the unity of interpretation within each of these Supreme Courts—the STF Plenary or the Special Court or the STJ Sections—having analysed the issue. Any of these interpretations may even become final and unappealable, each one acquiring the protection inherent to the *res judicata*[127]

When there is an interpretative disagreement that naturally shapes the establishment of precedents, a solution guided by a logical-argumentative perspective—which presupposes the potential equivocity of legal statements—favours legal

[122] Art. 5, item XXXVI, CRFB. In general, Ávila (2014). In particular, Marinoni (2016); Oliveira (2015); Marinoni and Mitidiero (2023), pp. 183–248; Mitidiero (2021), pp. 44–54.

[123] Arts. 525, § 15, and 535, § 8, CPC.

[124] Mitidiero (2021), pp. 44–54. For the record, I'm including below a few paragraphs of *Superação*.

[125] Guastini (2011), pp. 39 et seq. For an application of this suggested description of the law to justify the binding nature of the precedent, with the appropriate bibliographic indications, Mitidiero (2023), pp. 53–69.

[126] According to the summula 343 of the Supreme Court: "não cabe ação rescisória por ofensa a literal dispositivo de lei, quando a decisão rescindenda se tiver baseado em texto legal de interpretação controvertida nos tribunais" ("A rescissory action is not admissible due to a violation of a literal provision of a statute when the decision being rescinded was based on a legal text whose interpretation was disputed in the courts"). For a broad view on the subject, Marinoni and Mitidiero (2023).

[127] According to art. 5, item XXXVI, CRFB.

certainty by consolidating individual situations. This protects the possible and, therefore, equally legitimate jurisdictional interpretations consolidated prior to the establishment of precedents. Its theoretical framework rejects the normative univocity of the text or a purely declaratory-descriptive function of the jurisdiction, thus one can neither assume that the rule has always existed nor that the consolidation of the prevailing judicial interpretation in the Supreme Courts must be imposed on all cases without distinction. The precedent must obviously be enforced in the future—and all final and unappealable decisions subsequent to its existence that violate it must be reversed or vacated in the appropriate ways. It should not, however, be enforced retroactively; such application mistakenly presupposes the existence of an intrinsic and univocal meaning of the legislation and entails a clear violation of legal certainty.

Therefore, two elements must be considered in light of this problem. The first is that a solution that preaches the retroactivity of the precedent on the *res judicata* denies both the legal language's polysemic nature and the jurisdiction's autonomy in its interpretation and application. The second is that this solution denies force to the *res judicata*, making its protection always depend on a future and uncertain event—the confirmation of its content by a precedent in the Supreme Courts. Hence, at a time of general legal order instability, due to both the absence of a precedent that delimits the meaning of legislative statements and the factual-legal context in which they could be enforced, legal certainty, whose protection is guaranteed by *res judicata*, must be individually respected. It is an objective protection, which depends only on the *res judicata* having been established before the adoption of a judicial interpretation by the Supreme Courts.[128] Equality is achieved through isonomic treatment given to all who are in the same situation—those who benefit from the protection of *res judicata* have their legal spheres protected against the subsequent precedent, while those without the protection of *res judicata* are subject to the force of precedents.[129]

---

[128] According to Ávila (2014), pp. 366–369.

[129] The line followed by the STF in *Metabel v. Federal Government* (STF, Pleno, RE n. 590.809/RS, Rel. Min. Marco Aurélio, j. 22.10.2014, DJe 24.11.2014) and the STJ in *União v. Metalgrin* (STJ, 1ª Seção, AR n. 4.443/RS, Rel. Min. Herman Benjamin, Rel. para Acórdão Min. Gurgel de Faria, j. 08.05.2019, DJe 14.06.2019). This way of seeing the problem comes from a precedential development in the STF that spans from *Carrijo v. Goiás* (STF, Pleno, RE n. 89.108/GO, Rel. Min. Cunha Peixoto, j. 28.08.1980, DJ 19.12.1980), in which the summula n. 343, STF, was for the first time not enforced in constitutional matters, until *Bancários de Rio do Sul v. Banco de Santa Catarina* (STF, 2ª Turma, AgRg no RE n. 235.794/SC, Rel. Min. Gilmar Mendes, j. 22.10.2002, DJ 14.11.2002), its application being resumed in *Metabel*. In the STJ, *Rio do Sul* follows in *União v. Freire Engenharia* (STJ, 1ª Seção, EREsp n. 608.122/RJ, Rel. Min. Teori Zavascki, j. 09.05.2007, DJe 28.05.2007), also deciding not to enforce the summula n. 343, STF, in nonconstitutional matters in *Franco v. Federal* Government (STJ, 1ª Turma, REsp n. 1.026.234/DF, Rel. Min. Teori Zavascki, j. 27.05.2008, DJe 11.06.2008) and in *União v. Dimon do Brasil Tabacos* (STJ, Corte Especial, EREsp n. 687.903/RS, Rel. Min. Ari Pargendler, j. 04.11.2009, DJe 19.11.2009), its application being resumed in *União v. Sintrajusc* (STJ, 1ª Turma, REsp n. 1.458.607/SC, Rel. Min. Napoleão Nunes Maia Filho, j. 23.10.2014, DJe 03.11.2014) and *Metalgrin*. For a detailed discussion of these cases, Mitidiero (2021), pp. 44–54.

As an alternative to a motion for relief from judgment, the effects of *res judicata* may be neutralised through objection or[130] motion to stay execution.[131] The assumption is the same in both cases: a violation of the *ratio decidendi*—which also needs to be prior to the *res judicata*. It does not matter whether the precedent is constitutional or federal: for the sake of consistency, both the violation of the Constitution and that of the federal legislation may give rise to the declaration of unenforceability of the obligation protected by the *res judicata*.[132] The interested party has the burden of proving the offence by specifying the issues that must be compared and their material elements.[133] But the effect that can be obtained differs. The actions for relief from judgment promote the restoration to the previous state, including—if that is the case—the possibility of refunding an undue payment, objections and motions to stay execution merely prevent the execution from being continued based on an unenforceable obligation.[134]

Alongside cases in which the precedent is violated by *res judicata*, there are situations in which the *res judicata* expires due to a subsequent precedent. This can occur in the realm of relationships with an ongoing agreement[135] via the application of the maxim *rebus sic stantibus*. The establishment of precedents constitutes a supervening right that changes the normative framework of the relationship between the parties. Its establishment acts as a barrier, preventing the effects of *res judicata* from surpassing it. Subsequent facts are beyond the scope of *res judicata* and must be treated in accordance with the subsequent precedent.

Generally, the legal system attributes equal value to the words of people. Consequently, it is not sufficient to merely state that the subsequent *ratio decidendi* applies to the relationship with an ongoing agreement so that the effects of the *res judicata* cease. Where there are differing views on the situation, a third party must determine whether or not the *ratio* grasps the previous *res judicata*. Therefore, if the party wishes to declare the ineffectiveness of the *res judicata* based on the subsequent precedent, the burden of filing the appropriate motion for such purpose—in this case, an action aimed at declaring the ineffectiveness of the *res judicata*[136]—is on the party. Once this stage is reached, there is no obstacle to do so through an objection or

---

[130] Art. 525, §§ 12 and 14, CPC.

[131] Art. 535, §§ 5 and 7, CPC.

[132] Marinoni and Mitidiero (2023), pp. 57–60.

[133] *Retro*, items 2.2 and 3.1.

[134] Marinoni and Mitidiero (2023), pp. 60–61.

[135] Art. 505, item I, CPC. For a monography on this subject, Zavascki (2017), pp. 97 et seq.; Marinoni (2016); do Passo Cabral (2019); Oliveira (2015). For a perspective of the Italian legal literature, Caponi (1991).

[136] Art. 505, item I, CPC.

a motion of stay of execution. If it is possible to challenge the *res judicata* contrary to the precedent with those instruments, it is *a fortiori* possible to cease its effectiveness in the face of a subsequent precedent.

However, there are situations in which someone's words are given precedent: where public authorities and its various entities encompass one end of the relationship. Given the presumption of legitimacy of their acts, the government in general—or the tax authority in particular—can set aside the effects of *res judicata* in the face of a subsequent precedent without the need to file an action for that purpose. It is enough to notify the party through an administrative proceeding, indicating the consequences arising from the enforcement of the *ratio* to the case and enabling their defence. If the party wishes, they may file an action to discuss whether the *ratio* was well interpreted, whether it is appropriate to enforce it in order to put an end to the *res judicata* or in order to dispute the intended consequences. But, once the legitimacy of public administration acts is presumed, the burden of judicial initiative for the debate on the *ratio decidendi* is inverted.

As we near the end of our travels along the memory lane of the *ratio*, we have just a couple more things to consider before our journey is complete.

References

Abreu R (2015) Igualdade e Processo — Posições Equilibradas e Unidade do Direito. RT, São Paulo

Allen CK (1939) Law in the making, 3rd edn. Oxford University Press, Oxford

Alvaro de Oliveira CA (2010) Do Formalismo no Processo Civil — Proposta de um Formalismo-Valorativo, 4th edn. Saraiva, São Paulo

Andrews N (2013) On Civil Processes — Court Proceedings. Intersentia, Cambridge

Arruda Alvim T, Dantas B (2018) Recurso Especial, Recurso Extraordinário e a Nova Função dos Tribunais Superiores, 5th edn. Revista dos Tribunais, São Paulo

Aubert E (2020) Impugnação Especificada dos Fatos no Processo Civil. Revista dos Tribunais, São Paulo

Ávila H (2014) Teoria dos Princípios, 15th edn. Malheiros, São Paulo

Azzoni G (1991) Cognitivo e Normativo — il Paradosso delle Regole Tecniche. Franco Angeli, Milano

Caponi R (1991) L'Efficacia del Giudicato Civile nel Tempo. Giufrrè, Milano

Carnelutti F (1936) Sistema di Diritto Processuale Civile, vol 1. Cedam, Padova

Carpes A (2017) Ônus da Prova no Novo CPC — do Estático ao Dinâmico. Revista dos Tribunais, São Paulo

Corwin E (2008) The "Higher Law" — Background of American Constitutional Law. Liberty Fund, Indianapolis

Cramer R (2016) Precedentes Judiciais — Teoria e Dinâmica. Forense, Rio de Janeiro

de Paula Ramos V (2018) Ônus da Prova no Processo Civil — do Ônus ao Dever de Provar, 2nd edn. Revista dos Tribunais, São Paulo

de Oliveira PM (2015) Coisa Julgada e Precedente. RT, São Paulo

de Oliveira PM (2018) Segurança Jurídica e Processo — da Rigidez à Flexibilidade Procedimental. RT, São Paulo

Denti V (1999) Sistematica e Post-Sistematica nell'Evoluzione delle Dottrine del Processo. In: Sistemi e Riforme — Scritti sulla Giustizia Civile. Il Mulino, Bologna

Didier Júnior F (2010) Fundamentos do Princípio da Cooperação no Processo Civil Português. Coimbra Editora, Coimbra

Didier Júnior F (2015) Curso de Direito Processual Civil, vol 1, 17th edn. JusPodivm, Salvador
Didier Júnior F, da Cunha LC (2016) Curso de Direito Processual Civil, vol 3, 13th edn. JusPodivm, Salvador
Didier Júnior F, Braga PS, de Oliveira RA (2016) Curso de Direito Processual Civil, vol 2, 11th edn. JusPodivm, Salvador
Dinamarco C (2003) Instituições de Direito Processual Civil, vol 2, 3rd edn. Malheiros, São Paulo
do Passo Cabral A (2007) O Novo Procedimento Modelo (*Musterverfahren*) Alemão: uma Alternativa às Ações Coletivas. Revista de Processo 32(247):123–146
do Passo Cabral A (2019) Coisa Julgada e Preclusões Dinâmicas, 3rd edn. JusPodivm, Salvador
Domit O (2018) Interpretando Decisões e Precedentes — Proposta de uma Abordagem Antiformalista Moderada sobre a Interpretação das Decisões Judiciais Aplicada à Metodologia dos Precedentes. Doctoral thesis, UFRGS
Dotti R (2020) Tutela da Evidência. RT, São Paulo
Gascón Abellán M (2004) Los Hechos en el Derecho — Bases Argumentales de la Prueba, 2nd edn. Marcial Pons, Madrid
Gavazzi G (1970) L'Onere — Tra la Libertà e l'Obbligo. Giappichelli, Torino
Giannini L (2016) El Certiorari — La Jurisdicción Discrecional de las Cortes Supremas, vol 1–2. LEP, La Plata
Gometz G (2008) Le Regole Tecniche — una Guida Refutabile. ETS, Pisa
Guastini R (2011) *Interpretare e Argomentare*. Giuffrè, Milano
Jauernig O, Hess B (2011) Zivilprozessrecht, 30th edn. C. H Beck, München
Lessa G (2022) Precedentes Judiciais e Raciocínio Jurídico — Aplicação, Analogia e Distinção. RT, São Paulo
Marinoni LG (2016) Incidente de Resolução de Demandas Repetitivas. Revista dos Tribunais, São Paulo
Marinoni LG (2019) O STJ enquanto Corte de Precedentes, 4th edn. RT, São Paulo
Marinoni LG, Arenhardt SC, Mitidiero D (2022) Manual do Processo Civil, 6th edn. RT, São Paulo
Marinoni LG, Arenhart SC, Mitidiero D (2023) Curso de Processo Civil, vol 2, 9th edn. RT, São Paulo
Marinoni LG, Mitidiero D (2012) Repercussão Geral no Recurso Extraordinário, 3rd edn. RT, São Paulo
Mitidiero D (ed) (2019) *Accountability* e Transparência da Justiça Civil — Uma Perspectiva Comparada. RT, São Paulo
Mitidiero D (2020) O Ônus da Prova e seus Inimigos. Revista de Processo 45(306):17–47
Mitidiero D (2021) Superação para Frente e Modulação de Efeitos — Precedente e Controle de Constitucionalidade no Direito Brasileiro. RT, São Paulo
Mitidiero D (2022a) Cortes Superiores e Cortes Supremas — do Controle à Interpretação, da Jurisprudência ao Precedente, 4th edn. RT, São Paulo
Mitidiero D (2022b) Reclamação — entre a Autoridade da Decisão e a Eficácia do Precedente, 2nd edn. RT, São Paulo
Mitidiero D (2023) Precedentes — da Persuasão à Vinculação, 5th edn. RT, São Paulo
Mitidiero D (2024) Processo Civil, 2nd edn. RT, São Paulo
Motta O (2015) Justificação da Decisão Judicial — a Elaboração da Motivação e a Formação do Precedente. RT, São Paulo
Nörr KW (1976) Naturrecht und Zivilprozess. Mohr, Tübingen
Osna G (2023) Recursos. RT, São Paulo
Picardi N (1987) I. Processo Civil: c) Diritto Moderno. In: Enciclopedia del Diritto, v 36. Giuffrè, Milano
Robles L (2021) O Que Significa Violar uma Norma Jurídica? Uma Perspectiva Processual, RT, São Paulo
Robles L (2022) Qual Origem do Conceito de Processo? Revista de Processo 47(325):63–69
Scarparo E (2013) As Invalidades Processuais Civis na Perspectiva do Formalismo-Valorativo. Livraria do Advogado, Porto Alegre

Wróblewski J (1992) The Judicial Application of Law. (J. Wróblewski trans.). Kluwer, Dordrecht

Zaneti Júnior H (2017) O Valor Vinculante dos Precedentes — Teoria dos Precedentes Normativos Formalmente Vinculantes, 3rd edn. JusPodivm, Salvador

Zavascki T (2017) Processo Coletivo — Tutela de Direitos Coletivos e Tutela Coletiva de Direitos, 6th edn. RT, São Paulo

Part II
Obiter Dictum: When Does a Decision not Decide?

Chapter 5
By the Side of the Road

5.1 Simply Chit-Chat?

The third bank of the river, *al lado del camino* [by the side of the road], *al otro lado del río* [across the river]—Guimarães Rosa, Fito Páez, Jorge Drexler. References to the margins are ubiquitous: an aside, a comment in passing, idle talk. For me, these represent the *obiter dictum*. True, they are not synonymous but can serve as a useful heuristic: an approximation of its nature.

There was a time when every decision was a precedent, and its value was merely illustrative.[1] There was no obligation to consider, much less to follow the precedent.[2] This lack of binding or even persuasive authority meant there was no need differentiate the *ratio decidendi* from *obiter dictum*; they simply did not exist. Only when the following of precedent was characterised as a norm in the seventeenth century that the *ratio*—the "law of the case", the "general principles", of the "doctrine of the case", as it was known until the nineteenth century[3]—begins to emerge.[4] Inevitably, its negation, the notion of *obiter dictum* begins to unfold.

The first distinction between the *ratio decidendi* and *obiter dictum* is attributed to William Fulbeck.[5] In his 1600 book—*Direction*—a rarity that I was privileged to see at the *Old College* in Edinburgh, Fulbeck noted that it was necessary to distinguish

[1] For a history of the precedent in the Common Law tradition organised based on its strength (illustration, persuasion and binding), Mitidiero (2023a), pp. 29–43.

[2] Mitidiero (2023a), pp. 30–33; Mitidiero (2023b), pp. 27–28.

[3] It is very likely that the expression *ratio decidendi* was coined by Austin (1873), p. 97. More on the theme, Mitidiero (2023b), pp. 29–34.

[4] Duxbury (2008), pp. 67–68; Duxbury (2021), p. 8.

[5] Fulbeck (1829) (the recollection of Fulbeck's name appears, for example, in Duxbury 2008, p. 67).

D. Mitidiero, *Ratio Decidendi and Obiter Dictum*,
https://doi.org/10.1007/978-3-031-93152-9_5

between the "principal points" and the "bye-matters"[6] in judicial decisions. This differentiation was alluded to in *King v. Melling* (1671),[7] tried in the *King's Bench back*[8] when Sir Matthew Hale[9] was Chief of Justice. However, it was two more years, before this distinction was adopted by the courts. In *Bole v. Horton* (1673), tried in the *Common Pleas*, Chief Justice Sir John Vaughan[10] distinguished *judicial opinion* from *gratis dictum*. Stating "an opinion given in Court, if not necessary to the judgment given of record", is not "judicial opinion, nor more than a gratis dictum", but that "an opinion, though erroneous, concluding to the judgment, is a judicial opinion because delivered under the sanction of the judge's oath, upon deliberation".[11] In combining these pieces, his judgement states that the *ratio*—or *holding*, the preferred term in the United States[12]—constitutes the judicial opinion and deals with the principal points. The *obiter*, "*gratis dictum*", in turn, addresses the "bye-matters".

Obiter dictum—literally, *saying by the way*[13]—emerges as the antithesis of the *ratio decidendi*. The *ratio* is the concreteness of the matter, the reason behind a decision. In contrast, *obiter* appears as lateral commentary, a gratuitous remark, mere speculation. Perhaps a useful tool to break up the solemnity of the debate but, in general, not something to be taken too seriously.[14] It is the *ratio*, not the *obiter*, that matters for consideration in future cases.

Its domains are demarcated by exclusion,[15] thus the *obiter dictum* map is drawn *pari passu* to that of the *ratio decidendi*. The *ratio* is a norm formulated from the

---

[6]Fulbeck (1829), pp. 237/238. Fullbeck dealt with the subject in the last chapter of his book (Chapter IX, entitled "What method is to be used in handling and disposing matters of law", pp. 221 et seq., specifically as "observations upon the analysis", pp. 235 et seq).

[7]Duxbury (2021), p. 22. At the end of the seventeenth century, in fact, several judges would already allude to the *obiter dictum* (Duxbury 2021, p. 62, footnote n. 246).

[8]The *King's Bench* was one of the central courts of Common Law (also known as Westminster courts), alongside Common Pleas and Exchequer (more on the theme, Baker 2002, pp. 17/22; Langbein et al. 2009, pp. 118–122). Next to the Common Law courts, there was also the *Court of Chancery* in Westminster, which had been trying cases in Equity since at least the fourteenth century. In the nineteenth century in England and in the twentieth century in the United States, Common Law and Equity merged into a single system. For more on the theme, Baker (2002); Langbein et al. (2009).

[9]Sir Matthew Hale (1609–1676), *King v. Melling* (1671) (Duxbury 2021, p. 22). On Matthew Hale, the introduction by Gray (1971), by Mathew Hale, as well as Postema in Postema (2017).

[10]Sir John Vaughan (1603–1674), *Bole v. Horton* (1673) (Allen 1939, p. 198).

[11]Allen (1939), p. 198 (which removed the passages quoted from *Vaughan's Reports*, p. 382).

[12]The expression *ratio decidendi* is traditional in English Law, while the expression *holding* is more common in U.S. Law (Atiyah and Summers 1987, p. 124).

[13]Duxbury (2008), p. 68.

[14]Cardozo (1991), p. 29; Leval (2006), p. 1263. However, it is a mistake to imagine that the *obiter* is always chit-chatting, without relevant legal effects (*infra*, Chapter III, item 3.1).

[15]Dorf (1994); Abramowicz and Stearns (2005), p. 961. I will return to the subject to discuss the attempt of part of the legal scholars to blur the boundaries between the *ratio* and the *obiter* (*infra*, Chapter I, item 1.3).

reconstruction[16] of a Supreme Court case[17] decision[18] in which necessary[19] and sufficient reasons[20] operate on material facts[21] to determine, in whole or in part. In seeking the resolution to an identical or similar issue,[22] the *obiter dictum* is everything that has not been litigated and decided. It is what remains in the margins, by the side of the road, across the river. But, as with the *ratio*, its territory is carved out by interpretation.[23]

So, how do we construct these contours?

The *obiter* constitutes a logical-argumentative reconstruction, its object are certain reasons and certain facts. *Obiter dicta*—it's plural form—are judicial statements embodied in factual-legal reasons which are *irrelevant* to the solution of a given issue.[24] The qualification given by the Court is the result of an interpretative activity, therefore, this indicates on the side of the river that a statement falls. Yet, this is far from being decisive.

If you read the opinion of legal scholars regarding the *obiter dictum*, especially from the United Kingdom and the United States, you will realise that a common assumption is that both the *ratio* and the *obiter* have as their object the *case* faced by the court.[25] This point of view, besides reverting us to the amalgamation of decision and precedent, creates space for unnecessary discussions about what constitutes *ratio* or *obiter* in the light of the outcome of the decision. This approach is akin to the brush strokes of an afternoon bath by Georges Seurat. The lines between the two are blurred, more malleable and, thus, more susceptible to surplus manipulation.

---

[16] It's worth saying: an interpretation influenced by many factors (Llewellyn 2008, pp. 5, 7, 13/14, 65 and 71), which means that the text of the decision is taken as a framework capable of providing, in the face of its competing descriptions, a normative prescription (I'm using the distinction drawn by Stone 1959, pp. 600–601, to stress the difference between text *ratio* and norm *ratio*) through its logical-argumentative reconstruction (MacCormick 1987, pp. 155 and 169).

[17] Ram (1871), p. 102; Wambaugh (1894), p. 29.

[18] I'm considering that what makes the precedent are not the very words of the decision, but its spirit—as Lord Mansfield observed in 1762 in *Fisher v. Prince* (Allen 1939, p. 207).

[19] Cross and Harris (1991), p. 72. Incidentally, it is a widely used test by the *U.S. Supreme Court*—for example, *Seminole Tribe of Florida v. Florida*, 517 U.S. 44 (1996). By the way, the *Supreme Court*'s decisions have been published since 1875 in official collections called *U.S. Reports*. Before, they were published in *reports* that bore the names of their curators, which were: (i) Dallas (1789–1800); (ii) Cranch (1801–1815); (iii) Wheaton (1816–1827); (iv) Peters (1828–1842); (v) Howard (1843–1860); (vi) Black (1861–1862); (vii) Wallace (1863–1874). A *Supreme Court* decision is cited by case name, volume number, curator or *U.S.* name, first page, and year (Helminski 2005, pp. 847–848).

[20] Simpson (1961), pp. 163–168; MacCormick (1987), pp. 179–180.

[21] Goodhart (1937), pp. 2–9, 22 and 25.

[22] Mitidiero (2023b), pp. 69–70.

[23] Mitidiero (2023b), p. 92.

[24] Abramowicz and Stearns (2005), p. 979.

[25] Among others, Goodhart (1937), p. 22; Cross and Harris (1991), pp. 39 et seq.; Duxbury (2008), pp. 58 et seq.; Dorf (1994), pp. 2041 et seq; Abramowicz and Stearns (2005), pp. 1065 et seq.

To reconstruct the justification of reasons in a more accurate and reliable way, we must start with the distinction between decision from precedent[26]—civil procedure's double discourse that provides protection to the rights.[27] We must also recognise that the object of the *ratio* and the *obiter* is not the case, but the *issues* decided throughout the decision.[28] Within the confines of facts of the case, the Court may restrain its analysis, invoking reasons which speak only to the needs of the litigants, or it may take the opportunity to resolve the issue being tried[29] in a broader way. But, the *ratio* is not limited to the dispute between the parties. Some reasons are unnecessary for the solution of the litigants' case but fundamental for the solution of one of the issues brought to court. The case decision must not be mistaken for the precedent aimed at the unity of Law.[30] Because of this, seeing the issue as the object of the *ratio*—and, consequently, of the *obiter*—constitutes a more analytical and manageable approach. The Court must decide the case but can take advantage of it to resolve issues that go beyond the interest of the parties.[31] This autonomy of the issue as a parameter of the *ratio* and the *obiter* brings greater accountability, transparency and

[26] Decisions resolve a specifically delimited case, which may involve a concrete or abstract controversy. What matters is that decisions always have a particularised object: they are either the facts debated in court in light of the interpretation and application of certain norms or norms abstractly considered. Put more simply: decisions can judge a concrete case or a law in theory. The aim of the decision is to resolve a subjective or objective controversy. In either situation, there is a specifically delimited object about which the debate is established, and which will be resolved with its *provision*. An order is formed over a particularly characterised controversy. Precedents do not solve a case. Consubstantiating itself in a discourse elaborated from a reconstruction of certain reasons, precedents aim to give unity to the legal system. While the decision resolves a specific controversy from the past, the precedent gives a general direction for the future. Some features of the controversy—certain aspects of the concrete case or the specific law that was abstractly considered—are of no interest to the precedent, as is the provision that resolves it. What truly matters are the *facts*—which function as *reasons*—that led to the granting of meaning to the law. The basis for reconstruction is the constant *justification* of the case decision. The precedent is meant to give unity to the legal system, establishing the meaning of the law in a given context. Following this line of reasoning, precedents do not directly resolve cases but only indicate which road leads to the destination indicated by the Law in the face of an identical or similar issue. In other words, the precedent is the Law itself duly interpreted by the Supreme Courts from a given case. *Legis interpretatio legis vim obtinet*" (Mitidiero 2023b, pp. 23–24). Also reminding us that the interpretation of the law is the law itself in Brazilian legal literature, Jobim and Oliveira Júnior (2022), p. 69.

[27] Mitidiero (2022a); Mitidiero (2023a); Mitidiero (2023b); Mitidiero (2024a); Marinoni et al. (2023).

[28] Marinoni (2022), pp. 183–185; da Rosa de Bustamante (2012), p. 271; Zaneti Júnior (2017), p. 329; Mitidiero (2023a); Mitidiero (2023b). By the way, Dorf (1994), pp. 2041 et seq., took the right clue when theorising the *ratio* and the *obiter* in the light of the *"issue preclusion"*, taking the theme to the terrain of the resolution of the issues, but ended up not following it until the end when relating the decided issue and the result of the solution of the case (in this same misconception also Abramowicz and Stearns 2005, pp. 1065 et seq.).

[29] On the Court's alternatives to solve a case and its implications, Marinoni (2021), pp. 139 et seq. In American legal literature, by all, Sunstein (1999).

[30] Mitidiero (2023b), pp. 22–24.

[31] Mitidiero (2022a).

efficiency to the performance of the Courts and greater security for the work of the parties.

Yet, it is common to find decisions in the Federal Supreme Court determining a particular comment on an issue is *obiter dictum* as it was unnecessarily formulated for the solution of the case—for example, when the Court grants a preliminary argument of the appeal but still examines the "background issue".[32] If the *ratio* and the *obiter* are discourses linked to the unity of Law, and if their object is the solution to issues, one must reconsider this stance. As the Supreme Court moves in a terrain that goes beyond the litigants' interests, the confrontation of the issues by the Court—if they have been litigated, examined and consensual by the majority of the panel of judges—is capable of generating *ratio decidendi*, not a simple *obiter dictum*. Confronting an issue which is unnecessary to the resolution of the case may be an exercise that does not affect the parties, it can give the Law unity around the meaning of the issue faced. However, this depends on the depth of the debate, the completeness of the examination and the consensus reached by the group.

If the *ratio* is formed by necessary and sufficient reasons that act on legally relevant facts duly litigated and decided, then the starting point for identifying the *obiter dictum* is the inverse—it lies in the irrelevance of the reasons for the solution of issues.[33] They may be irrelevant from a substantive or procedural point of view. In the first case, the issues are irrelevant when: (i) they are not legal; (ii) they are lateral; or (iii) they are very broad. In the second, when: (i) not litigated; (ii) not considered; or (iii) not decided by consensus.

I begin with the judicial statements on *non-legal issues* in a decision.[34] These issues are irrelevant because they do not concern the world of Law. For instance, debating in Court whether the Brazilian football team was at its all-time best in 1982, 1994, or 2002, can only be seen as uncalled-for.

Legal statements about *facts that are not being tried* (that is, those that concern what is *aside*)[35] are also unnecessarily formulated. As the *ratio decidendi* is linked to the facts of the case, *hypothetical questions*, formulated spontaneously by the Court, touch upon the side issues—facts which are not claimed or litigated.[36] But these to do not refer to the issues being debated and decided and are, thus, immaterial. It is worth emphasing: statements are irrelevant because they are unnecessary and do not

---

[32] Por exemplo, União v. Companhia Agro Industrial de Goiana (STF, 2ª Turma, AgRg na Rcl n. 25.832/DF, Rel. Min. Ricardo Lewandowski, j. 18.12.2017, DJe 07.02.2018).

[33] Duxbury (2021), p. 26.

[34] Abramowicz and Stearns (2005), pp. 1065 et seq.

[35] Dorf (1994), pp. 2006–2007; Abramowicz and Stearns (2005), p. 1074; Stinson (2010), pp. 230–231. Also highlighting the laterality of the issue as a distinctive sign of the *obiter dictum* in Brazilian legal literature, Motta (2015), p. 197.

[36] Goodhart (1937), p. 22; Abramowicz and Stearns (2005), p. 1074. This does not mean, however, that hypothetical issues cannot constitute a litigious object of a procedure and, in this condition, give rise to the *ratio decidendi* on an issue. For a broad view on this theme, do Passo Cabral (2023).

serve to justify the reasons why the issue posed by the parties was decided in the way it was.[37] They are peripheral.[38]

A good example of an *obiter dictum* concerning a side issue in the *U.S. Supreme Court* can be found in *Bakke* (1978).[39] The case concerned the admissions program at the *David School of Medicine* at the *University of California*. Allan Bakke filed a lawsuit seeking a place at the University of California School of Medicine, asking the court to declare its admission program unconstitutional. As a white man, he claimed he was not admitted to the program due to his race, thus the admissions process violated the constitutional clause of equal protection. The Supreme Court's opinion, drafted by Justice Powell, held—on a five-justice majority—that reserving sixteen out of one hundred seats for racial minorities violated Bakke's right to equality, which guaranteed his admission. Consequently, reserving a specific number of seats for those of a particular racial background was prohibited.

However, the court noted that it may be possible to consider race as one of the factors for admission to university education. One part of the Court—led by Justice Stevens—understood that race could never be considered as a factor for admission, while the other—led by Justice Brennan—decided it was possible, and even vouched for the constitutionality of the program.[40] Notwithstanding his decision to allow race as a consideration for admission, Justice Powell understood that the program designed by the University of California School of Medicine was unconstitutional in its current formulation, due to the reservation of a certain number of seats.[41] He also mentioned—as an example—that the program used by Harvard University, in which race was just another factor to be weighed, would meet the requirements linked to the equal protection clause.[42] This allusion to the Harvard program as an example of an affirmative action compatible with the *Bill of Rights* is an example of *obiter dictum*, as the program was not being tried in this case.[43]

---

[37] Leval (2006), p. 1256.

[38] Kozel (2017), p. 72.

[39] *Regents of the University of California v. Bakke*, 438 U.S. 265 (1978). This case was analysed in depth by Abramowicz and Stearns (2005), pp. 961 et seq. (an essay, by the way, considered by many the most complete account of the *obiter dictum* in American legal literature, according to Michaels 2017, p. 678). The significance of *Bakke* was debated at length in *Grutter v. Bollinger*, 539 U.S. 306 (2003) and in *Gratz v. Bollinger*, 539 U.S. 244 (2003). *Bakke*, by the way, was overruled in *Students for Fair Admission v. Harvard*, 600 U.S. 181 (2023).

[40] Justices Burger, Stewart and Rehnquist adhered to Justice Stevens' reasons while Justices White, Marshall and Blackmun adhered to Justice Brennan's (Abramowicz and Stearns 2005, p. 963).

[41] For a full analysis of Justice Powell's opinion, Abramowicz and Stearns (2005), pp. 964–994.

[42] Abramowicz and Stearns (2005), p. 965.

[43] For a discussion on the status of the *"Harvard plan"* in *Bakke*, Abramowicz and Stearns (2005), pp. 989/990 (*"obiter"*) and 1077 (*"ratio"*—a position, by the way, defended by Abramowicz and Stearns).

In the Brazilian Federal Supreme Court, the case of *Santa Cruz do Sul* (2014)[44] offers another example. As its indexation reveals,[45] the Supreme Court examined two issues: (i) whether the PIS constituted a social security contribution for the purposes of art. 195, CRFB;[46] and (ii) whether the regulations required by art. 195, § 7, CRFB, may occur in an eclectic manner—partly by supplementary law, partly by ordinary law.[47] The Court affirmed both: its *ratio decidendi* is that the PIS constitutes a social security contribution and that there is a right to immunity under the terms of the complementary law (CTN) and the ordinary law (Law No. 8.212 of 1991).

Throughout Justice Fux's vote, there is a "digression[48] " regarding "education and social assistance institutions", characterising them as "private entities". However, at this time, the scope of the expression "charitable entities" for the purposes of immunity from social security contributions was not decided. The case makes no mention of charitable entities, no allusion to health charities and no reference to charitable entities governed by public law. These aspects of the issue were not decided in *Santa Cruz do Sul*; it was not on trial, for instance, whether a charity governed by public law could benefit from immunity from contributions. The decision emphasises that it consists of an "incidental issue, pending in the Supreme Court, the definitive decision of controversies about the concept of social assistance entity for the end of the declaration of the immunity discussed, such as those related to the requirement (or not) of the gratuity of the services provided, the understanding (or not) of charitable institutions of restricted clientele and private pension organizations".[49] Knowing whether you are before a charity for immunity purposes is a bye-matter in *Santa Cruz do Sul*: a matter not decided.

Likewise, broad[50] judicial statements are generally classified as *obiter dictum*. Their extensive nature prevents a direct connection with the facts of the case and the solution derived from them by the Court.[51] It's worth saying: such statements are irrelevant because they are unnecessary and do not serve to justify the reasons why

[44] *União v. Associação Pró-Ensino em Santa Cruz do Sul – APESC* (STF, Pleno, RE n. 636.941/RS, Rel. Min. Luiz Fux, j. 13.02.2014, DJe 04.04.2014).

[45] Tema 432, STF: "tax immunity for philanthropical entities in relation to PIS contribution".

[46] Synopsis of the appellate decision, item 6. In the body of the appellate decision, vote of Justice Luiz Fux, pages 6 and 7.

[47] Synopsis of the appellate decision, item 14. In the body of the appellate decision, vote of Justice Luiz Fux, pages 14 and 15.

[48] Appellate Decision, page 11. He speaks on digression to characterise the *obiter dictum* in Brazilian legal literature, Pugliese (2016), p. 80.

[49] Synopsis of the appellate decision, item 21. In the body of the appellate decision, vote of Justice Luiz Fux, page 17.

[50] Dorf (1994), p. 2007.

[51] *Cohens v. Virginia,* 19 U.S. (6 *Wheaton*) 264 (1821), reaffirmed numerous times—as, for example, in *Central Green Co. v. United States*, 531 U.S. 425 (2001) and *Central Virginia Community College v. Katz*, 546 U.S. 356 (2006).

the issue posed by the parties was decided in the way it was.[52] They are simply too vague.[53]

This type of remarks are often found in attempts to solve issues by invoking theories of justice—for example, those of Aristotle, Kant, Rawls, or Dworkin. Judicial reasoning that draws upon these theories does not automatically convert them into *rationes decidendi;* they may only be incorporated if they specifically resolve the issue faced.[54] This utilisation must establish a direct link between the proposition and the resolved issue. Beyond this, very general considerations, such as those normally elaborated by philosophers on justice, are only welcome at the *obiter's* table. The same logic applies to the views of legal scholars' that are cited in the reasons for judicial decisions.[55]

Whilst it may be relatively simple to catalogue a side issue as *obiter dictum*, this is not always the case when faced with a broad statement.[56] Consider, for example, the cases of *Roe* (1973)[57] and *Casey* (1992),[58] tried by the *U.S. Supreme Court*—in fact, later overruled by *Dobbs* (2022).[59] Jane Roe, a pseudonym for a pregnant woman, filed a lawsuit seeking permission to have an abortion outside the only parameters permitted under Texas law—to preserve the pregnant woman's life. In addition to declaring it unconstitutional, the Court took the opportunity to formulate the well-known three-trimester rule. In the first trimester, the decision on whether or not to abort is the woman's, based on the right to privacy,[60] and the State cannot prevent it. In the second, considering the health of the pregnant woman, she can, if she wants, regulate the right to abortion. In the third, in order to protect the potential right to life, the State may, willingly, regulate and even prohibit the right to abortion, except when necessary, according to adequate medical evaluation, to preserve the life or health of the pregnant woman.[61] *Roe* was reaffirmed in *Thornburgh* (1982),[62] *Akron* (1983),[63] and *Webster* (1989).[64]

---

[52] Leval (2006), p. 1256.

[53] Kozel (2017), p. 72.

[54] Abramowicz and Stearns (2005), p. 1071.

[55] Leval (2006), pp. 1267–1268.

[56] Michaels (2017), pp. 663 et seq., proposing a critical dialogue with Dorf (1994).

[57] *Roe v. Wade*, 410 U.S. 113 (1973).

[58] *Planned Parenthood of Southeastern Pennsylvania v. Casey*, 505 U.S. 833 (1992).

[59] *Dobbs v. Jackson Women's Health Organization*, 597 U.S. 215 (2022).

[60] Right to privacy, guaranteed by the due process clause, incidentally, which had already upheld the right of married persons to purchase and use contraceptive methods in *Griswold v. Connecticut*, 381 U.S. 479 (1965), later extended to unmarried persons in *Eisenstadt v. Baird*, 405, U.S. 438 (1972).

[61] For a summary of the case, Abramowicz and Stearns (2005), pp. 1078/1084.

[62] *Thornburgh v. American College of Obstetricians & Gynecologists*, 476 U.S. 747 (1982).

[63] *Akron v. Akron Center for Reproductive Health*, 462 U.S. 416 (1983).

[64] *Webster v. Reproductive Health Services*, 492 U.S. 490 (1989). Although *Webster* reaffirmed *Roe*, the Court declared constitutional the Missouri's legislation that imposed restrictions on the use of funds, facilities, and public officials to perform, assist, or counsel an abortion. For this reason, Michael Dorf sees in *Webster* a weakening of *Roe*'s *ratio*, notably by how Chief Justice Rehnquist described it (simple unconstitutionality of Texas legislation, without any allusion to the three-trimester rule) (Dorf 1994, p. 2008).

Given *Roe's* resolution, in *Casey*, *Planned Parenthood* brought action against certain provisions of the *Pennsylvania Abortion Control Act* of 1982—the need for consent from the husband, an informed consent, a twenty-four-hour waiting period, and, for minors, parental consent. In its decision, the Court stated that *Roe*'s *ratio decidendi* is limited to granting the right to abortion before the viability of the foetus' life outside the pregnant woman. The need for the husband's consent causes an undue burden for the married woman and was thus held to be unconstitutional. All other requirements were found to be constitutional. The identification of *Roe*'s *ratio* was necessary as there was no direct connection between the considerations made and the facts tried in the case.[65] But, in deciding *Casey*, the Court abandoned *Roe*'s three-trimester rule in favour of a more flexible one, thus allowing greater state regulation of the right to abortion. By limiting *Roe*'s *ratio* only to the unconstitutionality of Texas legislation, *Casey* relegated the three-trimester rule in the *obiter* drawer. It was considered unnecessary—without adherence, spare, too broad—for the solution of the facts alleged in *Roe*. Some legal scholars would contend that this serves as an example of a very broad statement.[66]

Many of the problems in differentiating the *ratio* from the *obiter* lie here—what degree a of breadth is sufficient to move a statement from one zone to another[67]? When examining the scope of the *ratio* for solving identical issues, everything outside the essential identity is *obiter*. The borders are (relatively) easy to identify. However, when determining the degree of generalisation sufficient to extend the *ratio* to resolve a similar issue, one must first define what the relevant similarities are. Only when this is complete can we know whether a statement goes beyond the parameters of the *ratio*.[68] Just as distinguishing identical issues from similar issues is essential to determining the *ratio*'s function, so too is it to understanding *obiter*'s behaviour. Careful attention must be paid to the steps to do so.

---

[65] For a summary of the case, Re (2014), pp. 1895–1897.

[66] Dorf (1994), pp. 2007–2008.

[67] It is Julius Stone's classical question, Stone (1946), pp. 187–189; Stone (1959), pp. 604–604, taken up, among several others, by Schauer (1987), pp. 576 et seq.; Schauer (2009), pp. 36 et seq.; Bayern (2009), p. 148; Michaels (2017), pp. 663 et seq.

[68] In my *Ratio* I proposed the following definition of identical issues: "identical issues are issues in which, abstracting one or all of the people involved, the value, time and place of the facts, there is normative congruence between all its essential elements, that is, its legally relevant elements. The *ratio* formed on an identical issue already judged serves as a precedent for another pending approval by means of subsumption. The identical issue is an issue already decided – it constitutes settled law'. As no issue is identical to the other, the matter of legal identity turns out to be a matter of abstraction of accidental elements and congruence among essential elements. It is an essential identity matter. Similar issues are issues in which, having abstracted their accidental elements, there is normative congruence at a certain level of generalisation among their essential elements. The *ratio* formed on the similar issue already tried serves as a precedent for another that is pending analysis, once having defined the level of generalisation in which they are in tune by means of analogy. The similar issue is not one already decided. It is a new issue, however close to the one already resolved—it constitutes a "case of first impression". The matter of legal similarity becomes, therefore, a matter of abstraction of accidental elements and congruence among essential elements at a certain level of generalisation. It is a matter of *relevant similarity*", Mitidiero (2023b).

Statements made as *obiter dicta*, in addition to being characterised by a substantive perspective (non-legal, lateral or very broad), can be denoted by a procedural one. If the *ratio* requires an issue decided by unanimity or by the majority of the panel,[69] then issues not litigated, not considered or not decided consensually can only draw up a seat at the *obiter dictum* table.

I start with the *non-litigated* issues, that is, with those that were not the object of the adversary proceeding between the parties and the Court.[70] The right to adversary proceedings is the most basic condition of a system concerned with the democratic administration of Justice.[71] From the core of the *due process*,[72] the substantial elements of the *ordo iudiciarius*[73] to the fundamental norms of the 2015 Code,[74] effective dialogue around the issues contended between the parties and the Court is always required.[75] In its creation of a path that signals the adversary proceeding within the Supreme Courts,[76] the 2015 Code prescribed this as a necessary condition in the formation of the *ratio*. Every decision must be preceded by an adversary proceeding.[77] Consequently, an issue that is not thoroughly debated by the parties in court ("investigated with care"[78]) cannot appear in the *ratio decidendi*. An issue which lacks this is, therefore, automatically relegated to the status of *obiter dictum*. Ideally, such debate—the absence of which renders the *ratio* formation unfeasible and pushes the issue to the *obiter* terrain—can mobilise society as a whole by considering the grounds brought to the Court by the *amici curiae* and the technical knowledge produced by experts in the field in public hearings.[79]

Even if litigated, some issues may not have been thoroughly considered and determined ("considered in its full extent"[80]). They may have only been mentioned

---

[69] Mitidiero (2023a), pp. 100–103; Mitidiero (2023b), pp. 69–85.

[70] Leval (2006), p. 1255.

[71] Millar (1923), p. 4; Calamandrei (1965), p. 678; Taruffo (1975), p. 407.

[72] Goodhart (1966).

[73] Nörr (1976), pp. 6/7.

[74] Mitidiero (2024a).

[75] Arts. 5, item LV, CRFB, and 9, 10, 485, § 1, item IV, and 1.022, item II, CPC.

[76] Arts. 1.035, § 4°, 1.036, § 6°, 1.037, item I, 1.038, items I, II and III, and § 3°, CPC. As you know, these provisions were designed for the regime of general repercussion and multiple appeals on the same point of law, but must be interpreted as requirements for forming and overruling precedents as a whole—that is, as a kind of instruction manual for the performance of the Supreme Courts—Marinoni and Mitidiero (2021), pp. 245–247; Mitidiero (2024a). By the way, they are obviously applicable to relevance, whose destiny is to supersede the repetitive appeals in the Superior Court of Justice (Mitidiero 2022b, pp. 116–117).

[77] Including all its elements, under penalty of undue surprise (arts. 5, item LV, CRFB, and 10, CPC – *INSS v. Santos*, STJ, 2ª Turma, REsp n. 1.676.027/PR, Rel. Min. Herman Benjamin, j. 26.09.2017, DJe 11.10.2017).

[78] *Cohens v. Virginia*, 19 U.S. (6 *Wheaton*) 264 (1821). In the same vein, Schauer (2008), pp. 1954/1955.

[79] Art. 1.038, items I and II, CPC.

[80] *Cohens v. Virginia*, 19 U.S. (6 *Wheaton*) 264 (1821).

within a decision, perhaps merely as a question, but lack an answer.[81] Some issues may have been considered, or even debated in Court, but not determined. In the absence of a decision, commentary about an issue can only be *obiter dictum*. The same logic applies if the issue, although litigated and decided, was not grounded—accompanied by reasons capable of justifying it. Moreover, if the reasons supporting the decision on the issue were not endorsed by at least the majority, its incorporation into the *ratio decidendi* cannot be justified. The *ratio* depends on adherence to the reasoning based on which a given issue was resolved. It does not matter whether an appeal was decided in this or that sense—what matters is whether the members of the panel faced and decided, with the same reasons, the issue examined unanimously or by the majority. If the courts, or at least its majority, does not adhere to the same reasoning, the issue must remain in the realm of *obiter dictum*.[82]

The absence of consideration, a debate or a decision indicates that a comment on an issue was made without due care ("completely investigated"[83]). This identifies it as *obiter*. Indeed, *Cohens* (1821)[84] determined everything that if is not properly debated, considered and decided is usually classified as *obiter*.[85] Its famous passage by Chief of Justice John Marshall states: "it is a maxim, not to be disregarded, that general expressions, in every opinion, are to be taken in connection with the case in which those expressions are used. If they go beyond the case, they may be respected, but ought not to control the judgment in a subsequent suit, when the very point is presented for decision. The reasoning behind this is obvious. The issue actually before the court is investigated with care, and considered in its full extent. Other principles which may serve to illustrate it, are considered in their relation to the case decided, but their possible bearing on all other cases is seldom completely investigated".[86] Consequently, the *obiter* does not hold the same prestige as the *ratio* ("may be respected, but ought not to control the judgment in a subsequent suit"), because it comes for free—one need not work for it.[87]

Court decisions do not come with an instruction manual.[88] Even if they did, I know few who would actually trouble themselves to read it (and I am not one of them). But, even if such a manual were provided, we are still presented with a

[81] Abramowicz and Stearns (2005), pp. 1065 et seq.

[82] Mitidiero (2023a); Mitidiero (2023b).

[83] *Cohens v. Virginia*, 19 U.S. (6 *Wheaton*) 264 (1821).

[84] *Cohens v. Virginia*, 19 U.S. (6 *Wheaton*) 264 (1821), reaffirmed—for instance—in *Green* (2001) and *Katz* (2006).

[85] Dorf (1994); Stinson (2010), pp. 225–228. Prior and detained debate, careful and thorough consideration and reasoned decision, therefore, are "procedural rule of law safeguards" (Killian 2013, pp. 3–7) for the definition or exclusion of the issue as part of the *ratio decidendi* or the *obiter dictum*, functioning as tests for proper interpretation and enforcement of the law.

[86] *Cohens v. Virginia*, 19 U.S. (6 *Wheaton*) 264 (1821).

[87] Leval (2006), p. 1263; Stinson (2010), p. 219. It's worth saying: the *obiter dictum* focuses on an issue that was not "completely investigated with care" and "considered in its full extent"—that's why it comes cheap. The mechanism of the case—the adversary proceeding and the grounds—did not charge the *obiter*.

[88] Abramowicz and Stearns (2005), p. 955.

problem. Court texts are lazy machines[89]—they require interpretation. Courts may appear to signal the *ratio*—and, indirectly, the *obiter*—with expressions such as "*we hold*",[90] summarising it in legal interpretations[91] or expressly using these labels. However, these are not conclusive. *Camargo* (2023)[92] offers a Federal Supreme Court example of express labelling. During the trial of the extraordinary appeal, the object of which was the constitutionality of the SENAR contribution, the Court—citing the *Dois Irmãos* case (1992)[93]—framed it as a general social contribution. When considering the second motion for clarification opposed to the decision,[94] the allusion to *Dois Irmãos* was suppressed and expressly labelled as *obiter dictum.*[95] Yet, interpreters would be nonetheless required to analyse which bank of the river the statements about the issues are located.

To know if a statement is *obiter*, one must interpret the decision to assess whether the issue on which it focuses is: (i) legal or not; (ii) central or lateral; (iii) adherent or very broad, and also examine whether or not it was: (i) previously and thoroughly debated; (ii) carefully considered; and (iii) duly decided and grounded. Statements on non-legal, lateral or very broad issues, not subject to prior and detained debate, careful consideration or grounded decision by unanimity or majority can only constitute *obiter dicta*—even if labelled as *rationes decidendi* by the Court. Now *obiter* is broadly defined, we can now turn to the following question: is it uniform concept, or do branches emerge from its trunk? Is every *obiter* mere chit-chat? Or can a greater purpose be found? I confess that studying the relationship between *ratio* and *obiter* reminds me of the painting of Goya in the Prado, *Saturn Devouring His Son*—do we cannibalise it out of fear of its potential? Some things are taken as axiomatic: a dog is "man's best friend" and "cats are not loyal" and so forth. But, that does not mean that these slogans contain unequivocal truth.

5.2 Ancient Trees

Classifications are like trees. If you traced back to their roots, you would find the oldest models. Actually, one—*Arbor Porphyriana*. The activity of categorising according to genus and species is at the origins of Western culture. First proposed

[89] Eco (2013), p. 34.

[90] Leval (2006), p. 1257; Michaels (2017), p. 666.

[91] Mitidiero (2023b), p. 84.

[92] *Camargo v. SENAR* (STF, Pleno, RE n. 816.830/SC, Rel. Min. Dias Toffoli, j. 17.12.2022, DJe 24.04.2023), indexed as Tema 801, STF.

[93] *União v. Petróleo Dois Irmãos* (STF, Pleno, RE n. 138.284/CE, Rel. Min. Carlos Velloso, j. 01.07.1992, DJ 28.08.1992).

[94] *Camargo v. SENAR* (STF, Pleno, ED nos ED no RE n. 816.830/SC, Rel. Min. Dias Toffoli, j. 12.09.2023, DJe 10.10.2023).

[95] *Infra*, Chapter II, item 2.1.

by Aristotle in the *Posterior Analytics* (fourth century BC) and utilised by Porphyrion (around the third century AD) to write the book that would serve as a prototype for the first dictionaries, in turn, encyclopaedias were the next evolutionary step. Classification is anchored to a common trunk and develops in different directions, thus inspiring the depiction of Porphyry's work as a tree.[96] All interesting facts that I was happy to discover and share with you here; how one can learn when investigating the possible classifications of the *obiter dictum*.

From the root of the *obiter*, the most common branching divides into "*gratis dictum*" and "*judicial dictum*".[97] The distinction is procedural: the first constitutes a statement formulated on an issue without prior debate, careful consideration or due justification, whilst the second paid the price of the adversary proceeding and the reasoning.[98] A hierarchy follows—*judicial dictum* is usually considered more *valuable* than the first.[99] It is the seminal lesson of *Humphrey's Executor* (1935):[100] the *judicial dictum* has a greater *weight* than the *gratis dictum*, although it falls far short of the authority of the *ratio*.

Another well-known subclassification—but which already presupposes a position in relation to the effects of the *obiter*—is the one that distinguishes the illustrative and persuasive.[101] While the distinction between "*free*" and "*judicial*" sees the *obiter* in the engine room of the procedure, the one between illustrative and persuasive sees it by its product: the illustrative *obiter* does not need to be faced by court, when alleged by the party, while the persuasive imposes the duty of consideration.[102] Although no *obiter* is binding, which is proper to the *ratio*, it moves from the terrain that goes from illustration to persuasion. The relevance of the *obiter* in relation to the subsequent issue is another method of subclassification. If it concerns the identical or similar issue, it is relevant. If not, irrelevant. As such, it is only the relevant *obiter* that is valuable, by this merit it holds *weight* for the solution of the subsequent issue.[103]

It is important when combining these three ways of viewing the *obiter dictum* to be aware of the dangers faced in its consideration—whether construed properly, as *obiter*, or improperly, disguised as *ratio*. Every now and then someone[104] invokes Félix Frankfurter in his *dissent* in *Rabinowitz* (1950) to remind us of this: one must

---

[96] I share a little of this story in Mitidiero (2024b), n. 348, whose source is Eco (2013a).

[97] For example, Coale and Couture (2007), p. 175; Stinson (2010), pp. 225–226 (who also calls "*judicial dictum*" "*considered dictum*"); McAllister (2011), pp. 168–169. A note: strictly speaking, the distinction that is made by *Common Law* jurists is between *obiter dictum* and *judicial dictum*. I took the liberty of placing the *obiter* as a genus and allocating the *gratis* as a species to avoid pointing out the *obiter* as both a genus and a species.

[98] *Humphrey's Executor v. United States*, 295 U.S. 602 (1935).

[99] Garner (2016), pp. 62–65; Duxbury (2021), pp. 94 et seq.

[100] *Humphrey's Executor v. United States*, 295 U.S. 602 (1935) (*infra*, Chapter III, item 3.1).

[101] *Infra*, Chapter III, item 3.1.

[102] Among many, Dorf (1994); Abramowicz and Stearns (2005), p. 1084.

[103] Duxbury (2021), pp. 83 et seq. (*infra*, Chapter III, item 3.3).

[104] For instance, Leval (2006), p. 1269.

avoid the "progressive distortion" that turns a hint into a suggestion, jumping from it to the level of the *dictum* to finally reach that of the *ratio* ("decision").[105]

In short: you must be careful not to buy a pig in a poke.[106]

The distinction between "*gratis*" and "*judicial*" related to the undertaking of the Court (the price paid for the statements themselves), the distinction between relevant and irrelevant concerns the applicability of the *obiter* to the issue at hand and the delineation between illustrative and persuasive concerns the effect that the *obiter* can have on a future decision. There is one final, lesser known, branching proposed by Marc McAllister in 2011. He distinguishes between "vibrant" ("vibrant *dicta*"), "opaque" ("dead *dicta*") or "controversial" ("divergent *dicta*").[107] The first is obiter that ascends to *ratio* status, the second is doomed to languish as *obiter*, whilst the third remains adrift in the sea of precedential controversies.[108]

An example of vibrant *obiter* is found in *J.L.* (2000).[109]

In this case, the police received anonymous tip that a young black man, dressed in a plaid shirt waiting at a bus stop, was carrying a firearm. Officers soon located a man matching the description. No gun was visible and nothing in his behaviour raised suspicion. The police proceeded to accost him and discovered an illegal weapon. The man, J.L., was subsequently charged with the possession of an illegal weapon. Although initially convicted the *U.S. Supreme Court*, overturned this due to the absence of evidence to corroborate police action. An anonymous tip is not sufficiently reliable information upon which to search him; this is the *ratio* of the case. In *obiter dictum*, however, the Court stated that anonymous and uncorroborated information can prove to be sufficiently reliable, provided that it involves facts that characterise a more significant public danger.[110] Since *J.L.*, its *obiter*—anonymous uncorroborated information, but involving emergencies with significant public danger—has been used to solve several cases.[111] As such, *J.L.*'s *obiter* became the *ratio* of other cases. It has been transformed and thrived.

Barktus (1959)[112] offers a good example of the opaque.

---

[105] *United States v. Rabinowitz*, 339 U.S. 56 (1950)—subsequently overruled, by the way, by *Chimel v. California*, 395 U.S. 752 (1969).

[106] Although I'm particularly fond of pigs at this point.

[107] McAllister (2011), pp. 163–164 and 185–202.

[108] McAllister (2011), pp. 163–164.

[109] *Florida v. J.L.*, 529 U.S. 266 (2000).

[110] This is the unanimous *opinion* passage that matters to us now: "*the facts of this case do not require us to speculate about the circumstances under which the danger alleged in an anonymous tip might be so great as to justify a search even without a showing of reliability. We do not say, for example, that a report of a person carrying a bomb need bear the indicia of reliability we demand for a report of a person carrying a firearm… In [this case], we [simply] hold that an anonymous tip lacking [sufficient] indicia of reliability… does not justify a stop and frisk whenever and however it alleges the illegal possession of a firearm*" (*Florida v. J.L.*, 529 U.S. 273/274 (2000), transcribed from McAllister 2011, p. 186).

[111] McAllister (2011), pp. 186–188.

[112] *Barktus v. Illinois*, 359 U.S. 121 (1959).

The United States Constitution protects against double criminal prosecution for the same fact ("double jeopardy clause"), the exception being the possibility of federal and state prosecution ("dual sovereignty" exception).[113] In *Barktus*, however, the *U.S. Supreme Court* alluded to a possible exception to the exception in *obiter dictum*: whenever the state authority is simply adopted as a federal tool to facilitate a second round; a mere "sham and cover". In this case, the subsequent is merely a repetition of the first and should not be allowed.[114] This *obiter* was not adopted by subsequent courts and remains so to this day—opaque, half erased, lacklustre.[115] It is unlikely that it will escape this to become *ratio*.

Finally, *Giles* (2008),[116] is an example of the controversial.

In *Crawford* (2004),[117] the *U.S. Supreme Court* ruled that a *testimonial statement* can only be admitted without the possibility of *cross-examination* in the *trial*, if the witness is no longer available and the defendant has been previously given the opportunity to be questioned.[118] An exception to this would be if the accused acted unlawfully to prevent the witness from attending the *trial*—for example, by means of intimidation. By merit of their illegal conduct, the accused has relinquished their right to confront the witness ("forfeiture by wrongdoing"). However, the strict application of *Crawford*'s renders it difficult to obtain convictions in particular cases. Especially so in those involving domestic violence—in which victims are reluctant, for different reasons, to testify. Therefore, the exception created by *Crawford* is much debated; was evidence the defendant sought to avoid testimony in court sufficient or is evidence of the specific intention of the defendant necessary for its configuration?

---

[113] *Fox v. State of Ohio*, 46 U.S. (5 *Howard*) 410 (1847)—reaffirmed several times, as, for example, in *Koon v. United States*, 518 U.S. 81 (1996).

[114] *Barktus v. Illinois*, 359 U.S. 123/124 (1959).

[115] McAllister (2011), pp. 190–193. À propos, Marc McAllister (McAllister 2011, pp. 188–189) further offers as an example of an opaque *obiter* the way that *Stack v. Boyle*, 342 U.S. 1 (1951) was dealt in *United States v. Salerno*, 481 U.S. 739 (1987). In *Salerno*, the *U.S. Supreme Court* ruled on the constitutionality of the norm that allows the arrest of the defendant before the *pretrial* on the basis of his dangerousness—in addition, therefore, to the traditional cases involving the risk of flight. In the opinion, the scope of *Stack* was discussed, in which it was decided that the setting of bail above that necessary to ensure the presence of the defendant in the *trial* is excessive and violates the Constitution. In deciding *Salerno*, the *U.S. Supreme Court* ruled that *Stack* did not face the issue of the possibility of adopting different grounds for imprisonment prior to the *trial* in all its implications and, for this reason, constitutes a simple *obiter dictum* for *Salerno*. It is clear, however, that this is an example of a distinct issue for a fact not considered (Mitidiero 2023b)—as *Stack*'s *obiter* does not coincide with the issue faced in *Salerno* (it is not an identical issue), it is impossible to know whether it was buried as *obiter* or whether it could have been enlightened as *ratio*.

[116] *Giles v. California*, 554 U.S. 353 (2008).

[117] *Crawford v. Washington*, 541 U.S. 36 (2004).

[118] "Cross-examination" is the possibility for the lawyer of one party to question the witness listed by the opposing party. "Trial" is the hearing to produce evidence and trial of the case. Although its object is civil proceeding, these definitions can be found and contextualized in Hazard et al. (2023).

This issue was examined by the *U.S. Supreme Court* in *Giles* and it was determined that evidence of intent is required. After resolving the case and summarising its reasons, the winning opinion faced the arguments of dissent, which proposed a less demanding standard for cases involving domestic violence. In *obiter*, the Court stated that, although leaving aside the evidence of the intention to prevent testimony could be particularly important to help women involved in abusive relationships, and although domestic violence is intolerable, one cannot override the right of the accused to carry out the cross-examination of a witness. However, it noted that the context of domestic violence gains greater importance in cases that culminate in murder. Here different abusive acts—such as preventing the victim from seeking help throughout the relationship, isolating the victim from family, friends or the police—can prove there is an intention that could confiscate the right of the defendant to confront the witness and make any previous statements of the victim admissible as evidence.[119] The meaning of this *obiter* is largely controversial[120] and it remains unresolved.

Taking a clear, and realistic perspective (a focus on what the Courts *do*—and not on what they *say*—as a means of understanding the operation of the *stare decisis* rule),[121] has a tripartite function: (i) informing our understanding of how *obiter* serves to signal where the developmental winds of Law blow;[122] (ii) to reconstruct characteristics that could determine its success in life;[123] and (iii) to enable the projection of criteria that could assist in this prediction.[124] In a critical dialogue with Shawn Bayern,[125] who sought to see in the simple intention of the Court the explanation for the life and death of the *obiter*, Marc McAllister proposed five criteria to anticipate its vicissitudes: (i) prestige or number of judges who endorsed the *obiter*; (ii) depth of the debate; (iii) demarcation of the line of precedents; (iv) intended scope; and (v) relationship between the facts of the case and the facts analysed in *obiter*.[126]

All very interesting, I know, but we are not ready to reap the fruits quite yet. We still have time to swing on some of those branches.[127] The *obiter dictum* is defined, and we have outlined four types of subclassification. However, there are others who

[119] *Giles v. California,* 554 U.S. 2.692–2.693 (2008).

[120] McAllister (2011), pp. 197–202.

[121] Oliphant (1928), pp. 74, 76 and 160–162; Llewellyn (2008), pp. 5, 7, 13/14, 65 and 71. For a broad view on this theme, Mitidiero (2023b).

[122] *Infra*, Chapter II, item 2.1.

[123] On top of that, some of these criteria can be used to size the weight that must be acknowledged to the *obiter dictum* (*infra*, Chapter III, item 3.2).

[124] McAllister (2011), p. 165.

[125] Bayern (2009), p. 158. By the way, Bayern understands that the court's intent can be determined by analysing the decision's context.

[126] McAllister (2011), p. 204.

[127] *Infra*, Chapter III, item 3.2.

would prefer to blur the boundaries between the *ratio* and the *obiter*, erasing the borders that we have erected between them.

Is that a better approach? Need we distinguish between the *ratio* and *obiter*?

5.3 Without Borders?

Those who pose this question defy the orthodoxy.

A basic, important and emblematic lesson, for the *first-year* law student, is the distinction between the *ratio* and *obiter*.[128] To undo this is no small feat. From Austin's *Lectures* (1861)[129] or Pollock's *First Book* (1896)[130] to Schauer's *Thinking like a Lawyer* (2009),[131] through Llewellyn's *Bramble Bush* (1930)[132] and Levi's *Introduction* (1949),[133] each rely upon this differentiation. That this separation does not exist is a contention of significant consequence. Distinguishing *ratio* and *obiter* promote the Rule of Law and the Democratic State; in the absence of this, the *stare decisis* rule is rendered nonfunctional. The ramifications are not relegated to the realm of semantics; significant real-life implications arise should the lines between *ratio* and *obiter* be erased.

So, how does this differentiation promote the Rule of Law?

First, it erects a fence around the reconstruction of law, entry is only permitted to the facts brought to court by the parties. In other words: the judicial reconstruction of the law is not done beyond what is necessary to resolve the issue presented. Here, the distinction promotes the separation of powers[134] and restrains, within the indispensable to face situations in need of protection, the powers of the jurisdiction to rebuild the law.[135]

Second, by determining the mandatory reasons that can be reconstructed in a decision and, thus, highlighting those to be put aside. In other words: the distinction signals which of the reasons are mandatory and which are not.[136] This promotes the principles of legal certainty, freedom and equality.[137] The definitions of *ratio* and *obiter* provide criteria from which it is possible to justify when a statement falls into

---

[128] Alexander (1989), p. 3. The *first year* is the mythical first year of American Law Schools, in which the students are immediately introduced to the need to study concrete cases—so to speak, it already begins in the hospital, serving the guys who need help. There is a very cool book that deals with Turow (1990).

[129] Austin (1873).

[130] Pollock (1918).

[131] Schauer (2009).

[132] Llewellyn (2008).

[133] Levi (2013).

[134] For a link between the Rule of Law and separation of powers, Sarlet et al. (2023), pp. 249–260; Mello (2023), pp. 121–127 and 133–137.

[135] Dorf (1994), pp. 2001 and 2067.

[136] Abramowicz and Stearns (2005), pp. 1018/1021 and 1023; Stinson (2010), p. 232.

[137] For a link between the Rule of Law, legal certainty, freedom and equality, Ávila (2021), pp. 195–199 and 224–229; Mitidiero (2023a), pp. 23–27.

one of the two fields: what must or must not be necessarily replicated for the solution of identical or similar issues. This allows the reaffirmation and coherent development of Law[138] and grants rationality to the interpretation and enforcement of the law as it sets parameters as to which side of the river a statement will fall.

And how does it promote the Democratic State?

The distinction ensures that the law enforced is not "bad law", that is, formed without prior and detained debate, careful consideration, and a due and grounded decision.[139] By drawing a distinctive line between the *ratio* and the *obiter*—and even between different species of *obiter dicta*—based on the right to adversary proceeding and on the duty to state reasons, the legal system requires a certain level of participation in the procedure so that certain reasons can reach a force capable of extrapolating it, either to compel to or to persuade for the solution of future issues.[140] Given this, it is apparent that the *stare decisis* rule depends on the distinction between *ratio* and *obiter*. If the *ratio* constitutes the norm and the *obiter* has—at most—persuasive effects, the promotion of legal certainty through proper interpretation and enforcement of the law—which obviously presupposes its identification—requires separating the chaff from the wheat. How is one to recognise what is decided and must remain—*stare decisis et quieta non movere*—if it is not possible to know what effectively compels, what simply persuades and what merely illustrates? The *stare decisis* is a nonstarter if the distinction between *ratio* and *obiter* fails.

The *ratio* and *obiter* are distinct concepts: conceived with, and integral to, the inception of our Law. They may reach the breadth of heaven as the controversies surrounding their exact contours arise, but their basic distinction is rooted in the darkness of earth. The abandonment of this may create a compelling entry to the pages of Brothers Grimm, Stevenson or Swift, but it has detrimental consequences for the day-to-day operation of the courts.

So, why would one seek to do so?

Why do people want to see the *ratio* and the *obiter* on a continuum? Why postulate an approach based on a spectrum of influence? Why do they want to erase the boundaries between them? I have some theories, but first we must understand why and how such ideas arose.

In 1989, Kent Greenawalt—after presenting the mainstream about the duo and problematising some of its aspects—concluded that the "*holding-dictum*" dichotomy does not properly capture the complexity of the practice of law in the United States.[141] In particular, noting the difficulty of defining the scope of the *ratio* in

---

[138] Specifically relating the justification activity with the cataloguing of statements in the field of *ratio decidendi* and *obiter dictum*, respectively, MacCormick (1987), pp. 155 and 169; Abramowicz and Stearns (2005), p. 961. Relating rationality, interpretation-activity (internal justification and external justification) and interpretation-result (coherence, universality and replicability), Mitidiero (2023a), pp. 60–68.

[139] Leval (2006), p. 1255; Stinson (2010), p. 228.

[140] For a link between Democratic State and participation, Canotilho (2003), pp. 98–100; Barroso (2023), p. 477; between participation, adversary proceeding and reasoning, Marinoni et al. (2023), p. 488; Mitidiero (2024a).

[141] Greenwalt (1989), p. 442.

the face of cases that require its generalisation for application.[142] The suggestion of this binomial insufficiency was taken up in 2003 by Thomas Fowler in an essay suggestively entitled *"Holding, Dictum… Whatever"*. He proposed that all the reasons contained in a decision constitute "good law", differing only in the intensity of the force that is accorded to each of them, Fowler suggested that the statements contained in a decision should not be valued as autonomous chapters, discriminated by the test of necessity, but as a continuum.[143] In 2009, Shawn Bayern voiced a similar perspective,[144] rebuking the notion of a "bright-line"[145] that distinguishes *ratio* from *obiter*. He suggested that the authority generated by the *ratio* is not sufficient to compel judges and courts to decide in accordance with the precedent. As it is always possible to extrapolate generalisations,[146] it is also possible to manipulate the facts, representing them in an uncharacterised way.[147] Hence all the reasons would end up in the same cauldron. Consequently, in 2017, Andrew Michaels concluded that it was impossible to consistently define *ratio* and *obiter*,[148] proposing an approach focused no longer on the "binary paradigm", but on a "spectrum of influence" of the ratios ("spectrum framework").[149]

My response…

First, the criticism of the manipulation of facts and reasons ignores the contingency that, considering that the *ratio* and the *obiter* are interpretative results, there is no way out for its rational reconstruction—intersubjectively controllable—outside the frames of justification, universalisation and replicability.[150] A culture of precedent demands the practice of candour, loyalty and transparency in the argumentation developed by the participants in the procedure.[151] The problem does not lie in recording raw facts and fitting fully pre-finished norms before interpretation, but rather in giving meaning to facts and texts endowed with legal authority. The possibility of error—intentional or not—is always lurking;[152] it is inherent to the human condition.

Second, the criticism of the definition of the scope of the *ratio* and the difficulty of determining an adequate level of generalisation turns a blind eye to the necessity of

---

[142] Greenwalt (1989), p. 438.

[143] Fowler (2003), pp. 140 and 161.

[144] Bayern (2009), p. 143.

[145] Bayern (2009), p. 156.

[146] Bayern (2009), p. 148.

[147] Bayern (2009), p. 165.

[148] Michaels (2017), p. 693.

[149] Michaels (2017), p. 670.

[150] With the appropriate bibliographical indications, Mitidiero (2023a); Mitidiero (2023b). It is not a coincidence that the reference to the *ratio* as the "arch of the bridge" depends precisely on justification as the basic scheme for its interpretative reconstruction.

[151] Emphasising the need for candour in argumentation, Abramowicz and Stearns (2005), pp. 1024/1025.

[152] Postema (2014), p. 92.

distinguishing identical and similar issues as possible targets of the *ratio*. This identification is key.[153] When solving an identical issue, the boundary between the *ratio* and the *obiter* is clearer. The *essential identity* leads to the solution of the issue by subsumption of the precedent ("settled law"). The *ratio* of the previous issue fits perfectly with the later issue—as our Common Law colleagues say, the *ratio* is "on all fours" with the issue.[154] What lies outside this fitting is *obiter*. When faced with a similar issue, the *relevant similarity* depends on defining how sufficient the analogy is to reach or not the issue still pending solution ("case of first impression"), this is a less secure path. However, this insecurity is concerned more the vagueness of the *ratio* itself—its scope—than the distinction between *ratio* and *obiter*. In other words, when resolving a similar issue, what is at stake is the extension of the *ratio* by analogy, not the colonisation of the *ratio* by the *obiter*. *Ratio* continues as *ratio*, *obiter* as *obiter*, although the ratio has had its scope expanded due to analogy. The generalisation does not weaken the distinction between *ratio* and *obiter*—it only expands, by analogy, the *ratio*.

Thirdly, the recognition of persuasive effects to a given class of *obiter* does not erase the distinction between *ratio* and *obiter*—on the contrary, it remains dependent on it. The *ratio* has a binding effect. The *judicial obiter*, a persuasive one. The *gratis dictum*, an illustrative one. Therefore, the graduation of the effects is far from denying the distinction between the *ratio* and the different types of *obiter dicta*—it, in fact, presupposes it. Otherwise, how do we associate the proper effects to each of them?

I hope this has convinced you of the importance of the distinction between *ratio* and *obiter*. Once the *obiter* is defined and properly classified, and its limits are defended, our next step is to figure out its function.

Creeeak.

Can you hear the wind-up bird?

References

Abramowicz M, Stearns M (2005) Defining Dicta. Stanford Law Rev 57(4):953–1036
Alexander L (1989) Constrained by precedent. South Calif Law Rev 63(1):1–63
Allen CK (1939) Law in the making, 3rd edn. Oxford University Press, Oxford
Atiyah PS, Summers R (1987) Form and substance in Anglo-American Law. Oxford University Press, Oxford
Austin J (1873) In: Campbell R (ed) Lectures on jurisprudence, vol 2. Linn, Jersey
Ávila H (2021) Teoria da Segurança Jurídica, 6th edn. Malheiros, São Paulo
Baker J (2002) An introduction to English legal history, 4th edn. Oxford University Press, Oxford
Barroso LR (2023) Direito Constitucional Contemporâneo, 11th edn. Saraiva, São Paulo
Bayern S (2009) Case interpretation. Florida State Univ Law Rev 36(2):125–175
do Passo Cabral A (2023) Jurisdição sem Decisão — *Non Liquet* e Consulta Jurisdicional no Direito Brasileiro. JusPodvm, São Paulo

[153] In the Common Law legal literature, Schauer and Spellman (2023), pp. 242–251; in Brazilian legal literature, Mitidiero (2023b) (for a definition of identical and similar issues, *retro*, note n. 68).
[154] Postema (2014), p. 91.

Calamandrei P (1965) Processo e Democrazia. In: Cappelletti M (ed) Opere Giuridiche, vol 1. Morano, Napoli
Canotilho JJG (2003) Direito Constitucional e Teoria da Constituição, 7th edn. Almedina, Coimbra
Cardozo B (1991) The nature of judicial process. Yale University Press, New Haven
Coale D, Couture W (2007) Loud rules. Pepperdine Law Rev 34(3):715–741
Cross R, Harris J (1991) Precedent in English Law, 4th edn. Oxford University Press, Oxford
da Rosa de Bustamante T (2012) Teoria do Precedente Judicial — A Justificação e a Aplicação de Regras Jurisprudenciais. Noeses, São Paulo
Dorf M (1994) Dicta and Article III. Univ Pa Law Rev 142(6):1997–2069
Duxbury N (2008) The nature and authority of precedent. Cambridge University Press, Cambridge
Duxbury N (2021) The intricacies of dicta and dissent. Cambridge University Press, Cambridge
Eco U (2013) Confissões de um Jovem Romancista (trans: Pen M). Cosac Naify, São Paulo
Eco U (2013a) Da Árvore ao Labirinto. In: Da Árvore ao Labirinto — Estudos Históricos sobre o Signo e a Interpretação (M. Dias M trans.) Record, Rio de Janeiro
Fowler T (2003) Holding, Dictum...Whatever. North Carolina Central Law J 25(2):139–162
Fulbeck W (1829) Direction or preparative to the study of the law — wherein is shewed what things ought to be observed and used of them that are addicted to the study of the law, 2nd edn. Clark, London
Garner B (ed) (2016) The law of judicial precedent. Thomson Reuters, St. Paul
Goodhart A (1937) Determining the Ratio Decidendi of a case. In: Essays in jurisprudence and the Common Law. Cambridge University Press, Cambridge
Goodhart A (1966) Law of the land. The University of Virginia, Charlottesville
Greenwalt K (1989) Reflections on holding and dictum. J Leg Educ 39(3):431–442
Hale M (1971) The history of the Common Law of England. Chicago University Press, Chicago
Hazard G Jr, Taruffo M, Mitidiero D (2023) A Justiça Civil — dos Estados Unidos ao Brasil. RT, São Paulo
Helminski F (2005) Reports, Supreme Court. In: Hall K (ed) The Oxford companion to the Supreme Court of the United States, 2nd edn. Oxford University Press, Oxford
Jobim M, Oliveira Júnior Z (2022) Súmula, Jurisprudência e Precedente — da Distinção à Superação, 3rd edn. Livraria do Advogado, Porto Alegre
Killian R (2013) Dicta and the rule of law. Pepperdine Law Rev 41(1):1–20
Kozel R (2017) Settled versus right — a theory of precedent. Cambridge University Press, Cambridge
Langbein J, Lerner R, Smith B (2009) History of the Common Law — the development of Anglo-American legal institutions. Aspen, New York
Leval P (2006) Judging under the constitution: dicta about dicta. N Y Univ Law Rev 81(4): 1249–1282
Levi E (2013) An introduction to legal reasoning. The University of Chicago Press, Chicago
Llewellyn K (2008) The Bramble Bush — the classic lectures on the law and law school. Oxford University Press, Oxford
Maccormick N (1987) Why cases have rationes and what these are. In: Goldstein L (ed) Precedent in law. Oxford University Press, Oxford
Marinoni LG (2021) Processo Constitucional e Democracia. RT, São Paulo
Marinoni LG (2022) Precedentes Obrigatórios, 7th edn. RT, São Paulo
Marinoni LG, Mitidiero D (2021) Recurso Extraordinário e Recurso Especial — do *Jus Litigatoris* ao *Jus Constitutionis*, 3rd edn. RT, São Paulo
Marinoni LG, Arenhart SC, Mitidiero D (2023) Curso de Processo Civil, vol 1, 8th edn. RT, São Paulo
Mcallister M (2011) Dicta redefined. Willamette Law Rev 47(2):161–210
Mello CA (2023) Direito Constitucional — Teoria da Constituição e Direitos Fundamentais. Tirant lo Blanch, São Paulo
Michaels A (2017) The holding-dicta spectrum. Arkansas Law Rev 70(3):661–706
Millar RW (1923) The formative principles of civil procedure. Illinois Law Rev 18

Mitidiero D (2022a) Cortes Superiores e Cortes Supremas — do Controle à Interpretação, da Jurisprudência ao Precedente, 4th edn. RT, São Paulo
Mitidiero D (2022b) Relevância no Recurso Especial. RT, São Paulo
Mitidiero D (2023a) Precedentes — da Persuasão à Vinculação, 5th edn. RT, São Paulo
Mitidiero D (2023b) *Ratio Decidendi* — Quando uma Questão é Idêntica, Semelhante ou Distinta? RT, São Paulo
Mitidiero D (2024a) Processo Civil, 2nd edn. RT, São Paulo
Mitidiero D (2024b) Entre Listas, Dicionários e Enciclopédias — da Gaveta da Cozinha ao Processo Civil. Revista de Processo 49(348):495–510
Motta O (2015) Justificação da Decisão Judicial — a Elaboração da Motivação e a Formação do Precedente. RT, São Paulo
Nörr KW (1976) Naturrecht und Zivilprozess. Mohr, Tübingen
Oliphant H (1928) A return to Stare Decisis. Am Bar Assoc J 14
Pollock F (1918) A first book of jurisprudence for students of the Common Law, 4th edn. MacMillan and Co., London
Postema G (2014) Law's system: the necessity of system in Common Law. N Z Law Rev 1:69–105
Postema G (2017) Matthew Hale — on the law of nature, reason & common law. Oxford University Press, Oxford
Pugliese W (2016) Precedentes e a *Civil Law* Brasileira. RT, São Paulo
Ram J (1871) The science of legal judgment — a treatise designed to show the materials whereof, and the process by which, the Courts of Westminster Hall construct their judgments and adapted to practical and general use in discussion, and determination of questions of law, 2nd edn. Baker, New York
Re R (2014) Narrowing precedent in the Supreme Court. Columbia Law Rev 114(7):1861–1911
Sarlet I, Marinoni LG, Mitdiero D (2023) Curso de Direito Constitucional, 12th edn. Saraiva, São Paulo
Schauer F (1987) Precedent. Stanford Law Rev 39(3):571–605
Schauer F (2008) Authority and authorities. Virginia Law Rev 94(8):1931–1961
Schauer F (2009) Thinking like a lawyer. Harvard University Press, Cambridge
Schauer F, Spellman B (2023) Precedent and similarity. In: Endicott T, Kristjánsson HD, Lewis S (eds) Philosophical foundations of precedent. Oxford University Press, Oxford
Simpson AWB (1961) The Ratio Decidendi of a case and the doctrine of binding precedent. In: Guest AG (ed) Oxford essays in jurisprudence. Oxford University Press, Oxford
Stinson J (2010) Why dicta becomes holding and why it matters. Brooklyn Law Rev 76(1):219–264
Stone J (1946) The province and function of law. PTY, Sidney
Stone J (1959) The ratio of the Ratio Decidendi. Mod Law Rev 22(6):597–620
Sunstein C (1999) One case at time — judicial minimalism on the Supreme Court. Harvard University Press, Cambridge
Taruffo M (1975) La Motivazione della Sentenza Civile. Cedam, Padova
Turow S (1990) O Primeiro Ano — Como se Faz um Advogado (A. B. Pinheiro de Lemos trans.). Record, Rio de Janeiro
Wambaugh E (1894) The study of cases — a course of instruction in reading and stating reported cases, composing head-notes and briefs, criticising and comparing authorities, and compiling digests, 2nd edn. Little, Brown and Company, Boston
Zaneti Júnior H (2017) O Valor Vinculante dos Precedentes — Teoria dos Precedentes Normativos Formalmente Vinculantes, 3rd edn. JusPodivm, Salvador

Chapter 6
The Wind-Up Bird Chronicle

6.1 *Creeeak*

Murakami is a staple of life. I have read every book translated and it is a passion I share with Victoria—have you read *Norwegian +Wood*? She has. *Kafka on the Shore,* one of my favourites, is hidden in the first paragraph of the *Civil Procedure*; it also appears on several pages of *Como Escrevo*. A good old friend. His book, *The Wind-Up Bird Chronicle*, published between 1994 and 1995 in Japan before finally arriving in Brazil in 2017, employs *creeeak* as sound to signal flow, maturation, transformation. My adoption of this onomatopoeia may be unusual, but I hope it will be effective. It is said that Chico Buarque was tasked to set to music *paralelepípedo* ("cobblestone"), a Portuguese word that is demanding even to write. A challenge he rose to and, as it is said, the rest is history—one of the most emblematic sambas of the time, *Diretas Já,*[1] was born. Sometimes, unorthodoxy is required.

Creeeak is a way to highlight something—the drawing a yellow marker. *Obiter dictum* offers a comparable effect. It broadcasts a two-fold signal, transmitted to all participants in the justice system.[2] First, indicating the direction that the Law can develop;[3] it encourages the evolution of the Law in a coherent way,[4] a smooth transition into new terrain,[5] and can even create a spark to fuel institutional dia-

[1] "Diretas Já!" was a Brazilian civil movement in the early 1980s that demanded direct presidential elections after two decades of military dictatorship (1964–1985). Chico Buarque played a prominent role in the movement, using his platform as a popular musician and cultural icon.

[2] *Carey v. Musladin*, 549 U.S. 70 (2006), mentioned—along with *Local 28 Sheet Metal Workers v. EEOC*, 478 U.S. 421 (1986)—by Bayern (2009), p. 161.

[3] Dorf (1994), p. 2053, note n. 199.

[4] Leval (2006), p. 1253; Bayern (2009), p. 143.

[5] Mitidiero (2023a), pp. 145–146; Mitidiero (2021), pp. 63–64; do Passo Cabral (2023), p. 111.

D. Mitidiero, *Ratio Decidendi and Obiter Dictum*,
https://doi.org/10.1007/978-3-031-93152-9_6

logue.[6] Second, its demarcation reaffirms the *ratio decidendi*; it can sweep away any interpretative doubts, as well as to clarify what the *ratio* is and, if there is a dispute between different *rationes,* to solve an issue still pending analysis.[7] It is a method to resolve apparent antinomies.

It's worth closely examining both of these functions—a signal as to the developmental direction of Law and a method of appraising the *ratio decidendi* in cases of interpretative doubts.

I confess that I was initially inclined to tackle the *obiter dictum* and dissent simultaneously,[8] although soon realised that *obiter* offered ample challenge for one book. Yet, these two subject naturally pair, both hope to grow up to be like the *ratio.* However, the *obiter* is an affirmation capable of living peacefully with the *ratio* or seeks to smoothly pave its overruling, while the dissent is its enemy: it seeks to dethrone the *ratio*, take its place, behead it in the public square—preferably with a quick and single overruling. It is no coincidence that, while lateral comment occur within the winning opinion, the concurring opinion or the dissent, is always written in a separate opinion.[9] It is the opposition of the *ratio decidendi.* Hence, we cannot confuse *obiter dictum* with dissent, nor *see* the dissent as a species of *obiter dictum.* They are distinct entities. Yet, as noted, they share a common goal. *Obiter* and dissent want—to make use of a classic expression by Benjamin Cardozo—each in their own way, to be the "voice of a new day".[10] Their presence allows us to foresee the Court's concern with an issue pending decision or already decided with a *ratio* that won but failed to attain unanimity. They signal where the wind may blow, thus highlighting possible paths upon which the Law may embark. They are breadcrumbs leading us to a future *ratio.*[11]

Examples abound,[12] but a few here will suffice.

Although not the subject of concern here, I have included dissents—particularly because I think the Brazilian Law should adopt it.[13] Justice Harlan's dissents in *Civil*

[6] Marinoni (2021), pp. 139 et seq.

[7] Leval (2006), pp. 1252–1253.

[8] Proba-bly influenced by Neil Duxbury, who did something similar to this in Duxbury (2021) (only similar, because they are two stand-alone essays published together).

[9] "Opinion" is the way in which the decision of the *U.S. Supreme Court* is alluded to. Usually, Justices do not write a separate vote for each case—if they agree, they only adhere to the Court's opinion. If they want to emphasise any specific aspect, however, they can suggest to the opinion writer to incorporate any particular line of argument or they can write a separate concurring opinion. In order, however, to express opposition to the *ratio*, they can only write a dissent opinion, which is necessarily formulated separately, also to allow a more visible confrontation between the two (McLauchlan 2005; Garner 2005, pp. 706–710).

[10] Cardozo (1991), p. 79 (also mentioned by Llewellyn 2008, p. 66).

[11] Duxbury (2021), p. 56.

[12] Speaking of which, I found those examples in Fisher (1988), p. 188.

[13] As I've been suggesting since Mitidiero (2022), pp. 127–128.

Rights Cases (1883) and in *Plessy* (1895) won in *Brown* (1954) and *Jones* (1968).[14] Likewise, the formulation by Justice Holmes in *Lochner* (1905)—always remembered[15]—had its day in the sun in *Parrish* (1937).[16] Justice Stone's in *Gobitis* (1940) and in *Barnette* (1943).[17] We now turn to the ratio. Previously discussed, the fate of the *obiter dictum* in *J.L* (2000)[18] is an ascension to ratio that serves as an example of developing Law in a coherent way. Likewise, in *Bakke* (1978), the lateral comment that the Harvard admission program met the requirements of "equal protection", as race was only one of the considered factors to be valued;[19] this was adopted as a *ratio* in *Grutter* (2003) and in *Gratz* (2003).[20] It was so prestigious that, when the U.S. Supreme Court decided to overrule *Bakke, Grutter,* and *Gratz* in *Students* (2023),[21] it chose to do so in a case where Harvard's own program was being challenged.

The debate of the Federal Supreme Court regarding the definition of *service* for the purposes of levying the tax on services of any nature (ISSQN), evolving over the

[14]The *Civil Right Cases*, 109 U.S. 3 (1883), constitute the set of five cases (*United States v. Stanley, United States v. Ryan, United States v. Nichols, United States v. Singleton and Robinson and Wife v. Memphis & Charleston R. R. Co.*) in which the U.S. Supreme Court ruled that Congress, in enacting the *Civil Rights Act* of 1875 (which authorised all people, regardless of race or colour, to stay in hotels, access public transportation and attend theatres), did not prohibit the practice of acts of discrimination by individuals (Currie 1985, pp. 398–401). In *Plessy v. Ferguson*, 163 U.S. 537 (1896), the U.S. Supreme Court ruled as constitutional the possibility that the States imposed racial segregation in public places ("separate but equal"). *Plessy* was overruled by *Brown v. Board of Education of Topeka*, 347 U.S. 483 (1954), while the *Civil Rights Cases* by *Jones v. Alfred H. Mayer and Co.*, 392 U.S. 409 (1968) (Currie 1990, pp. 40–41 and 377–381).

[15]For example, by Cardozo (1991), p. 79 (which, by the way, made up the majority in *Parrish*).

[16]In *Lochner v. New York*, 198 U.S. 45 (1905), the U.S. Supreme Court ruled as unconstitutional a statute of the State of New York that limited a baker's working day to ten hours a day or sixty hours a week, on the grounds that it violated the right to freedom of contract (Currie 1990, pp. 48–50). *Lochner* was overruled by *West Coast Hotel Co. v. Parrish*, 300 U.S. 379 (1937) (Currie 1990, pp. 236–238).

[17]In *Minersville School District v. Gobitis*, 310 U.S. 586 (1940), the U.S. Supreme Court ruled that public schools could force their students to salute the American flag and recite the pledge of allegiance, notwithstanding any conscientious objections (in this case, from Jehovah's Witness students). *Gobitis* was overruled by *West Virginia State Board of Education v. Barnette*, 319 U.S. 624 (1943) (Currie 1990, pp. 266–267 and 317–320).

[18]*Florida v. J.L.*, 529 U.S. 266 (2000) (*retro*, Chapter I, item 1.2).

[19]*Regents of the University of California v. Bakke*, 438 U.S. 265 (1978) (*retro*, Chapter I, item 1.1).

[20]*Grutter v. Bollinger*, 539 U.S. 306 (2003) and *Gratz v. Bollinger*, 539 U.S. 244 (2003) were tried on the same day. In the first case, it was decided that the admission program of the University of Michigan Law School was constitutional because, besides favouring applications from people belonging to not sufficiently represented minorities, it considered other individual factors to value them. In the second, it was decided that the admission program at the University of Michigan was unconstitutional because it automatically associated points with applications from minority groups.

[21]*Students for Fair Admission v. Harvard*, 600 U.S. 181 (2023).

cases of *Ideal* (2000),[22] *Cândido Randon* (2017)[23] and *Venbo* (2020),[24] offers fertile terrain for exploring the *obiter*'s functions.

In *Venbo*, the Supreme Court ruled that "it is constitutional to levy a Tax on Services of Any Nature (ISS) on franchise agreements (items 10.04 and 17.08 of the services lists provided for in the Annex to Complementary Law 116/2003)". Throughout the trial, the development of the definition of *service* from *Ideal* to *Cândido Randon* emerged, thus preparing for the decision of *Venbo*. The ensuing debates of *Venbo* demonstrated that *Ideal* distinguished between the obligations of giving and doing in defining *service*. Justice Gilmar Mendes recalled the votes of Justices Marco Aurélio and Celso de Mello in *Ideal*, noting that "the passage is illustrative of the Court's *ratio decidendi* in this and other trials of the same content. Consequently, leasing could not be taken as a service; it is an obligation to give, not to do".

Venbo then highlights the broader concept of *service* employed in *Cândido Randon*—it sought to abandon the distinction between *giving* and *doing* as a sufficient reason to categorise an activity. Justice Gilmar Mendes's observes: "nonetheless, as the activities carried out by the health plan operators were considered of a mixed nature (that is, they encompass both 'giving' and 'doing'), it cannot be said that there has been—yet—a total overruling of the understanding that the ISS is only levied on obligations to do, and not on obligations to give. It can be established, however, that, according to the understanding of the Federal Supreme Court, the ISS levies on activities that represent both obligations to do and mixed obligations, which also include obligations to give".

The *obiter* is found in the adverb: yet. *Cândido Randon* indicated that the understanding of *service* may be altered in the future—just three years later this transpired in *Venbo*. The *obiter* forewarns.

The waves of the obiter can ripple beyond the court; indeed, the justice system is not confined to the Judicial Branch. The Legislative Branch and the Executive Branch also have the duty to protect the rights, acting within their functions to legislate and govern according to the Constitution.[25] The signals sent of the Supreme Courts can, and should, be equally received by all. An *obiter* that promoted a dialogue between the U.S. Supreme Court and the U.S. Congress occurred in *Dobbs* (2022). Justice Thomas stated that the same reasons used to overrule *Roe* (1973) and *Casey* (1992) by *Dobbs* would also serve to overrule *Obergefell*

[22] *Ideal Transportes e Guindastes v. Santos* (STF, Plenário, RE n. 116.121/SP, Rel. Min. Octávio Gallotti, Rel. para Acórdão Min. Marco Aurélio, j. 11.10.2000, DJ 25.05.2001), which, by the way, originated the binding summula n. 31.

[23] *Hospital Cândido Randon v. Cândido Randon* (STF, Plenário, RE n. 651.703/PR, Rel. Min. Luiz Fux, j. 26.04.2017, DJe 26.04.2017).

[24] *Venbo v. Rio de Janeiro* (STF, Plenário, RE n. 603.136/RJ, Rel. Min. Gilmar Mendes, j. 28.05.2020, DJe 16.06.2020).

[25] Marinoni et al. (2023).

(2015),[26] which recognised the possibility of same-sex marriage. Congress promptly received the memo and, in the same year, enacted the *Respect for Marriage Act*, which protected the right to equal consideration and respect in the context of affective relationships between people of the same sex.

In addition to its precognitive function, the obiter can clarify the *ratio* in cases of interpretive doubts; it helps to draws the line between an issue already analysed ("settled law") and another still pending decision ("case of first impression") or define the scope of two or more *rationes* in apparent antinomy. In *VDA Logística e Transporte* (2023),[27] obiter served to reaffirm a previous *ratio*. To identify the issue pending analysis,[28] the Superior Court of Justice first clarified the *ratio* of an issue already decided[29] and took with it the opportunity to reaffirm and delimit its contours. Such statements are important, not only as they dispel doubts about the content and authority of the *ratio*, but also about the moment of its formation—which can define, for example, whether one would subject a certain *res judicata* to the action for relief from judgment or not. Likewise, in *Camargo* (2023)[30] *obiter dictum* cemented the authority of the *ratio*. In reference to *Dois Irmãos* (1992),[31] the Supreme Court recognised that the issue of the proper fitting of the contribution to SENAR had already been resolved in another case—even though it initially appeared to be a lateral issue.

Despite the intimation that the *obiter* is simply chit-chat, it nonetheless possesses a number of important functions in the legal system. It would be a travesty to lose it from the court decisions.[32] But, if one understands the *ratio* and the *obiter* as interpretative reconstructions, it's vital to make sure that its use is physiological, that is, corresponding to its proper function. Imperatively, one must resist the pathological development of the *obiter*.

---

[26] *Obergefell v. Hodges*, 576 U.S. 644 (2015).

[27] *Fazenda Nacional v. VDA Logística e Transporte* (STJ, 1ª Seção, REsp n. 1.945.110/RS, Rel. Min. Benedito Gonçalves, j. 26.04.2023, DJe 12.06.2023, catalogued as Tema 1.182).

[28] It's worth saying: whether or not the other tax benefits of ICMS (such as, for example, reduction of tax base, reduction of tax rate, tax exemption, immunity and deferral) can be excluded from the tax base of corporate income tax (IRPJ) and social contribution on net profit (CSLL) and, if they can, under what circumstances.

[29] It's worth saying: the possibility of excluding the presumed ICMS credit from the IRPJ and CSLL tax base, defined in *Fazenda Nacional v. Cotriguaçu* (STJ, 1ª Seção, EREsp n. 1.517.492/PR, Rel. Min. Og Fernandes, Relatora para o Acórdão Mina. Regina Helena Costa, j. 08.11.2017, DJe 1°.02.2018).

[30] *Camargo v. SENAR* (STF, Pleno, RE n. 816.830/SC, Rel. Min. Dias Toffoli, j. 17.12.2022, DJe 24.04.2023), catalogued as Tema 801, STF.

[31] *União v. Petróleo Dois Irmãos* (STF, Pleno, RE n. 138.284/CE, Rel. Min. Carlos Velloso, j. 01.07.1992, DJ 28.08.1992).

[32] do Passo Cabral (2023), pp. 105–111.

6.2 Obitering

I'm a fan of metaphors. As I note in *Como Escrevo*,[33] having been round the block a few times, I now allow myself some freedom to use them. The opposition between "physiological time" and "pathological time" is a differentiation I raise in *Civil Procedure*.[34] An eloquent articulation: it is one of the first things I thought of when considering the misuse of the *obiter dictum*.

When the *obiter* is used to signal the development of the Law or delimit the *ratio* in cases of doubt, this is a healthy interplay between the *ratio* and *obiter:* a physiological functioning. Like any system, however, the absence of care can render sickness. Three inflictions are most common: (i) the colonisation of the *ratio* by the *obiter*; (ii) the manufacture of the *ratio* by the *obiter*; and (iii) the corrosion of the *ratio* by the *obiter*. These forms of "*obitering*":[35] colonising, manufacturing and corroding the *ratio* are the *obiter*'s pathologies. A alongside inconsistent distinctions[36] and anticipatory overruling,[37] they are a violation of legal system.

The *obiter* colonises the *ratio* when it eclipses it, thus leaving propositions that would determine the solution of an issue in the shadow of irrelevance. The condition of the *obiter* renders a necessary and sufficient proposition of the *ratio* unduly lowered. An example of this kind can be found in how the U.S. Supreme Court dealt with *Barnette* (1943)[38] in[39] *Rust* (1991). *Barnett* determined that public schools cannot force their students to salute the flag and recite the pledge of allegiance, because it offends the right to free speech clause. Speaking on behalf of the Court, Justice Jackson pointed out: "if there is any fixed star in our constitutional constellation, it is that no official, high or petty, can prescribe what shall be orthodox in politics, nationalism, religion, or other matters of opinion or force citizens to confess

[33] Mitidiero (2023b).

[34] Mitidiero (2024), in which I stick by Pisani (2015), pp. 595 et seq.

[35] The expression is from Marshall (1997), p. 516.

[36] According to Luiz Guilherme Marinoni, there is an inconsistent distinction when "the court leaves aside a previous understanding without revoking the precedent that shelters it" (Marinoni 2022a, p. 245), doing so, however, based on "inconsistent distinctions in relation to the social propositions that justify the precedent". For Marinoni, however, this technique is "compatible with the principles that govern the way the precedents are instituted and modified by the Courts" (Marinoni 2022a, p. 248).

[37] According to Luiz Guilherme Marinoni, "anticipatory overruling" occurs when there is "anticipation of the probable revocation of a precedent by the Supreme Court" (Marinoni 2022a, p. 259). That is: when a Court of Justice, in the face of signals issued by a Supreme Court, believes that there will be an overruling of a precedent and, for this reason, feels free to overrule it based on this assumption. For Marinoni, however, this technique is compatible with Brazilian Law (Marinoni 2022a, pp. 267–268).

[38] *West Virginia State Board of Education v. Barnette*, 319 U.S. 624 (1943).

[39] *Rust v. Sullivan*, 500 U.S. 173 (1991).

by word or act their faith therein".[40] According to legal scholars,[41] this is *Barnette*'s *ratio*. In *Rust*, however, it was held that the government can determine the transfer of funds to certain private institutions under the condition that they adopt the same opinion disseminated by it—in this case, determine the transfer of funds to medical clinics under the condition that their doctor's express disagreement or remain silent about the possibility of abortion. Essentially, if the government provides finance, it can prescribe what can or cannot be said.[42] Of course, the issues in *Barnette* and *Rust* are not identical, but similar. However, if *Barnette*'s *ratio* can be individualised as noted above, then it is certain that *Rust* violated it. Moreover, as both issues involve government funding (public schools and public health policies), it would be difficult to even imagine them as a distinct issue for a fact not considered. *Rust* construed *Barnette*'s *ratio* as *obiter*, thus relegating it to a broad and simple comment.

Inversely, the *obiter* manufactures the *ratio* when it illegitimately supersedes it. Here a lateral or nonspecific comment is unduly raised to the status of *ratio decidendi*. In *Parents Involved in Community Schools v. Seattle* (2007),[43] the debate between Justice Roberts, who led the majority, and Justice Breyer, in dissent, is an example in which the former accuses the latter of labelling the *obiter* as *ratio*.[44] In this case, the U.S. Supreme Court ruled that it is unconstitutional to use race as a factor in composing the student body, in an attempt to mirror the racial composition of the neighbourhood as a whole, unless thus is a means of repairing a history of segregation. The dissenting opinion argued that the meaning of *Swann* (1971)[45] was ignored, advocating a rigid opposition between *ratio* and *obiter*. Justice Roberts, speaking on the behalf of the majority, stressed that Justice Breyer adopted a selective view of the cases discussed, thus seeking to incorporate *Swann*'s *dicta* as part of its *ratio*.

This "art of surreptitiously manufacturing the law,[46]" is hardly a well-kept secret of the U.S. Supreme Court. In a 2013 essay, Ryan Killian recalled a warning memo Justice Powell drafted for his consultants: "I know from experience that [Justice William Brennan] has a demonstrated ability (that I admire) to shape future decisions by the inclusion of general language unnecessary to the present opinion but apparently free from serious objection.[47]" He also recalled that "[he] learned to watch for the seemingly innocuous casual statement or footnote—seeds that would be exploited to their logical extreme in later cases".[48] As an example, Killian mentioned

---

[40] *West Virginia State Board of Education v. Barnette*, 319 U.S. 624, 642 (1943).

[41] Dorf (1994).

[42] Dorf (1994).

[43] *Parents Involved in Community Schools v. Seattle*, 551 U.S. 701 (2007).

[44] Stinson (2010), p. 229, note n. 55. For other examples involving the attempt to label the *obiter* as *ratio*, Stinson (2010), pp. 233–240.

[45] *Swann v. Charlotte-Mecklenburg Board of Education*, 402 U.S. 1 (1971).

[46] Killian (2013), p. 16.

[47] Killian (2013), p. 16.

[48] Killian (2013), p. 16.

the note written by Justice Brennan in *Shapiro* (1969)[49] and cited by himself in *Goldberg* (1970)[50]—furthermore, this reflects another comment formulated by himself in *Sherbert* (1963).[51]

These acts of colonising and manufacturing are endeavours that keep up appearances. They violations to the legal system, but disguise this by respecting the settled meaning of the propositions. To colonise and manufacture, their interpreters seek only to throw obiter from one side of the river to the other; it is a practice of rechristening. Like relabelling a bottle of wine, the art is in the qualification: the necessary and sufficient proposition is denoted as a lateral comment or broad statement. However, corroding the *ratio* is a more intrusive exercise. It is by far the most insidious form of *obitering*. It involves deliberately appending a meaning to the *ratio* which it different from what was established. It is a way of manipulating the content of the *ratio* by changing the meaning of the propositions. This is no simple change of labels—the wine has been replaced.

Imagine a horse race—perhaps at the *Palio di Siena*, the *Hipódromo de Palermo* in Buenos Aires or the *Paris Longchamp*. As with all legal texts, the text of a decision is susceptible to several possible interpretations.[52] These different interpretations of the decision that fit the frame are the possible descriptions of the *ratio*—the descriptive *ratio*—each represents a bet. The winning *ratio*—the one in which the norm is embodied—is the horse that wins the race: the prescriptive *ratio*.[53] When the *ratio* is corroded by the *obiter*, the winning *ratio* is usurped by a loser. The photo of the finish line is doctored. Furthermore, the Court that that performs the photoshop knows exactly what they are doing.

Such manipulations were denounced by Christopher Peters in 2008[54] and by Barry Friedman in 2010.[55] Peters discuss the dangers of under-the-table overruling, whilst Friedman raises how stealth overruling corrodes the *ratio*. However, in 2014[56] and 2016[57] a new perspective was asserted. Richard Re sought to defend this form of *obitering*, arguing that a narrow and deliberately unfaithful reading of the *ratio* ("narrowing") was appropriate.[58] According to Re, one could always adopt

[49] *Shapiro v. Thompson*, 349 U.S. 618 (1969).

[50] *Goldberg v. Kelly*, 397 U.S. 254 (1970).

[51] *Sherbert v. Verner*, 374 U.S. 398 (1963).

[52] Although some interpretations, together with the decision, could already be considered out of the race—Mitidiero (2023a); Mitidiero (2023c).

[53] By invoking the expressions *descriptive ratio* and *prescriptive ratio*, I am obviously referring to Stone (1959), pp. 600–601. For the context and implication of his lessons on the definition of *ratio*, Mitidiero (2023c), pp. 52–60 and 69–85.

[54] Peters (2008).

[55] Friedman (2010).

[56] Re (2014).

[57] Re (2016).

[58] Although it shares the same name, Richard Re's suggestion is not to be confused with the test of *Marks v. United States*, 430 U.S. 188 (1977), which is usually used as a criterion for interpreting the *ratio* when there is no majority. For a broad view on this theme, Marinoni (2023a), pp. 142–149.

a narrow and deliberately unfaithful reading of the *ratio* which aligns with a coherent and integral understanding of the Law—in accordance with the "first principles" of the legal system.[59] The legitimacy of this "narrowing"[60] derives from an allegiance to them; the undertaking of such an interpretative adjustment comes in the package of the Supreme Court, the Courts of Appeal, and the Trial's Courts.[61] For Re, a time machine is at the permanent disposal of the courts to resize an earlier interpretation in light of the principles.[62] One is always at liberty to re-do the crossing line photo. The *ratio* could be legitimately eroded—"narrowing", in its terminology—by the *obiter* in four situations: (i) to correct, through trial and error, a mistaken *ratio* ("experimental narrowing");[63] (ii) to adjust a very broad *ratio* ("narrowing rules");[64] (iii) to prepare the *overruling* of the *ratio* ("narrowing to overrule");[65] and (iv) to invite the courts to wear out the *ratio* ("aspirational narrowing").[66]

Examples of "experimental narrowing" include *Flast* (1968),[67] the *ratio* of which recognised the taxpayer's legitimacy to act ("standing") by proposing an action to challenge any unconstitutional program authorised by Congress—in this case, a program that allocated funds to finance the activity of religious schools. In *Schlesinger* (1974)[68] and *Richardson* (1974),[69] the U.S. Supreme Court set aside the *Flast's* broader test for one in which measured legitimacy and was limited it to programs involving the violation of the clause prohibiting the imposition of a religion by the Congress ("establishment clause"). Furthermore, in *Valley Forge* (1982),[70] it held necessary to show more than simply violating the prohibition of religion clause for configuring the taxpayer's legitimacy to act. In *Hein* (2007),[71] it was decided that *Flast* does not apply to cases of government expenditure carried out without specific legislative authorisation. Finally, *Winn* (2011)[72] determined that *Flast* applies to contrasting government expenditures, but not to challenging tax benefits.

---

[59] Re (2014), pp. 1874, 1889 and 1911. The echo of Dworkin's lessons—Dworkin (1986)—, is, by the way, evident in his thinking.

[60] Re (2014), p. 1889.

[61] Re (2014); Re (2016).

[62] Re (2014), p. 1889.

[63] Re (2014), pp. 1889–1895.

[64] Re (2014), pp. 1895–1902.

[65] Re (2014), pp. 1903–1907.

[66] Re (2014), pp. 1907–1910.

[67] *Flast v. Cohen,* 392 U.S. 83 (1968).

[68] *Schlesinger v. Reservists Committee to Stop the War*, 418 U.S. 208 (1974).

[69] *United States v. Richardson*, 418 U.S. 166 (1974).

[70] *Valley Forge Christian College v. Americans United for Separation of Church and State*, 454 U.S. 464 (1982).

[71] *Hein v. Freedom from Religion Foundation*, 551 U.S. 587 (2007).

[72] *Arizona Christian School Tuition Organization v. Winn*, 563 U.S. 125 (2011).

Other examples of "narrowing rules" can be observed in *Casey* (1992),[73] *Boumediene* (2008),[74] *Gant* (2009)[75] and *Miller* (2012).[76] *Casey* limited *Roe*'s three-trimester rule (1973).[77] *Boumediene* recognised the right to *habeas corpus* for foreigners in American custody in other countries, leaving aside what was decided in *Eisentrager* (1950).[78] *Gant* limited *Belton* (1981)[79]—from the consolidated interpretation that the driver's arrest authorises the police search inside the car compartments to the understanding that the search is only authorised if the police reasonably fear that the driver may return to the car to remove a weapon. And *Miller* limited *Harmelin* (1991)[80] by deciding that the imprisonment of a young person without the possibility of parole is unconstitutional.

Actions of "*narrowing to overrule*" are found in *Citizens United* (2010).[81] In dealing with restrictions on campaign financing, *Citizens United* carried out a more restricted reading of *Austin* (1990),[82] *McConnell* (2003)[83] and *Wisconsin* (2007).[84] This sparked some courts to restrict its reach as a strategy of resistance thus paving the way for its revocation.[85] Likewise, examples of "*aspirational narrowing*" can be found in *United States v. Windsor* (2013).[86] Here, it was ruled that federal law—in this case, the *Defense of Marriage Act* of 1996—cannot prohibit same-sex marriage.[87] In his dissent, however, Justice Roberts sought not only to demarcate the limits of *Windsor*'s *ratio* but also to encourage other courts to moderate its reach.[88]

Although the analysis of each case raises an interesting debate, I am more concerned here with the conceptual underpinning of Re's proposal. The need for development, correction of directions and exploration of new routes are impositions of the life of Law. Inevitable paths we take in its evolution., but this is not without costs. The price paid is the specific justification around the wear and tear of a certain

---

[73] *Planned Parenthood of Southeastern Pennsylvania v. Casey*, 505 U.S. 833 (1992).
[74] *Boumediene v. Bush*, 553 U.S. 723 (2008).
[75] *Arizona v. Gant*, 556 U.S. 332 (2009).
[76] *Miller v. Alabama*, 567 U.S. 460 (2012).
[77] *Retro*, Chapter I, item 1.1.
[78] *Johnson v. Eisentrager*, 339 U.S. 763 (1950).
[79] *New York v. Belton*, 453 U.S. 454 (1981).
[80] *Harmelin v. Michigan*, 501 U.S. 957 (1991).
[81] *Citizens United v. FEC*, 558 U.S. 310 (2010).
[82] *Austin v. Michigan State Chamber of Commerce*, 494 U.S. 652 (1990).
[83] *McConnell v. FEC*, 540 U.S. 93 (2003).
[84] *FEC v. Wisconsin Right to Life* (2007).
[85] Re (2014), pp. 1905–1907.
[86] *United States v. Windsor*, 570, U.S. 744 (2013).
[87] In *Obergefell v. Hodges*, 576 U.S. 644 (2015), the right to same-sex marriage was recognised by the *U.S. Supreme Court*—which was also recognised a few years later by Congress in the *Respect for Marriage Act of* 2022.
[88] Re (2014), pp. 1908–1909.

solution[89] and, when applicable, the protection of all those who relied on the previous precedent ("prospective overruling").[90] Re's proposal, in authorising the denial of the consolidated meaning of the precedent in the name of "first principles", can only be understood as an attempt to deny its own mandatory effectiveness—and that, therefore, of positive law itself. An appeal to coherence and integrity as instances of correction of the precedent, moreover, proves the objective of weakening its authority, seeking to assimilate it to a simple example.[91] The corrosion of the *ratio* by the *obiter*, is and remains as, the pure and simple violation of the *ratio*.

The summary of the matter is as follows.

The dissolution of the *ratio* in the waters of the *obiter* impedes the good law in the determination of an issue. The opposite—which unduly transforms the *obiter* into *ratio*—creates space of a decision underpinned by bad law. In both cases, the unity of Law is weakened, and the parties are denied the opportunity to have their issues resolved by it. The Rule of Law is at fault with them. The State is in debt to the Law.

There are three reasons why this occurs.

The first is that Civil Justice does not always run with the same program: the definitions of *ratio* and *obiter* are not universal. Its users employ different apps, they read different instruction manuals.[92] Different commands are provided about what to do in the face of certain propositions and issues. Confusion compounds. If—for convenience, lack of skill or distinct convictions—the line distinguishing the *ratio* and the *obiter* is changed and the result of this change is put back on the market, there is a ripple effect that feeds the confusion between the relevant and irrelevant reasons in a judicial decision.[93]

The second that an emphasis is placed on the words of a decision to the detriment of its reasons. An old lesson: Lord Mansfield in *Fischer v. Prince* (1762) states that "the reason and spirit of cases make law, not the letter of precedents".[94] One recently echoed by the U.S. Supreme Court in *Reiter* (1979): "the language of an opinion is not always to be parsed as though we were dealing with language of a statute".[95] Decisions can be attributed meaning to their words without checking the context in which they are used.[96] This happens not only due to the immense caseload[97] with which Civil Justice deals every day, but also to the way in which jurisprudential research is carried out on judicial websites (a type of "Google-search mode",

[89] Art. 927, § 4, CPC.

[90] Art. 927, § 3, CPC. For a broad view on this theme, with the appropriate bibliographical indications, Mitidiero (2021).

[91] With the appropriate bibliographical indications, Mitidiero (2023a).

[92] Stinson (2010), p. 240.

[93] Stinson (2010), pp. 241–242.

[94] Lord Mansfield in *Fisher v. Prince* (1762) (Allen 1939, p. 207).

[95] *Reiter v. Sonotone Corporation*, 442 U.S. 330 (1979).

[96] Stinson (2010), pp. 245–248.

[97] Stinson (2010), pp. 248–249.

presents the immense risk[98] of one buying an "electronically manufactured law"[99]). Moreover, most users of the system often devote inadequate time and attention to research (hence they simply pinch a few words and phrases rather than analyse the case as a whole and reformulate it).[100]

The third is that some judges seek, behind an opaque window, the exercise of greater power than that conferred by the facts of the case at stake. This occurs when very broad or lateral comments are carefully planted and then collected as if they represented more than they do. This planting of *obiter* and harvesting of *ratio* stealthily directs the development of the Law[101] and can only contribute to its confusion.

Underpinning our assumption is the assumption that *obitering* is a pathology of the Law. It is worth explicitly outlining why this is so. The *obiter* weighs less than the *ratio*; it is formed in an environment without well-defined facts ("concreteness"[102]), without adversary proceeding ("investigated with care"[103]) and without broad and deep consideration ("considered in its full extent"[104]). In other words: no debate and no appropriate judicial scrutiny ("insufficient judicial scrutiny"[105]). It arises in the absence of the "procedural Rule of Law safeguards".[106] Adversary proceeding and statement of reasons on well-defined facts entail significant costs. They gear up the procedure. This is the price one pays for the *ratio*. The *obiter*, in turn, comes for free—and, since it comes for free, the court does not pay much attention to it ("the court paid no price, and consequently paid little attention"[107]). That's why the *obiter*, as a rule, generates bad law.

Nevertheless, Pierre Leval warned, in 2006, that the pathology of *obitering* is endemic in US courts.[108] What can be done to prevent this from happening here too?

---

[98] Stinson (2010), pp. 250–255.

[99] Kuh (2008).

[100] Stinson (2010), pp. 258–260.

[101] Killian (2013), pp. 16–18. For a broad view on this theme, da Rosa de Bustamante (2018), pp. 708–745.

[102] Leval (2006), p. 1257. By the way, the concreteness of the material facts has been recognised since Arthur Goodhart (Goodhart 1937b, pp. 2–9, 22 and 25) as a fundamental anchor for the characterisation of the *ratio decidendi* and is signalled by Michael Abramowicz and Maxwell Stearns, (Abramowicz and Stearns 2005, p. 1055), as one of the essential lines to distinguish *ratio* and *obiter*.

[103] *Cohens v. Virginia*, 19 U.S. (6 *Wheaton*) 264 (1821). In the same vein, Schauer (2008), pp. 1954–1955.

[104] *Cohens v. Virginia*, 19 U.S. (6 *Wheaton*) 264 (1821).

[105] Leval (2006), pp. 1262–1263.

[106] Killian (2013), pp. 3–6.

[107] Leval (2006), p. 1263; Stinson (2010), p. 219.

[108] Leval (2006), p. 1255.

6.3 How to Avoid It?

Our discussion has revealed the dual personality of *obiter dictum*: the dichotomy of Dr. Jekyll and Mr. Hyde is at play. In its public persona it contributes to the development of the Law and signals the *ratio*. But, behind closed doors it assumes an insidious role, operating on the margins of the legal system (the *obitering*).[109] I will soon consider how Civil Justice has an ally in Dr. Jekyll to promote the unity of the legal system.,[110] but I am first concerned with how we prevent Dr. Jekyll from taking his potion.

To draw a line between *ratio* and *obiter*, one must pay attention to three different activities that involve the pair: forming, communicating and interpreting. The formation of decisions by the Supreme Courts and the Courts of Justice and, in the latter case, when they act to standardise the caselaw. The communication of precedents and uniform caselaw in the electronic repositories maintained by the Courts. The interpretation of the propositions contained in the decisions.

I begin with the Courts' methodology in deciding issues.

The Supreme Courts aims to give unity to the Law through precedents,[111] whilst the Courts of Justice standardises caselaw through the incidents of *assunção de competência*[112] and resolves claims on the same point of law.[113] Thus, the individualisation, the debate and the decision regarding the grounds—the reasons—which serve for the solution of an issue must be seen as a priority by the panel of judges.[114] Consequently, the interpretative activity must be grounded in the issues at stake, one by one, for the resolution of the issue. This approach, however, faces a historic challenge. Traditionally, the Supreme Courts have adopted, as a decision-making method, the *seriatim*, which generates plural decisions; the Courts of Justice follows suit. The U.S. Supreme Court previously employed the same approach. Yet,

---

[109] I know the reference is obvious, but I can't help but indicate the reading of the Companhia das Letras edition *of O Médico e o Monstro – O Estranho Caso do Dr. Jekyll e Sr. Hyde* (1886), by Robert Louis Stevenson (1850–1894), translated by Jorio Dauster with preface by Luiz Alfredo Garcia-Roza (1936–2020). I add this note not only to mention Stevenson's book, which was a wonder to re-read these days after so long, but also to take the opportunity to indicate the several crime novels by Garcia-Roza, one of my favourite Brazilian writers. If you don't know any, I suggest you start with the first one: Garcia-Roza (1996).

[110] *Infra*, Chapter III.

[111] Arts. 102, item III, and § 3, and 105, item III, and §§ 2 and 3, CRFB, and 489, § 1, items V and VI, 926 and 927, CPC. For a constitutionally appropriate reading of these provisions, Marinoni (2022a); Mitidiero (2023a); Zaneti Júnior (2017).

[112] Art. 947, CPC. The incident of *assunção de competência* is a legal device provided for in the Brazilian Code of Civil Procedure, aimed at preventing or resolving disputes on a point of law concerning which there are no repetitive cases and guiding the members of the court and the judges under its authority.

[113] Arts. 976 to 987, CPC.

[114] For more on the distinction between the function of the Supreme Courts and the Courts of Justice, Mitidiero (2022); Marinoni (2019); Arruda Alvim and Dantas (2018), Robles (2021); Marinoni et al. (2023); Mitidiero (2024).

at the beginning of the 19th century a new method was adopted: decisions were made *per curiam*. This generates collegiate decisions by institutional vote.[115] This development in U.S. Supreme Court, meant that two methodologies of decision-making coexisted: that of plural decisions and that of collegiate decisions.[116]

Plural decisions—also known as fragmented decisions or decisions by aggregation—are those in which the non-necessity of facing the points and issues of the case in the light of the same grounds generates the impression that the panel of judges is the simple sum of individual positions on a given point or issue. Each judge casts his or her vote separately. Consequently, plural decisions tend to have competing grounds rather than shared grounds, that is, different grounds that serve the solution of the same issue. It requires precise identification of the issue and identification of the grounds, but not a separate vote on each of the grounds. What matters is the agreement on the provision, with a minor issue being the consensus regarding the grounds used to obtain it. Furthermore, the same fragmentation that occurs in relation to the concurrent grounds also occurs when the judges that make up the panel diverge: the divergent vote is usually given without any concern for the confrontation of the grounds already supported by the other members of the panel. It consists of a simple aggregation of another ground in the appellate decision.

Conversely, a collegiate decision is focused on the solution of the case and the search for the provision. Here, the formation of the *ratio decidendi* and the signals of the *obiter dicta* take a backseat. Collegiate decisions are those that allow the panel of judges to be seen as a single whole, insofar as they contain shared grounds (the "opinion")—there may still be dissenting opinions within the appellate decision. Collegiate decisions present a debate that involves the same grounds on the same issues—it is from this community in the debate that the *ratio decidendi* of the decision can be more easily assessed, distinguishing it from the *obiter dictum*. As a result, the issue is always examined in the light of the grounds agreed upon by the panel. If these are unanimously adopted, there are shared grounds. If only part of the panel agrees, there is majority grounds. The decision is not the sum of individual votes, but by a vote written by a single member of the panel capable of mirroring the entire debate, including dissenting reasons—the vote is institutional. Collegiate decisions require the precise identification of the issue and a separate vote on each of the issues in the light of the different grounds on which they may eventually be decided, notwithstanding that everything is written and presented to the public in a single vote. The issues must be identified, so too must the grounds upon which it can be resolved. As such, a vote must be cast on each of these grounds. Any emphasis on some of the grounds that formed the majority can be made separately on a concurrent ground, if any member of the panel so wishes. Moreover, in collegiate decisions, even the dissent is anchored to the grounds upon which the issues revolve. Dissenters are expected to do so on the grounds employed by the majority; they must

[115] Fisher (1988), p. 183.

[116] The first monograph on the subject by a Brazilian legal scholar is by Marinoni (2023a).

cast a true dissent and, thus, demonstrate why the shared *ratio decidendi* cannot prevail.

This method of plural decisions can be used for the resolution of cases before the Courts of Justice—which, as a rule, are engaged in the provision of protection of rights through the fair decision of the case. The method of collegiate decisions, in turn, is the most suitable for confronting issues before the Supreme Courts—aimed at the provision of protection of rights through the unity of Law by precedents.[117] Likewise, when the Courts of Justice seek to standardise the caselaw by resorting to the incidents of *assunção de competência* and to the resolution of multiple claims on the same point of law, they would ideally employ a collegiate decision. Here, what matters is the need to identify the reasons underlying the decision of a particular issue. This will serve as a guide of how such issues should be tried in the future—and not the decision of the specific case.

Although a legislative reform is not necessary for decision-making—considering Brazilian Law is sufficiently open in this regard[118]—some change to the Internal Regulations of the Courts would undoubtedly be welcome.[119] The STF took a step in the right direction when they started to listen first to the oral arguments of the parties and then deliberate.[120] Ideally, however, the rapporteur would first present the case and a draft vote so that the parties could make their oral arguments, and the deliberation would then revolve around this debate. At the end of the trial, the rapporteur could present the issues decided, the respective grounds and the position of each judge in a single vote. The option would be open for each judge to, if they felt necessary, present their own concurring vote and dissenters would necessarily present theirs separately. I have no doubt that this would not only increase the parties' participation rate, fostering judicial accountability, but, most pertinently, would also facilitate the identification of the *ratio* and consequently the *obiter* in the decisions.

But, once the issues are decided, another challenge arises: the communication of the Courts with their users. Courts may communicate with their audience by attempting (or not) to summarise their reasons at the time they analyse certain issues. They can also index—with a greater or lesser degree of detail—the topics faced. Traditionally, the *ratio* is reconstructed by the judges and courts in charge of

---

[117] Criticising how decisions are made at the House of Lords of the United Kingdom, which at the time performed the role of the Supreme Court, and as a suggestion to the Australian High Court, Patton and Sawer (1947), pp. 483–485. In the same vein, regarding how decisions are made at the STF and the STJ, Marinoni (2023a).

[118] Art. 941, CPC, in the interpretation defended in Marinoni and Mitidiero (2018), pp. 239–242.

[119] On the role of internal regulations, de Oliveira (2019).

[120] Solution proposed by Justice Luís Roberto Barroso as President of the Court, which began with designating a session for oral arguments on 18.10.2023 on the case *Nispeche da Silva v. Rayes Pereira* (STF, Pleno, ARE n. 1,309,642/SP, Rel. Min. Roberto Barroso), which dealt with the constitutionality of the regime of mandatory separation of property for the marriage of people over 70 (seventy) years old, and another session for its disposition on 01.02.2024.

interpreting and enforcing the precedent.[121] This is the English tradition, recalled, for example, by Viscount Dunedin at the House of Lords in 1928 when he tried the *Great Western Ry case. Co. v. Owners of S. S. Mostyn*. He stated that it is not the court's duty to indicate the *ratio* to the others.[122] In some cases,[123] and in some theoretical elaborations one may feel a certain softening.[124] Here, the court charged with the precedent formation will endeavour make the *ratio* more explicit. However, the general rule is to reconstruct it retrospectively. With eyes in the rearview mirror, judges and courts interpret the decision-making texts on which the *rationes decidendi* are based. Therefore, those comments on the sidelines are also apprehended in the same way: what is not included in the reconstruction of the *ratio* is left on side of the road as *obiter*.

However, there is a peculiarity[125] in Brazilian Law—the concept of legal interpretation. Legal interpretations are a summary of the *ratio*. Like the summula, it is an express statement of the Court: its elder sister.[126] As an element of the court's effort to formulate the *ratio*, these legal interpretations cannot be disregarded.[127] They are an act of compassion: an attempt to improve communication—within the court, with other courts, and with all participants of the justice system.[128] In constructing an outline, boundaries between the *ratio* and the *obiter* are drawn. It defines what is not a part of its core. But we must also be careful to not overvalue legal interpretations. They can only be read in the light of the *ratio*,[129] not in place of it. Even when a Supreme Court formulates a legal interpretation to fit the *ratio*, one must keep in mind that legal interpretations may not mirror it.[130] Legal interpretation is a statement without facts, elaborated without the boundaries offered by their context.

---

[121] Alvim (2012), p. 44.

[122] Goodhart (1937a), p. 75.

[123] As in the *R. v. Moloney* case, tried in 1985 by the House of Lords, and cited by MacCormick (1987), p. 178, and as is the rule in the proceedings of the Supreme Court of Ohio in the United States due to the "syllabus rule", which seeks to mirror the decision's *ratio* (Stinson 2010, p. 246, note 133). In a similar sense, Passanante (2018), pp. 254 et seq., traces the tendency of the Italian *Corte di Cassazione* to claim the power to indicate which—among their decisions—is considered to have precedential force.

[124] Eisenberg (1988), pp. 54–55, who proposes the "announcement approach" for the definition of the *ratio decidendi*, that is, its announcement or proclamation by the court that decided the case from which the precedent originated.

[125] Domit (2016), p. 155; Monnerat (2019), p. 409.

[126] On summulas and their development in Brazilian Law, Mitidiero (2023a).

[127] So much so that Stinson (2010), p. 262, expressly suggests the identification of the *ratio* by the Court itself as one of the strategies that should be adopted to improve the performance of the *ratio* and *obiter* distinction in forensic practice.

[128] The *legal interpretations* and the *themes* that index them are, therefore, also ways of organising the work of the Supreme Courts, by recording it—so to speak—*ad perpetuam rei memoriam* (Marchiori 2022, p. 54).

[129] Mitidiero (2023a). Analogically, art. 926, § 2, CPC.

[130] Garner (2016), p. 59; Mitidiero (2023a), p. 104; Lessa (2022), p. 153.

Equally, when the *ratio* is summarised in a legal interpretation or summula, the *obiter* must also be weighed in relation to the *ratio*, not these mere statements.

The precedents of the Supreme Courts and the uniform caselaw of the Courts of Justice—public goods of the highest importance[131]—are freely available via electronic repositories maintained by those Courts. An essential service, of great quality, which elevates the Brazilian Civil Justice to a prominent position from the point of view of legal comparison.[132] This service helps to enable the distinction between the issues that have already been faced and the ones that are pending analysis. In other words: which ones can count as an already formed *ratio* ("settled law"), and which ones are unresolved ("cases of first impression"). Generally, a search of the caselaw repositories gives access to both a summary of the case and its decision. Also noted are the relevant legislation, the opinions of jurists and the cited decisions. This is immensely valuable to anyone seeking a decision on an identical or similar issue or seeking one that distinguished certain issues. However, this may be further improved—in the interest of distinguishing the *ratio* from the *obiter*—by adding a summary of the relevant facts of the case and including links to similar issues—both already determined or pending analysis. The more precise the indexing, the clearer the boundary between the *ratio* and the *obiter*.

Our discussion draws to a close.

Once decisions are made *per curiam* and detailed reporting is made public, what remains is to determine what has been captured to expand the territory of the *ratio* and what remains in the *obiter*'s no man's land. This is when definitions are of utmost importance. Here, definitions are inversely related; what is not claimed as the *ratio*'s, is found in the definition of *obiter*. In his classic essay on the *obiter dictum*, Michael Dorf highlights that the boundaries between *ratio* and *obiter* are usually blurred when the Court in charge of interpreting the precedent proceeds to reconstruct it; what he deems a moment of "recharacterization".[133] To ensure borders remain clear, one must have in hand the touchstone by which the propositions and issues will be examined and organised—this is provided by the definition of *obiter*.

The reconstruction of reasons is inherent to interpretation[134]—its nature is not found on the pages of mathematics books.[135] But this does not mean that the interpreter is free to ignore the minimal meaning of the words[136] or change the position and status of an issue throughout a debate or in a decision.[137] The

[131] Amrani Mekki (2019), p. 169, with express reference to the work led by Loïc Cadiet in France to promote "open data" as an essential part of promoting "open justice".

[132] Mitidiero (2019).

[133] Dorf (1994), p. 2030 (with the same meaning, by the way, Dorf speaks of "reconceptualization" right after, Dorf 1994, p. 2034).

[134] Tarello (1980), pp. 9–10 and 61–63; Guastini (2011), p. 8; Chiassoni (2007), p. 142; Ávila (2014), pp. 51–55.

[135] Holmes Jr. (1963), p. 5.

[136] Respect for the minimal meaning of words is one of the fundamental rules of interpretation: Hesse (1999), pp. 29–30; Ávila (2019), p. 38.

[137] Dorf (1994), pp. 2035–2037.

interpretation of a decision rationally fails if it mistakenly identifies what *ratio* is and what *obiter* is, universalising the *obiter* in place of the *ratio* or failing to replicate the *ratio* because it mistakes the *ratio* for *obiter*. This is an inherent danger to the practise. To thwart this risk, one must test the statements contained in the decision in the light of the definition of *obiter*. The *obiter*'s bench test lies in the justification: the parties justify in their claims, and the courts justify in their decisions, that certain propositions and issues should or should not be characterised as *obiter dicta* based on its definition.[138] As is the wisdom of the Sorting Hat, where you do not fit determines where you do. The queen of the deck is drawn—her essential traits apparent, she offers a mould which distinguishes her from the king.

Let's reiterate the basic parameters established.

Substantively, the *obiter* constitutes a comment on an issue that is (i) non-legal; (ii) lateral to what is being debated; or iii) very broad, unable to lead directly to the solution of an issue. Procedurally, it constitutes a comment on an issue that is: (i) not litigated; (ii) not considered; and (iii) not decided or grounded.[139] Hence, statements on non-legal, lateral or very broad issues, not subject to prior and detained debate, careful consideration or grounded decision by unanimity or majority constitute *obiter dicta*. Each of these items, in turn, constitutes tests capable of directing a proposition to one or another corner of the library. If all goes according to plan (collegiate decision, detailed communication and proper interpretation), we may enter a world where the *obiter* does not consume its potion and Dr. Jekyll—and I apologise to Stevenson for that—may win.

But... what for purpose?

What positive effects can we get from the *obiter*?

References

Abramowicz M, Stearns M (2005) Defining Dicta. Stanford Law Rev 57(4):953–1036

Allen CK (1939) Law in the making, 3rd edn. Oxford University Press, Oxford

Amrani Mekki S (2019) Responsabilité et Transparence de la Justice Civile. In: Mitidiero D (ed) *Accountability* e Transparência da Justiça Civil — Uma Perspectiva Comparada. RT, São Paulo

Arruda Alvim T (2012) Precedentes e Evolução do Direito. In: Arruda Alvim T (ed) Direito Jurisprudencial. RT, São Paulo

Arruda Alvim T, Dantas B (2018) Recurso Especial, Recurso Extraordinário e a Nova Função dos Tribunais Superiores, 5th edn. Revista dos Tribunais, São Paulo

Ávila H (2014) Teoria dos Princípios, 15th edn. Malheiros, São Paulo

Ávila H (2019) Constituição, Liberdade e Interpretação. Malheiros, São Paulo

Bayern S (2009) Case interpretation. Florida State Univ Law Rev 36(2):125–175

Cardozo B (1991) The nature of judicial process. Yale University Press, New Haven

---

[138] So is the *ratio*'s: MacCormick (1987), pp. 155 and 169; Schauer (2009), p. 53; Mitidiero (2023c).

[139] *Retro*, Chapter I, item 1.1.

Chiassoni P (2007) Tecnica dell'Interpretazione Giuridica. Il Mulino, Bologna
Currie D (1985) The Constitution in the Supreme Court — the first hundred years (1789 – 1888). University of Chicago Press, Chicago
Currie D (1990) The Constitution in the Supreme Court — the second century. Chicago University Press, Chicago
da Rosa de Bustamante T (2018) Obiter Dicta Abusivos: Esboço de uma Tipologia dos Pronunciamentos Judiciais Ilegítimos. Revista Direito GV São Paulo 14(2):707–745
de Oliveira PM (2019) Regimentos Internos como Fonte de Normas Processuais. JusPodivm, Salvador
do Passo Cabral A (2023) Jurisdição sem Decisão — *Non Liquet* e Consulta Jurisdicional no Direito Brasileiro. JusPodivm, São Paulo
Domit O (2016) *Iura Novit Curia* e Causa de Pedir. RT, São Paulo
Dorf M (1994) Dicta and Article III. Univ Pa Law Rev 142(6):1997–2069
Duxbury N (2021) The intricacies of dicta and dissent. Cambridge University Press, Cambridge
Dworkin R (1986) Law's Empire. Harvard University Press, Cambridge (Mass.)
Eisenberg M (1988) The nature of the Common Law. Harvard University Press, Cambridge
Fisher L (1988) Constitutional dialogues — interpretation as political process. Princeton University Press, Princeton
Friedman B (2010) The wages of stealth overruling (with particular attention to Miranda v. Arizona). Georgetown Law J 99(1):1–63
Garcia-Roza LA (1996) O Silêncio da Chuva. Companhia das Letras, São Paulo
Garner B (2005) Opinions, Style of. In: Hall K (ed) The Oxford companion to the Supreme Court of the United States, 2nd edn. Oxford University Press, Oxford
Garner B (ed) (2016) The Law of Judicial Precedent. Thomson Reuters, St. Paul
Goodhart A (1937a) Three cases on possession. In: Essays in jurisprudence and the Common Law, 2nd edn. Cambridge University Press, Cambridge
Goodhart A (1937b) Determining the Ratio Decidendi of a case. In: Essays in jurisprudence and the Common Law. Cambridge University Press, Cambridge
Guastini R (2011) *Interpretare e Argomentare*. Giuffrè, Milano
Hesse K (1999) Grundzüge des Verfassungsrechts der Bundesrepublik Deutschland, 20th edn. C. H. Müller, Heidelberg
Holmes OW Jr (1963) The Common Law. Harvard University Press, Cambridge
Killian R (2013) Dicta and the rule of law. Pepperdine Law Rev 41(1):1–20
Kuh KF (2008) Electronically manufactured law. Harv J Law Technol 22
Lessa G (2022) Precedentes Judiciais e Raciocínio Jurídico — Aplicação, Analogia e Distinção. RT, São Paulo
Leval P (2006) Judging under the constitution: dicta about dicta. N Y Univ Law Rev 81(4): 1249–1282
Llewellyn K (2008) The Bramble Bush — the classic lectures on the law and law school. Oxford University Press, Oxford
Maccormick N (1987) Why cases have rationes and what these are. In: Goldstein L (ed) Precedent in law. Oxford University Press, Oxford
Marchiori M (2022) A Atuação do Poder Judiciário na Formação de Precedentes Definitivos — Experiências e Desafios. JusPodivm, Salvador
Marinoni LG (2019) O STJ enquanto Corte de Precedentes, 4th edn. RT, São Paulo
Marinoni LG (2021) Processo Constitucional e Democracia. RT, São Paulo
Marinoni LG (2022a) Precedentes Obrigatórios, 7th edn. RT, São Paulo
Marinoni LG (2023a) Julgamento nas Cortes Supremas, 3rd edn. RT, São Paulo
Marinoni LG, Mitidiero D (2018) Comentários ao Código de Processo Civil, vol 15, 2nd edn. RT, São Paulo
Marinoni LG, Arenhart SC, Mitidiero D (2023) Curso de Processo Civil, vol 1, 8th edn. RT, São Paulo

Marshall G (1997) What is binding in a precedent. In: Maccormick N, Summers R (eds) Interpreting precedents — a comparative study. Ashgate, Dartmouth

McLauchlan W (2005) Opinions, assignment and writing. In: Hall K (ed) The Oxford companion to the Supreme Court of the United States, 2nd edn. Oxford University Press, Oxford

Mitidiero D (ed) (2019) *Accountability* e Transparência da Justiça Civil — Uma Perspectiva Comparada. RT, São Paulo

Mitidiero D (2021) Superação para Frente e Modulação de Efeitos — Precedente e Controle de Constitucionalidade no Direito Brasileiro. RT, São Paulo

Mitidiero D (2022) Cortes Superiores e Cortes Supremas — do Controle à Interpretação, da Jurisprudência ao Precedente, 4th edn. RT, São Paulo

Mitidiero D (2023a) Precedentes — da Persuasão à Vinculação, 5th edn. RT, São Paulo

Mitidiero D (2023b) Como Escrevo — Confissões de um Jovem Processualista, 2nd edn. RT, São Paulo

Mitidiero D (2023c) *Ratio Decidendi* — Quando uma Questão é Idêntica, Semelhante ou Distinta? RT, São Paulo

Mitidiero D (2024) Processo Civil, 2nd edn. RT, São Paulo

Monnerat F (2019) Súmulas e Precedentes Qualificados — Técnicas de Formação e Aplicação. Saraiva, São Paulo

Passanante L (2018) Il Precedente Impossibile — Contributo allo Studio del Diritto Giurisprudenziale nel Processo Civile. Giappichelli, Torino

Patton G, Sawer G (1947) Ratio Decidendi and Obiter Dictum in Appellate Courts. Law Q Rev 63(4):461–485

Peters C (2008) Under-the-table overruling. Wayne Law Rev 54:1067–1104

Pisani AP (2015) Lezioni sul Processo Civile, 6th edn. Jovene, Napoli

Re R (2014) Narrowing precedent in the Supreme Court. Columbia Law Rev 114(7):1861–1911

Re R (2016) Narrowing Supreme Court precedent from below. Georgetown Law J 104:921–971

Robles L (2021) O Que Significa Violar uma Norma Jurídica? Uma Perspectiva Processual. RT, São Paulo

Schauer F (2008) Authority and authorities. Virginia Law Rev 94(8):1931–1961

Schauer F (2009) Thinking like a lawyer. Harvard University Press, Cambridge

Stinson J (2010) Why dicta becomes holding and why it matters. Brooklyn Law Rev 76(1):219–264

Stone J (1959) The ratio of the Ratio Decidendi. Mod Law Rev 22(6):597–620

Tarello G (1980) L'Interpretazione della Legge. Giuffrè, Milano

Zaneti Júnior H (2017) O Valor Vinculante dos Precedentes — Teoria dos Precedentes Normativos Formalmente Vinculantes, 3rd edn. JusPodivm, Salvador

Chapter 7
May the Force Be with You

7.1 Illustrating, Persuading

In 1921, in his famed *Storrs Lecture* at Yale, Benjamin Cardozo—direct heir to Oliver Wendell Holmes Jr. and one of the most influential Justices of the U.-S. Supreme Court—recorded his astonishment at the trust placed, especially by judges, in the *obiter dictum*.[1] A real mystery.[2] More than eighty years later, Pierre Leval—judge at the Court of Appeals of the Second Circuit—, in his *Madison Lecture* at New York University, expressed his doubts on the viewpoint; is the *obiter* truly insignificant[3]? Is it simply chit-chatting, or does it possess hidden strength?

As the literature on *obiter* highlights, although safe in the knowledge only the *ratio* is mandatory, the court does, on occasion, feel obliged to consider the *obiter dictum* in their decisions.[4] In the fashion of *Star Wars*, the force is strong with some *dicta*.[5] Later, we will consider an exercise of connecting the dots which allows us to identify, in practice, when the pull of one *obiter* is stronger than the other—criteria which will make our endeavours tidier.[6] For now, however, we are concerned with defining what composes this strange force and how it generates the pull of *obiter dictum.*

The boundaries of the *obiter* are determined by its opposition. Naturally, I begin with an examination of its effects by recalling those of the *ratio*. There are different ways to tell the story of the precedent in Common Law. A well-known attempt begins with the development of the *Reports*—specifically portrayed by T. Ellis

[1] Cardozo (1991), p. 29.

[2] Cardozo (1991), p. 29.

[3] Leval (2006), p. 1255.

[4] Greenwalt (1989), p. 432.

[5] Coale and Couture (2007), pp. 725, note 61, and 727–728.

[6] *Infra*, Chapter III, item 3.2.

D. Mitidiero, *Ratio Decidendi and Obiter Dictum*,
https://doi.org/10.1007/978-3-031-93152-9_7

Lewis between 1930 and 1932[7] and of John Dawson in 1968.[8] When writing *Precedentes* in 2016, I chose a different approach, seeking to reconstruct its history through highlighting the evolving effects over time: *illustrate*, *persuade* and *bind*.[9] From the thirteenth century to the end of the sixteenth century, English judges cited precedents in their decisions in order to explain the law applicable to the case.[10] It was a way of illustrating the Law, returning it to principles invoked in previous decisions. Decisions were synonymous with precedents.[11] However, no judge was obliged to consider a precedent, let alone follow it.[12] The precedent illustrated the Law but did not embody it. It carried no weight.

By the late sixteenth century and the early seventeenth century, the landscape changed; a path for new perspective on precedent was paved, the effects of which rippled into the late nineteenth century. Many interesting factors contributed to this development, but we do not have the space to explore them here.[13] The result was that the precedent shall be invoked as a reason for deciding an issue, provided that it complies with the Common Law. It became considered a proof of the right's existence—the "best proof",[14] as in 1628 Edward Coke emblematically stated in the subtitle of his *The First Part of the Institutes of the Laws of England*. Consequently, judges were obliged to consider the precedent when deciding an issue, and it was only possible to set it aside—as William Blackstone would say in 1765—if it was "patently absurd or unfair".[15] The precedent proved that right existed, thus it should be considered and adopted to resolve an issue encompassed by the precedent unless the judge could show that it met Blackstone's criteria. Its function was now persuasive; the court had to consider it to be correct in order to follow it.

The late nineteenth century saw another evolution. Due to a campaign launched by Jeremy Bentham in the name of legal certainty, the improvement of *Law Reports* and the judicial reforms of 1873 and 1875, the House of Lords was able to confront the notion of the precedent possessing a binding force.[16] Following debates in a series of cases,[17] in *London Tramways Co. v. London County Council* (1898), the House concluded that they were obliged—as well as all other courts submitted to

[7]Lewis (1930a), n. 46, Lewis (1930b), n. 46, Lewis (1931), n. 47, and Lewis (1932), n. 48. In general, it is possible to divide the evolutionary stages of judicial repositories into four: (i) *Year Books* (1290–1535); (ii) *Named Reports* (1535–1765); (iii) *Authorized Reports* (1765–1865); and (iv) *Law Reports* (1865 onwards) (Lewis 1930a, p. 207, n. 46).

[8]Dawson (1986), pp. 50 et seq.

[9]Mitidiero (2023a), pp. 29–43.

[10]Hogue (1986), pp. 200–201.

[11]Duxbury (2008), p. 32.

[12]Berman (2003), p. 273.

[13]Duxbury (2008), pp. 33–34.

[14]Coke (1823).

[15]Blackstone (1979), p. 70.

[16]Evans (1987), pp. 64–72.

[17]They are: *Velley v. Burder* (1837), *Bright v. Hutton* (1852), *Attorney General v. Dean and Canons of Windsor* (1860) and *Beamish v. Beamish* (1861) (Evans 1987, pp. 54–57).

it—to consider and follow its own precedents, regardless of whether or not it agreed with the solution contained therein.[18] *Stare decisis et non quieta movere.* The precedent embodied the right, having to be considered and adopted for the solution of the issue provided for therein.

The *ratio* in English Law, therefore, transversed the realms of illustrative to binding force. A similar fate befell the precedent in U.S. Law.[19]

In Brazil, the strength of the precedent derives from the role of the STF and STJ as Supreme Courts (no longer as courts of control and caselaw, but of interpretation and precedents),[20] the meaning of interpretation (neither mere declaration, nor pure creation, but normative reconstruction)[21] and the meaning of the verb "observe" used by the legislator.[22] It is a major debate, but—to summarise it—I assume here that the precedent is a mandatory legal norm, duly contextualised by facts, which constitutes the instrument by which the principles of legal certainty, freedom and equality are promoted and respected in Brazilian Law. It is not, therefore, a simple means of managing repeated cases. It is not a fortuitous path, limited to civil proceedings, but an institute that opens itself up to the *grande sertão* of the primary sources of Law in Brazil.

On this approach, *observing* the *ratio decidendi* means considering, interpreting and, in the face of an identical or similar issue, enforcing the norm in which the precedent is embodied for its solution, regardless of adherence to its content.[23] *Observing* the *ratio* means—all things considered—to be bound by it, obliged to enforce it for the resolution of an issue. Observing implies a duty to consider,

---

[18]By the way, it was only in 1966, through a Practice Statement, that the House of Lords granted themselves the right to overrule its own precedents. In text: *"Their Lordships regard the use of precedent as an indispensable foundation upon which to decide what is the law and its application to individual cases. It provides at least some degree of certainty upon which individuals can rely in the conduct of their affairs, as well as a basis for orderly development of legal rules. Their Lordships nevertheless recognize that too rigid adherence to precedent may lead to injustice in a particular case and also unduly restrict the proper development of the law. They propose, therefore, to modify their present practice and, while treating former decisions of this House as normally binding, to depart from a previous decision when it appears right to do so. In this connection they will bear in mind the danger of disturbing retrospectively the basis on which contracts, settlements of property and fiscal arrangements have been entered into and also the especial need for certainty as to criminal law. This announcement is not intended to affect the use of precedent elsewhere than in this House"* (cited from Duxbury 2008, pp. 126–127).

[19]Mitidiero (2023a), p. 130, with emphasis on the cases *Burnet v. Coronado Oil & Gas Co.*, 285 U.S. 393 (1932), and *Cooper v. Aaron*, 358 U.S. 1 (1958).

[20]Arts. 102, item III, and 105, item III, CRFB, in the suggested reading, among others, in Mitidiero (2022).

[21]With the appropriate bibliographical indications, Mitidiero (2023a); Mitidiero (2023).

[22]Art. 927, *caput*, CPC, in the suggested reading, among others, in Mitidiero (2023a); Mitidiero (2023).

[23]For more on the different operations required for enforcing the *ratio* in the face of identical and similar issues, Mitidiero (2023).

interpret and, if applicable, enforce.[24] Hence the question: if obligation is an effect exclusive to the *ratio*, what is the draw of the *obiter*?

Time to revisit the basics: *Cohens* (1821)[25] and *Humphrey's Executor* (1935).[26]

Cohens determined that propositions which go beyond the settled issue ("beyond the case") do not oblige ("ought not to control the judgment in a subsequent suit") but must be considered ("may be respected").[27] Axiomatically, only propositions that are considered can be respected: without mandatory consideration there is no possibility of adoption. From this, we can conclude that the proper effect of the *obiter* is to persuade. There is a duty to consider the *obiter*, but no concurrent duty to follow it.[28] The court must take it into account but can escape it by demonstrating the reasons why they do not accept it. This is not an uncommon understanding; a number of legal scholars—abroad[29] and here in Brazil[30]—also link this persuasive effect[31] to the *obiter*.

In *Humphrey's Executor*, however, a delineation was drawn. The command of the force can vary; not every *obiter* is created equal.[32] One must distinguish "*gratis*" from "*judicial dictum*". The first is produced without prior debate, careful consideration or grounded decision, whilst the second had the proceeding machine working in its favour[33]—and, therefore, "may have great weight".[34] The force is stronger: its effects are apparent.

The combined reading of *Cohens* and *Humphrey's Executor*, however, indicates the need to dig a little deeper into the land of distinctions between "*gratis*" and "*judicial dictum*" to explore their effects. Are there other criteria, in addition to the

---

[24] Marinoni and Mitidiero (2018), pp. 65–66; Mitidiero (2023a), p. 116, note 108; Mitidiero (2024).

[25] *Cohens v. Virginia,* 19 U.S. (6 *Wheaton*) 264 (1821).

[26] *Humphrey's Executor v. United States*, 295 U.S. 602 (1935).

[27] I invoke once more the classic passage of the Chief of Justice Marshall in *Cohens*: *"it is a maxim, not to be disregarded, that general expressions, in every opinion, are to be taken in connection with the case in which those expressions are used. If they go beyond the case, they may be respected, but ought not to control the judgment in a subsequent suit, when the very point is presented for decision. The reason of this maxim is obvious. The question actually before the court is investigated with care, and considered in its full extent. Other principles which may serve to illustrate it, are considered in their relation to the case decided, but their possible bearing on all other cases is seldom completely investigated*" – *Cohens v. Virginia*, 19 U.S. (6 *Wheaton*) 264 (1821).

[28] Pollock (1918), p. 242.

[29] In English Law, Duxbury (2021), p. 48; Michelon (2023), pp. 118–119; in US law, Dorf (1994), pp. 2000 and 2026; Abramowicz and Stearns (2005), p. 1084.

[30] In a monograph, Cruz e Tucci (2004), p. 177; Perrone (2008), p. 126; Marinoni (2022), p. 168; de Macedo (2019), p. 275; Henriques Filho (2021), p. 226; Miranda (2022), pp. 74/75; do Passo Cabral (2023), p. 111. In more comprehensive works, Didier Júnior et al. (2021), p. 570; Carvalho (2022), p. 45.

[31] Although the truth is they do not always bother to distinguish mandatory effect from persuasive effect and to define what persuading means.

[32] Duxbury (2021), p. 77.

[33] *Retro*, Chapter I, item 1.1.

[34] *Humphrey's Executor v. United States*, 295 U.S. 602 (1935).

procedural ones, that allow associating the duty to consider—the persuasive effect—to the *obiter*? Are there alternative criteria available which can determine when an *obiter dictum* may be considered or can be safely set aside?

7.2 Connect the Dots

In one of his best-known texts, Arthur Goodhart differentiated between precedent in English Law and caselaw in French Law based on their effects—the former was mandatory whilst the latter was persuasive.[35] The year was 1934. Many developments have occurred since, but at the time, this was the crux of it.[36] I raise this simple demarcation for a good reason. The Roman-Canonical tradition has always worked in the field of caselaw with the idea of persuasion.[37] This is a notion that can be analysed in terms of degree; an issue can be more or less persuasive. Thus, searching for criteria capable of measuring the credibility of caselaw is not a foreign activity to Civil Law scholars. Accordingly, one can search for criteria to weigh the *obiter*, from this the duty arises to consider it (or not) in subsequent decisions. There are, thus, along with the distinction drawn in *Humphrey's Executor*, other criteria capable of helping measure the credibility of the *obiter* and its consequent association to the persuasive effect.

Casting our gaze backwards allows one to note that the reconstructions made by Italian legal scholars on precedent and the accompanying argumentative scheme elaborated by German scholars, are particularly influential in Brazilian scholarship. Several examples are to hand, but here it is sufficient—since they represent a certain perspective on the theme—to limit our examination to the works of José Rogério Cruz e Tucci,[38] from 2004, Thomas da Rosa de Bustamante,[39] from 2012, and Humberto Theodoro Júnior and Érico Andrade, from 2021.[40]

I'll start with the Italian scholars;[41] their efforts concern the "*diritto giurisprudenziale*" and their concern with this topic has endured decades. When I lived in Pavia, I came across a little-known book written by Gian Antonio Micheli in Oxford in 1938—probably the first on the topic published in Italy ("*Contributo allo Studio della Formazione Giudiziale del Diritto – 'Case Law' e 'Stare Decisis'*").[42]

[35] Goodhart (1934), p. 42.

[36] For more on the historical development of the theme, Mitidiero (2023a).

[37] Taruffo (1994), pp. 411–430; Taruffo (2007), pp. 709–725.

[38] Cruz e Tucci (2004).

[39] da Rosa de Bustamante (2012).

[40] Theodoro Júnior and Andrade (2021).

[41] For more on the influence of Italian Civil Procedure scholars on Brazilian scholars, with the appropriate bibliographic indications, Taruffo and Mitidiero (2018); Pasqualotto (2022).

[42] Micheli (1938).

More popular musings include the works of Luigi Lombardi's, published in 1967[43] and Gino Gorla, published in 1970[44] and 1990.[45] The most influential works are, perhaps, those by Giovanni Orrù, from 1983,[46] by Michele Taruffo, published between 1994 and 2018,[47] and by Luca Passanante, from 2018.[48] These authors have made their mark on the Brazilian civil procedure.[49] As a friend of mine has said to me—they have passed the immigration check.

Regarding the reconstruction of the *obiter's* persuasive effects, I am most interested in the impartations of Giovanni Orrù. He suggests, as a recognition rule of caselaw, the criterion of "normative effectiveness".[50] Having classified this into three major species,[51] Orrù observed that authority is gained due to: (i) the intrinsic strength of the argumentation adopted; (ii) the prestige of who is judging; (iii) the position of the court; and (iv) the accordance with the literature.[52] The roots of this construction are key to understanding it. In reading his *Richterrecht*, it is clear that Orrù's arguments are influenced by the works of Josef Esser and Martin Kriele, as well of that of Luigi Lombardi. That's only natural; we do not create our own scaffolding. The basis of his argument can be found in a popular book by Esser, published in 1956. Dealing with the role of principles in the construction of Law in the Roman-Canonical tradition and in Common Law, Esser observed that certain *dicta*—and this is the exact expression used by him—may have greater or lesser authority due to: (i) the position of the court; (ii) the prestige of the judge; and (iii) the strength of the argument.[53] Of course, Esser's systematisation also drew upon material found elsewhere, including—not by chance—that of the Common Law tradition. In his *Grundsatz und Norm*, Esser attributes his ideas to Julius Stone and Thomas Holland.[54] Upon reading this, I attempted to skip ahead and sought the first work dedicated specifically to the precedent with an open defence of its binding

[43] Lombardi (1975).

[44] Gorla (1981).

[45] Gorla (1990).

[46] Orrù (1983) (which, by the way, has a preface by Luigi Lombardi).

[47] Among which stand out, in what concerns us now, Taruffo (1994), pp. 411–430, and Taruffo (2007), pp. 709–725 (the first, by the way, dedicated to a volume of studies in honour of Gino Gorla).

[48] Passanante (2018).

[49] Orrù, Taruffo and Passanante are often quoted in Cruz e Tucci (2004), and in Theodoro Júnior and Andrade (2021).

[50] Orrù (1983), pp. 60–62.

[51] Orrù (1983), pp. 62–65. They are: (i) authorised decision (*"opinione autorizzata"*, which may or may not be considered); (ii) decision with authority (*"opinione autorevole"*, which must be considered, and its non-application must be justified); and (iii) mandatory decision (*"opinione autoritativa"*, which must be considered and mandatorily enforced).

[52] Orrù (1983), pp. 67–71.

[53] Esser (1961), p. 255.

[54] Esser (1961), p. 255, note 267. Of Stone (1946), and of Holland (1916).

character:[55] *The Science of Legal Judgment*, published in 1834 in England and in 1871 in the United States by James Ram.[56] To the victor, the potatoes—to use a Machado de Assis expression.[57]

James Ram also devotes several pages to the weight of the *obiter*. In considering how to determine the weight of a decision ("of estimating authorities"),[58] Ram divided his argument into three parts: (i) the value of each court's decisions;[59] (ii) the circumstances that can increase its value;[60] and (iii) those that can decrease it.[61] Writing at a time when the English courts were still shrouded in mystery—the Judicature Acts that whipped it into shape arrived in 1873, 1875 and 1876[62]—Ram first clarified that the decisions made at the House of Lords had a greater weight than any other.[63] He then nominally listed more than forty famous Common Law judges, among them, Littleton, Coke, Hale and Mansfield, drawing upon the status attributed to them by others.[64] He argued that the weight of a decision is proportional to the notoriety of each one's knowledge in a particular branch of law, their personality or their path.[65] Finally, he observed that a decision that was not grounded, timidly grounded, not debated by the panel of judges or not supported by an effective adversary proceeding between the parties had less weight.[66] In other words, Ram weighed decisions according to (i) the position of the court; (ii) the prestige of the judge; and (iii) the quality of the argument. An unsurprising turn of events.

These criteria are perhaps akin to reclaimed wood furniture, only lightly touched by the patina of time. Largely unaltered, despite traversing several borders. James Ram in 1834 in England, Josef Esser in 1956 in Germany, Giovanni Orrù in 1983 in Italy—not to mention MacAllister in 2011 in the United States—also invoke the authority of the courts, the quality of the judges and the depth of the debate as

[55] Freda (2012), p. 18. Also highlighting the importance of Ram's book, Evans (1987), p. 46.

[56] Ram (1871) (the first edition was published in London by Maxwell—this second edition has John Townshend's additions and notes).

[57] The expression "To the victor, the potatoes!" ("Ao vencedor as batatas!") comes from Machado de Assis' novel *Quincas Borba* and humorously conveys the idea that the spoils of victory are reserved for the strongest.

[58] Ram (1871), pp. 283–322.

[59] Ram (1871), pp. 283–299.

[60] Ram (1871), pp. 299–316.

[61] Ram (1871), pp. 316–322.

[62] Mitidiero (2023a), p. 41.

[63] Ram (1871), pp. 283–284.

[64] Ram (1871), pp. 300–304. For example: "Hale: 'one of the ablest and most learned judges that ever adorned the profession'; 'as correct, as learned, and as humane a judge, as ever graced a bench of justice'; 'one of the greatest and best men who ever sat in judgment'" (Ram 1871, p. 300).

[65] Ram (1871), pp. 305 and 307.

[66] Ram (1871), pp. 316–319.

elements to weigh the persuasive effect of caselaw.[67] We cannot be surprised at their arrival in Brazilian literature;[68] they are ideas that resist the winds of change.

Let us turn to the German's approach. Here, I'm interested in the rules of argument elaborated by Robert Alexy in 1978 regarding the use of the precedent[69] and their subsequent use by Brazilian scholars.[70] Before examining them, however, it's worth taking a few steps back and considering how this argumentation theory developed and became so prominent. Alexy's theory seeks to answer to a problem posed by Kelsen in 1934 in his *Reine Rechtslehre*; a cumulation of a transatlantic dialogue. Writing in Austria in 1934, Kelsen closed his *Reine Rechtslehre* by demonstrating that the interpretation of a text carries with it more than one possibility of application.[71] It is indeterminate, yet determinable. The legislator provides a frame within which the judge decides what meaning should be attached to the text and applied to the solution of a specific case. His arrival at this conclusion, however, prompted the realisation that the greatest challenge one faced would be the promotion of the principle of legal certainty.[72]

Holmes—a key figure in the philosophy of Law in Common Law in the twentieth century[73]—reached similar conclusions, attributing a key role to judges in defining the meaning of law. Writing in the United States in 1881, he opens *The Common Law* with the assertion that law is not pure logic, but also the fruit of experience.[74] In 1897, in *"The Path of the Law"*, he outlines his main goal as the ability to predict judicial behaviour—what is *done* by the courts.[75] For authors like Karl Llewellyn, writing in 1930, this abstract discreditation of legal norms as instruments to guide judicial decisions was but a step[76].

However, it is problematic to interweave these strands into the theory of Law tapestry.

Whilst it is necessary to understand the practical contours of a judge's decision-making, legal theory demands that norms operate, that the Law is binding in nature. The history of modern argumentation theory begins at this intersection; an attempt to tackle these, seemingly contradictory, challenges. It began with an effort to distinguish decision from justification, and then escalated to the distinction between internal and external justification, the link between justification and grounding, and the elaboration of the first argumentation theories. Such movement, from the publication of Richard Wasserstrom's book in the U.S. in 1961 to the dissemination

---

[67] McAllister (2011), p. 204.

[68] Ataíde Júnior (2012), p. 88; de Macedo (2019), pp. 275–276; Carvalho (2022), pp. 32–33.

[69] Alexy (1978), pp. 334–341.

[70] Cruz e Tucci (2004), pp. 296–299; da Rosa de Bustamante (2012), pp. 307 et seq.

[71] Kelsen (2000), p. 348. Before Kelsen, by the way, Merkl (1916), pp. 535–556, n. 42, already observed that the absence of univocal solutions in Law is the rule.

[72] Kelsen (2000), p. 354. I tell this story in more detail in Mitidiero (2023a).

[73] Duxbury (1995), pp. 9/64; Postema (2011), pp. 43–77.

[74] Holmes Jr. (1963), p. 5.

[75] Holmes Jr. (1897).

of the works of Neil MacCormick in the U.K. and Robert Alexy in Germany—both in 1978—is what set the argumentation theory in stone. The resulting cultural melting pot is what Manuel Atienza, in 1991, called the standard argumentation theories.[76]

Let's do this.

Richard Wasserstrom took the first step to demonstrate that invoking norms in the decision proves that it is bound the Law. In 1961, when he published *The Judicial Decision – Toward a Theory of Legal Justification*, he brought the distinction between "context of discovery" and "context of justification"[77] to the field of Law. Accordingly, he distinguished "decision context" from "justification context", demonstrating that reasons outside the law may influence decision-making, but cannot be used its justification.[78] In response to the realists, he attempted to refocus the debate about the interpretation of the law on what was *said* in the decision. What really mattered were the reasons capable of justifying the decision; these are the domain of Law.

Ten years later Jerzy Wróblewski expanded upon this. He restructured the understanding of judicial reasoning to be more organised and intersubjectively controllable. In "*Legal Decision and its Justification*",[79] he drew the distinction between internal and external justification. The former relating to the court's logical reasoning (how one uses, for example, deduction, induction and abduction to reach their conclusions), whilst the latter concerning the selection of the material used in the decision (how the court carries out the argumentation necessary to resolve the case).[80] Likewise, in 1975, Michele Taruffo weighed in. In *La Motivazione della*

---

[76] Atienza (1991).

[77] In epistemology, the distinction first appears with Carnap (1974), its elaboration being useful to the later developments of Popper (1935), and Reichenbach (1961) (all according to Kochem 2021, pp. 60–66).

[78] Wasserstrom (1961).

[79] Wróblewski (1971), n. 14. Such distinction is one of the foundations of Wróblewski's thought, especially in the 1988 *Sadowe Stosowanie Prawa*, whose English version was prepared by Wróblewski in Edinburgh in 1989 and revised by Neil MacCormick and Zenon Bankowski (Wróblewski 1992, pp. 209/262).

[80] In *Precedentes*, I wrote that "de um lado, uma decisão apresenta justificação interna sempre que o dispositivo decorre logicamente da fundamentação e que essa contempla todos os fundamentos arguidos pelas partes. Na justificação interna, portanto, interessa a correção lógica e a completude da fundamentação da decisão. Daí que a justificação interna é uma justificação formal que responde à necessidade de não contradição no discurso jurídico. É o campo em que a lógica atua no processo interpretativo, no qual o julgador raciocina de forma dedutiva para solução das questões. De outro, uma decisão tem justificação externa sempre que as premissas adotadas na decisão são adequadas. A justificação externa, portanto, concerne à adequação das escolhas das premissas empregadas na justificação interna. Nessa linha, constitui uma justificação material que responde à necessidade de adoção de razões suficientes para tomada de decisão, envolvendo o exame tanto de normas como de fatos, na medida em que entre ambos existe uma absoluta implicação. É o campo em que a argumentação atua no processo interpretativo, no qual o julgador individualiza, valora e decide de forma não dedutiva. Como campo próprio da argumentação jurídica, entram em consideração na justificação externa, por exemplo, as normas jurídicas, as normas sobre interpretação, as normas

Sentenza Civile, he suggested distinguishing decision, internal justification and external justification to draw the profile of the reasoning of decisions, scrutinizing their minimum content.[81] Utilising these parameters, he presented a frame for reasoning in judicial decisions.

Hereafter, assessing whether a decision is rational and consistent with the Law relates to the legal reasons—those that are used to justify the different interpretative decisions the judge must take when resolving a case—invoked. The evaluation of the decision depends on its reasoning; its justifying reasons is what makes possible to control it intersubjectively.[82] This is reflected in Pierluigi Chiassoni's *Tecnica dell'Interpretazione Giuridica*, published in 2007: interpreting and enforcing the law is synonymous with its reasoning.

The work of Wasserstrom, Wróblewski, and Taruffo collectively demonstrated the importance of norms in judicial decision-making. The organisation of external justification—the way in which argumentation should develop is a task—that was undertaken by Neil MacCormick[83] and Robert Alexy.[84] Through their respective dialogues, (MacCormick with Hart,[85] Alexy with Kelsen[86]), they sought to solve the problem of the indeterminacy of the law by invoking criteria capable of guiding the argument,[87] making it more rational and secure.[88] Both were received as important

---

preferenciais argumentativas e as construções doutrinárias empregadas na decisão. Em outras palavras, encontra-se no âmbito da justificação externa o material que se encontra à disposição do intérprete para consecução do processo interpretativo" (Mitidiero 2023a, pp. 64–65).

[81] For example, Taruffo (1975). By the way, the minimum required is as follows: (i) the enunciation of the choices developed by the judicial body for the, (i.i) individualisation of the applicable rules, (i.ii) verification of the allegations of fact, (i.iii) legal qualification of the factual support, (i.iv) legal consequences resulting from the legal qualification of the fact; (ii) the establishment of the context of the links of implication and coherence between the statements, and (iii) the justification of the statements based on criteria that show the respective rationality (Taruffo 1975, p. 467).

[82] Chiassoni (2007), p. 142.

[83] MacCormick (1978). MacCormick, by the way, will get back to this subject in MacCormick (2005).

[84] Alexy (1978).

[85] Hart (2012).

[86] Kelsen (2000).

[87] This is the most appropriate reading of the purpose, sometimes distorted, of these authors' works. As Cláudio Michelon Jr. observes, "a expressão 'princípio jurídico' tem tido uma presença frequente em decisões judiciais e na doutrina brasileiras. A expressão foi popularizada entre os profissionais e teóricos do direito no Brasil a partir de uma leitura direta ou, frequentemente, indireta de autores como Ronald Dworkin e Robert Alexy. Ironicamente, um conceito que foi originalmente elaborado como uma forma de estabelecer critérios de racionalidade que limitam a discricionariedade judicial é mais comumente associado no Brasil a um instrumento que permite ao juiz mais liberdade em relação à lei e ao direito posto. De fato, os princípios são muitas vezes utilizados por tribunais e doutrinadores como uma forma de eliminar dificuldades postas por regras complexas e/ou que destoam da concepção de justiça do juiz ou escritor. Na maior parte da América Latina os princípios dworkinianos foram recebidos não tanto como uma reação à crítica *realista* ao formalismo na argumentação jurídica, mas como uma forma de reação ao próprio *formalismo* interpretativo tardio que, segundo alguns, caracterizava a região. No caso particular do Brasil, a

contributors to the debate.[89] Hence, I now return to Alexy's lessons. For him, the precedent (*"Präjudiz"*) is central to the argument. The party have the burden and, the judge the duty, to argue against its solution if they do not wish to follow it.[90] Failing this, the precedent must be prioritised in resolving the case. In recognising this persuasive activity, Alexy sought to honour both the principle of universalisation of decisions (*"Universalisierbarkeitsprinzip"*)[91]—which plays in favour of maintaining the precedent—and the claim to correct the decisions (*"Anspruch auf Richtigkeit"*)[92]—which plays against it.

If the *ratio decidendi* is mandatory, it is appropriate to recognise the persuasive effect to the *obiter dictum*, carrying these theoretical constructions to its domain. As such, certain *dicta* must be considered in the justification of decisions; the court can only ignore its force when presenting good reasons to do so.

The question now arises: which *dicta*? By what criteria do we recognise them?

7.3 The Empire Strikes Back

As we have established, the obiter has a twofold function. It can signal the development of the Law or delimit the *ratio* in case of interpretative doubts. It is true that, in these employments, it may be lured to the dark side, directed to the path of *obitering* and subverting the principles that underpin the Rule of Law.[93] However, if it stays in its lane, it has the potential reinforce its borders or the ratio or, it may even

inserção dos princípios na argumentação jurídica faz parte da segunda geração de ataques ao formalismo jurídico, que se segue à primeira geração composta pelo amplo espectro de teorias relacionadas direta ou indiretamente ao chamado 'direito alternativo'. Essa segunda onda de ataque ao formalismo atingiu o seu alvo e o paradigma formalista de argumentação não é mais a regra no Brasil (se é que um dia foi). Todavia, o ataque ao formalismo atingiu muito mais do que o seu alvo declarado. O que se coloca em questão a partir do modo como os princípios jurídicos vêm sendo utilizados tanto na doutrina como na prática do direito brasileiro é a própria noção de que o direito é algo criado dinamicamente pela comunidade política e não algo derivado de um conjunto abstrato e vago de bens ou valores por especialistas que têm um *insight* privilegiado sobre como esses bens e valores fundamentais devem conformar nossas instituições e decisões políticas. Ou seja, o que está em jogo é a legitimidade democrática desse arranjo institucional" (Michelon 2011, pp. 261–262). Also on this theme, Amato (2023), pp. 358 et seq.

[88] Ávila (2019), pp. 38–40.

[89] Cruz e Tucci (2004), pp. 296/299; da Rosa de Bustamante (2012), pp. 307 et seq.

[90] Alexy (1978), p. 339.

[91] Alexy (1978), p. 335. In Brazilian literature, Pessoa (2014); Cunha (2021).

[92] Alexy (1978), p. 336.

[93] *Retro*, Chapters 4, item 4.3, and 5, item 5.2.

become *ratio*. It ceases to be a young Padawan. However, for the *obiter* to perform this functionality, it must first have something to say—it must be "valuable[94]". This worthiness comes when it's relevant to the interpretation of the issue at stake; when it can reveal a path that offers a resolution. Secondly, it cannot be any simple commentary: it requires a degree of status.

Thus, we return the crux of the matter; how does the *obiter* obtain credibility?

There are various factors at play: the Courts' position, its underwriters' calibre and the quality of the proceeding's;[95] elements that we identified just a few pages ago. As such, two paths to legitimacy are available. The first runs through the Supreme Courts—the STF and the STJ. Their function is to give unity to the Law; they both pacify and develop it.[96] Consequently, their *obiter dicta* showcase how their Justices face the issues presented to them. It is unsurprising that Common Law scholars attribute persuasive value to the *obiter dicta* of the Supreme Courts.[97] It is a criterion that honours the *obiter* for its pedigree—"*auctoritas, non veritas facit legem*".[98] These origins are sufficient to mandate the consideration of *obiter*. Alternatively, its credibility may derive from the quality of the argument: signalled by the status of its underwriters or demonstrated in the careful debate in which it supported the proceeding. As a friend of mine says: what matters is the argument's authority, not the authority's argument. Here, the value of the *obiter* derives from the inverse maxim "*veritas, non auctoritas facit legem*",[99] those who claim or invoke it are required demonstrate its quality. How so? By invoking the reputation of those who sign it, the caselaw and the support received by legal scholars.

[94] Duxbury (2021), p. 83.

[95] Ram (1871), pp. 283–322 (*retro*, Chapter 6, item 6.2).

[96] Unity of Law "is the state of affairs in which the law provides security for the exercise of freedom and respect for equality", having as its "object the resolution of interpretative disagreements concerning longstanding issues that have already received the legislator's attention or the resolution of interpretative disagreements regarding new issues that have not yet been addressed by the legislator." (Mitidiero 2024, p. 245). Looking back, when seeking to pacify its interpretation, unity is retrospective; looking forward, when seeking to develop law, unity is prospective (Mitidiero 2022, pp. 79 and 108–117).

[97] Dorf (1994), pp. 2000 and 2026; Abramowicz and Stearns (2005), p. 1084; Duxbury (2021), p. 48.

[98] For a classic text, Hobbes (1991), pp. 183–200.

[99] Coke (1823), L.2, C.4, Sect. 108, vol. I, in which it points to *Magna Charta* as a "confirmation or restitution of the Common Law" and as "source of the other acts of Parliament". The debate between Hobbes and Coke is very interesting and represents a key moment in the development of Law. It can be found in an imaginary dialogue written by Hobbes and published posthumously which is worth checking out: Hobbes (1971), especially pp. 54–55. These two maxims, moreover, are generally opposed by legal scholars to illustrate the debate between morality and Law (for example. Ferrajoli 2007, p. 115; Zaneti Júnior 2017, pp. 102–108).

The hallmark of these values—its relevance and credibility—warrants the consideration of *obiter dictum*. The court can only avoid this if they can present good reasons to leave the *obiter* aside. This demonstrates the persuasive assumption of the obiter: it is an ally of *ratio* in promoting the unity of Law. It also derives value from its ability to rouse interest in a broader debate, serving as a point of support—for example—for the opposition of divergence motions in the Supreme Courts. However, if it fails to meet this criteria, it may still illustrate the Law, but it does not need to be considered and hardly raises sufficient interest to autonomously legitimise a round of appeals.

For instance, in *Rio de Janeiro Refrescos v. Minas Gerais* (2023) the STJ decided: "the plea rendered in *obiter dictum* on the merits of the special appeal does not characterise the decisional divergence, since it is only an argumentative reinforcement".[100] To determine such divergence, what matters is whether an issue was faced in a valuable, relevant, noteworthy way, given that the appeal of divergence motions aims precisely at the granting of unity to Law. With the divergence motions, the goal is, therefore, to make Law move in the same direction, avoiding false clues and confusing signs. Therefore, what is decisive for admitting or not the divergence motions in relation to the *obiter dictum* lies in the court's argument considering its value. That is where its importance stems from as a signal sent by it to civil society and to the legal community. That is where its value to represent the divergence is taken from.

You must have realised, finally, that I argue that the pair *ratio* and *obiter* can generate three—and not just two—effects. The *ratio* has a binding, mandatory effect. The valuable *obiter*, a persuasive one, which must be considered but not necessarily adopted. The non-valuable, illustrative one, which allows it to be considered and adopted or not. The problem involving the *ratio* and the different species of *obiter dicta* is not only solved in the dilemma of following or not following[101] them, but also in that of considering or not considering them. There are situations in which there is no duty to follow it, but there is a duty to consider it, which is precisely the case of the valuable *obiter*, endowed with a persuasive effect. Hence the opportunity to distinguish things when trying to transpose—attentively to the peculiarities of the Roman-canonical tradition—the effects of each of them.

In short: when valuable, the *obiter* has a persuasive effect. It must be considered and adopted, unless better reasons are invoked. And because it is an ally for the promotion of the unity of Law, it can even be invoked to characterise decisional divergence. Not being so, it has a merely illustrative effect: it does not have to be considered and it does not characterise it.

---

[100] *Rio de Janeiro Refrescos v. Minas Gerais* (STJ, 1ª Seção, AgInt no EREsp n. 2,051,752/MG, Rela. Mina. Regina Helena Costa, j. 29.08.2023, DJe 31.08.2023).

[101] As understood, however, by Schauer (2009), pp. 69–70.

References

Abramowicz M, Stearns M (2005) Defining Dicta. Stanford Law Rev 57(4):953–1036

Alexy R (1978) Theorie der juristischen Argumentation. Suhrkamp, Frankfurt im Main

Amato L (2023) Teoria Geral do Direito. Fórum, Belo Horizonte

Ataíde Júnior JR (2012) Precedentes Vinculantes e Irretroatividade do Direito no Sistema Processual Brasileiro. Juruá, Curitiba

Atienza M (1991) Las Razones del Derecho — Teorías de la Argumentación Jurídica. Centro de Estudios Constitucionales, Madrid

Ávila H (2019) Constituição, Liberdade e Interpretação. Malheiros, São Paulo

Berman H (2003) Law and revolution, vol 2. Harvard University Press, Cambridge

Blackstone W (1979) Commentaries on the Laws of England (1765-1769). The University of Chicago Press, Chicago. v 1

Cardozo B (1991) The nature of judicial process. Yale University Press, New Haven

Carnap R (1974) Der logische Aufbau der Welt, 4th edn. Felix Meiner, Hamburg

Carvalho F (2022) Comentários ao Código de Processo Civil, vol 19. Saraiva, São Paulo

Chiassoni P (2007) Tecnica dell'Interpretazione Giuridica. Il Mulino, Bologna

Coale D, Couture W (2007) Loud rules. Pepperdine Law Rev 34(3):715–741

Coke E (1823) The First Part of the Institutes of the Laws of England — or a Commentary upon Littleton, vol 1. Clarke, Pheney and Brooke, London

Cruz e Tucci JR (2004) Precedente Judicial como Fonte de Direito. RT, São Paulo

Cunha G (2021) Precedentes Obrigatórios e Jurisprudência Vinculante. Marcial Pons, São Paulo

da Rosa de Bustamante T (2012) Teoria do Precedente Judicial — A Justificação e a Aplicação de Regras Jurisprudenciais. Noeses, São Paulo

Dawson J (1986) Oracles of the law. William Hein, New York

de Macedo LB (2019) Precedentes Judiciais e Direito Processual Civil, 3rd edn. JusPodivm, Salvador

Didier Júnior F, Braga PS, de Oliveira RA (2021) Curso de Direito Processual Civil, vol 2, 16th edn. JusPodivm, Salvador

do Passo Cabral A (2023) Jurisdição sem Decisão — *Non Liquet* e Consulta Jurisdicional no Direito Brasileiro. JusPodvm, São Paulo

Dorf M (1994) Dicta and Article III. Univ Pa Law Rev 142(6):1997–2069

Duxbury N (1995) Patterns of American jurisprudence. Oxford University Press, Oxford

Duxbury N (2008) The nature and authority of precedent. Cambridge University Press, Cambridge

Duxbury N (2021) The intricacies of dicta and dissent. Cambridge University Press, Cambridge

Esser J (1961) Principio y Norma en la Elaboración Jurisprudencial del Derecho Privado (trans: Valentí Fiol E). Bosch, Barcelona

Evans J (1987) Change in the doctrine of precedent during the nineteenth century. In: Goldstein L (ed) Precedent in law. Oxford University Press, Oxford

Ferrajoli L (2007) Principia Iuris, vol 1. Laterza, Roma

Freda D (2012) "Una Dispotica Creazione" — Il Precedente Vincolante nella Cultura Giuridica Inglese dell'Ottocento. Giappichelli, Torino

Goodhart A (1934) Precedent in English and Continental Law. Law Q Rev 50:40–65

Gorla G (1981) La Giurisprudenza. Diritto Comparato e Diritto Comune Europeo. Griuffrè, Milano

Gorla G (1990) Precedente Giudiziale. In Enciclopedia Giuridica Treccani. Treccani, Roma

Greenwalt K (1989) Reflections on holding and dictum. J Leg Educ 39(3):431–442

Hart H (2012) The concept of law, 3rd edn. Oxford University Press, Oxford

Henriques Filho RA (2021) Identificação dos Precedentes Judiciais. Thoth, Londrina

Hobbes T (1971) A dialogue between a philosopher and a student of the Common Laws of England. Chicago University Press, Chicago

Hobbes T (1991) Leviathan. Cambridge University Press, Cambridge

Hogue A (1986) Origins of the Common Law. Liberty Fund, Indianapolis

Holmes OW Jr (1897) The path of the law. Harv Law Rev 10:457–478

Holmes OW Jr (1963) The Common Law. Harvard University Press, Cambridge
Kelsen H (2000) *Reine Rechtslehre.* Österreich, Wien
Kochem R (2021) Fundamentando Decisões — Uma Doutrina Lógico-Argumentativa. Thoth, Londrina
Leval P (2006) Judging under the constitution: dicta about dicta. N Y Univ Law Rev 81(4): 1249–1282
Lewis TE (1930a) The history of judicial precedent — I. Law Q Rev 46:207–224
Lewis TE (1930b) The history of judicial precedent — II. Law Q Rev 46:341–360
Lewis TE (1931) The history of judicial precedent — III. Law Q Rev 47:411–427
Lewis TE (1932) The history of judicial precedent — IV. Law Q Rev 48:230–247
Lombardi L (1975) Saggio sul Diritto Giurisprudenziale. Giuffrè, Milano
Maccormick N (1978) Legal reasoning and legal theory. Oxford University Press, Oxford
Maccormick N (2005) Rhetoric and the Rule of Law. Oxford University Press, Oxford
Marinoni LG (2022) Precedentes Obrigatórios, 7th edn. RT, São Paulo
Marinoni LG, Mitidiero D (2018) Comentários ao Código de Processo Civil, vol 15, 2nd edn. RT, São Paulo
Mcallister M (2011) Dicta redefined. Willamette Law Rev 47(2):161–210
Merkl A (1916) Zum Interpretationsproblem. Grünhutsche Zeitschrift für das Privat- und Öffentliche Recht der Gegenwart 42. Alfred Hölder, Wien
Micheli GA (1938) Contributo allo Studio della Formazione Giudiziale del Diritto — "Case Law" e "Stare Decisis". Treves, Pavia
Michelon C (2011) Princípios e Coerência na Argumentação Jurídica. In: Macedo Júnior RP, Barbieri CHC (eds) Direito e Interpretação — Racionalidades e Instituições. Saraiva, São Paulo
Michelon C (2023) The uses of precedent and legal argument. In: Endicott T, Kristjánsson HD, Lewis S (eds) Philosophical foundations of precedent. Oxford University Press, Oxford
Miranda VV (2022) Precedentes Judiciais — Construção e Aplicação da *Ratio Decidendi.* Revista dos Tribunais, São Paulo
Mitidiero D (2022) Cortes Superiores e Cortes Supremas — do Controle à Interpretação, da Jurisprudência ao Precedente, 4th edn. RT, São Paulo
Mitidiero D (2023) *Ratio Decidendi* — Quando uma Questão é Idêntica, Semelhante ou Distinta? RT, São Paulo
Mitidiero D (2023a) Precedentes — da Persuasão à Vinculação, 5th edn. RT, São Paulo
Mitidiero D (2024) Processo Civil, 2nd edn. RT, São Paulo
Orrù G (1983) Richterrecht — Il Problema della Libertà e Autorità Giudiziale nella Dottrina Tedesca Contemporanea. Giuffrè, Milano
Pasqualotto V (2022) Processo Civil Comparado — do Direito Comparado à Comparação no Processo Civil. RT, São Paulo
Passanante L (2018) Il Precedente Impossibile — Contributo allo Studio del Diritto Giurisprudenziale nel Processo Civile. Giappichelli, Torino
Perrone P (2008) Precedentes — O Desenvolvimento Judicial do Direito. Renovar, Rio de Janeiro
Pessoa P (2014) Legitimidade dos Precedentes — Universabilidade das Decisões do STJ. Revista dos Tribunais, São Paulo
Pollock F (1918) A first book of jurisprudence for students of the Common Law, 4th edn. MacMillan and Co., London
Popper K (1935) *Logik der Forschung.* Springer, Wien
Postema G (2011) Legal philosophy in the twentieth century: the Common Law world. Springer, Dordrecht
Ram J (1871) The science of legal judgment — a treatise designed to show the materials whereof, and the process by which, the Courts of Westminster Hall construct their judgments and adapted to practical and general use in discussion, and determination of questions of law, 2nd edn. Baker, New York
Reichenbach H (1961) Experience and prediction. Phoenix Books, Chicago
Schauer F (2009) Thinking like a lawyer. Harvard University Press, Cambridge

Taruffo M (1975) La Motivazione della Sentenza Civile. Cedam, Padova
Taruffo M (1994) Dimensioni del Precedente Giudiziario. Rivista Trimestrale di Diritto e Procedura Civile 48(2):411–430
Taruffo M (2007) Precedente e Giurisprudenza. Rivista Trimestrale di Diritto e Procedura Civile 61(3):709–725
Taruffo M, Mitidiero D (2018) A Justiça Civil — da Itália ao Brasil, dos Setecentos a Hoje. RT, São Paulo
Theodoro Júnior H, Andrade É (2021) Precedentes no Processo Brasileiro. Forense, Rio de Janeiro
Wasserstrom R (1961) The judicial decision — toward a theory of legal justification. Stanford University Press, Stanford
Wróblewski J (1971) Legal decision and its justification. Logique et Analyse 14
Wróblewski J (1992) The judicial application of law (trans: Wróblewski J). Kluwer, Dordrecht
Zaneti Júnior H (2017) O Valor Vinculante dos Precedentes — Teoria dos Precedentes Normativos Formalmente Vinculantes, 3rd edn. JusPodivm, Salvador

Chapter 8
Final Thoughts

For me, the closing passage represents a twofold test. First, an evaluation of whether I have remained faithful to the propositions of my introduction. Second, an assessment as to whether the strands of my argument are suitably developed to be interwoven and create the final summation.

In one hand, the *ratio decidendi*, as imprinted on the passage of *Common Law* history, enables us to distinguish it from the decision and to discern a general normative nature capable of resolving identical, similar and distinct issues. Identity, similarity and distinction are methods which aim to transverse the gaps between issues. They are aimed at promoting the principles of legal certainty, freedom and equality, which, in the language of *Common Law*, are usually associated with the rules of *stare decisis* and "treat like cases alike". Thus, both the identical treatment of identical and similar issues and the distinct treatment of distinct issues can be achieved, developing *Common Law* in a way that can be coherent and universalised.

Based on this debate, it's possible to define the *ratio*, among us, as a rule formulated from the decision of a case by a Supreme Court in which necessary and sufficient reasons operate on relevant facts to determine, wholly or partly, the solution of an identical ("settled law") or similar ("case of first impression") issue. The text of the decision provides the raw material of our endeavour; it erects a framework capable of providing, amongst its competing descriptions, a normative prescription through its logical-argumentative reconstruction.

To identify the *ratio*, interpreting it so as to enforce it, one must follow three steps. First, to distil the accidental from the essential elements, this allows us to identify what was applicable to the resolution of the decided issue. The factual-legal propositions—the necessary and sufficient reasons—related to positions and things of a given situation are essential elements. The people, the time, the place and the value involved are, in principle, accidental. The essential elements are those relevant to defining the *ratio*. Second, to specify the issue decided, comparing it with the issue pending decision. It's necessary to identify what was decided ("settled law") to then justify identity (congruence of essential elements and abstraction of accidental ones), similarity (congruence of essential elements at a certain level of generalisation

D. Mitidiero, *Ratio Decidendi and Obiter Dictum*,
https://doi.org/10.1007/978-3-031-93152-9_8

and abstraction of accidental ones) or distinction (absence of congruence of any essential elements or existence of congruence marked by a fact not previously considered). Third, to reconstruct the rule to demonstrate that its relevant elements support identity, similarity or distinction. Identical issues are resolved by settled law. In turn, cases of first impression (characterised by similar or distinct issues due to unconsidered facts), enter the realm of settled law with the concurrent expansion or constriction of the *ratio*. The *ratio* has no bearing on issues which are totally distinct.

In the other hand, *obiter dicta* are statements on non-legal, lateral or very broad issues, not subject to prior and detained debate, careful consideration or grounded decision or by unanimity or majority. They aim at signalling the development of Law or weigh the *ratio* in case of interpretative doubts. If the script is followed, then *obiter* is a worthy ally in promoting the unity of Law. But, if one deviates, then the *obiter* thwarts our ability to reach a sound decision on issues brought before the court. *Obitering* flourishes and the law fails. Furthermore, not all *obiter* is born equal, we must distinguish between what is valuable for the solution of an issue (and, for this reason, has a persuasive effect: it must be considered, yet it does not need to be adopted) and the one that does not (and it has a merely illustrative effect: it does not need to be considered, let alone adopted).

My hope is that I have passed the test. Perhaps I will hear your verdict someday.

Table of Cases

I American Cases

I.I. New York Court of Appeals

- *Adams v. New Jersey Steamboat Company* (1896)
- *Carpenter v. New York N.Y. N. H. H. R. R.* (1891)
- *People v. Vandewater* (1928)

I.II. New York Supreme Court

- *Hullet v. Shift 33 N. Y.* 571 (1865)

I.III. U.S. Supreme Court

- *Akron v. Akron Center for Reproductive Health*, 462 U.S. 416 (1983)
- *Arizona v. Gant*, 556 U.S. 332 (2009)
- *Arizona Christian School Tuition Organization v. Winn*, 563 U.S. 125 (2011)
- *Austin v. Michigan State Chamber of Commerce*, 494 U.S. 652 (1990)
- *Barktus v. Illinois*, 359 U.S. 121 (1959)
- *Boumediene v. Bush*, 553 U.S. 723 (2008)
- *Brown v. Board of Education of Topeka*, 347 U.S. 483 (1954)
- *Burnet v. Coronado Oil & Gas Co.*, 285 U.S. 393 (1932)
- *Carey v. Musladin*, 549 U.S. 70 (2006)
- *Central Green Co. v. United States*, 531 U.S. 425 (2001)
- *Central Virginia Community College v. Katz*, 546 U.S. 356 (2006)

D. Mitidiero, *Ratio Decidendi and Obiter Dictum*,
https://doi.org/10.1007/978-3-031-93152-9

- *Chimel v. California*, 395 U.S. 752 (1969)
- *Citizens United v. FEC*, 558 U.S. 310 (2010)
- *Civil Right Cases*, 109 U.S. 3 (1883)
- *Cohens v. Virginia,* 19 U.S. (6 *Wheaton*) 264 (1821)
- *Cooper v. Aaron*, 358 U.S. 1 (1958)
- *Crawford v. Washington*, 541 U.S. 36 (2004)
- *Dobbs v. Jackson Women's Health Organization*, 597 U.S. 215 (2022)
- *Eisenstadt v. Baird*, 405, U.S. 438 (1972)
- *Flast v. Cohen,* 392 U.S. 83 (1968)
- *FEC v. Wisconsin Right to Life* (2007)
- *Florida v. J.L.*, 529 U.S. 266 (2000)
- *Fox v. State of Ohio*, 46 U.S. (5 *Howard*) 410 (1847)
- *Giles v. California*, 554 U.S. 353 (2008)
- *Goldberg v. Kelly*, 397 U.S. 254 (1970)
- *Gratz v. Bollinger*, 539 U.S. 244 (2003)
- *Griswold v. Connecticut*, 381 U.S. 479 (1965)
- *Grutter v. Bollinger*, 539 U.S. 306 (2003)
- *Harmelin v. Michigan*, 501 U.S. 957 (1991)
- *Hein v. Freedom from Religion Foundation*, 551 U.S. 587 (2007)
- *Humphrey's Executor v. United States*, 295 U.S. 602 (1935)
- *Johnson v. Eisentrager*, 339 U.S. 763 (1950)
- *Jones v. Alfred H. Mayer e Co.*, 392 U.S. 409 (1968)
- *Koon v. United States*, 518 U.S. 81 (1996)
- *Local 28 Sheet Metal Workers v. EEOC*, 478 U.S. 421 (1986)
- *Lochner v. New York*, 198 U.S. 45 (1905)
- *Marks v. United States*, 430 U.S. 188 (1977)
- *New York v. Belton*, 453 U.S. 454 (1981)
- *McConnell v. FEC*, 540 U.S. 93 (2003)
- *Miller v. Alabama*, 567 U.S. 460 (2012)
- *Minersville School District v. Gobitis*, 310 U.S. 586 (1940)
- *Obergefell v. Hodges*, 576 U.S. 644 (2015)
- *Parents Involved in Community Schools v. Seattle*, 551 U.S. 701 (2007)
- *Planned Parenthood of Southeastern Pennsylvania v. Casey*, 505 U.S. 833 (1992)
- *Plessy v. Ferguson*, 163 U.S. 537 (1896)
- *Regents of the University of California v. Bakke*, 438 U.S. 265 (1978)
- *Reiter v. Sonotone Corporation*, 442 U.S. 330 (1979)
- *Roe v. Wade*, 410 U.S. 113 (1973)
- *Rust v. Sullivan*, 500 U.S. 173 (1991)
- *Schlesinger v. Reservists Committee to Stop the War*, 418 U.S. 208 (1974)
- *Seminole Tribe of Florida v. Florida*, 517 U.S. 44 (1996)
- *Shapiro v. Thompson*, 349 U.S. 618 (1969)
- *Sherbert v. Verner*, 374 U.S. 398 (1963)
- *Stack v. Boyle*, 342 U.S. 1 (1951)
- *Students for Fair Admission v. Harvard*, 600 U.S. 181 (2023)

- *Swann v. Charlotte-Mecklenburg Board of Education*, 402 U.S. 1 (1971)
- *Thornburgh v. American College of Obstetricians & Gynecologists*, 476 U.S. 747 (1982)
- *United States v. Rabinowitz*, 339 U.S. 56 (1950)
- *United States v. Richardson*, 418 U.S. 166 (1974)
- *United States v. Salerno*, 481 U.S. 739 (1987)
- *United States v. Windsor*, 570, U.S. 744 (2013)
- *Valley Forge Christian College v. Americans United for Separation of Church and State*, 454 U.S. 464 (1982)
- *Webster v. Reproductive Health Services*, 492 U.S. 490 (1989)
- *West Coast Hotel Co. v. Parrish*, 300 U.S. 379 (1937)
- *West Virginia State Board of Education v. Barnette*, 319 U.S. 624 (1943)

II Brazilian Cases

II.I. Supremo Tribunal Federal

- *Bancários de Rio do Sul v. Banco de Santa Catarina* (STF, 2ª Turma, AgRg no RE n. 235.794/SC, Rel. Min. Gilmar Mendes, j. em 22.10.2002, DJ 14.11.2002)
- *Caixa Econômica Federal v. Instituto Brasileiro de Defesa do Consumidor* (STF, Pleno, RE n. 1.101.937/SP, Rel. Min. Alexandre de Moraes, j. em 08.04.2021, DJe 14.06.2021)
- *Camargo v. SENAR* (STF, Pleno, RE n. 816.830/SC, Rel. Min. Dias Toffoli, j. em 17.12.2022, DJe 24.04.2023)
- *Carrijo v. Goiás* (STF, Pleno, RE n. 89.108/GO, Rel. Min. Cunha Peixoto, j. em 28.08.1980, DJ 19.12.1980)
- *Fundação Universidade Federal de Rondônia v. Sousa Leitão* (STF, 1ª Turma, AgRg no RE n. 597.872/RO, Rel. Min. Marco Aurélio, j. em 03.06.2014, DJe 26.08.2014)
- *Hospital Cândido Randon v. Cândido Randon* (STF, Plenário, RE n. 651.703/PR, Rel. Min. Luiz Fux, j. em 26.04.2017, DJe 26.04.2017)
- *Ideal Transportes e Guindastes v. Santos* (STF, Plenário, RE n. 116.121/SP, Rel. Min. Octávio Gallotti, Rel. para Acórdão Min. Marco Aurélio, j. em 11.10.2000, DJ 16.06.2001)
- *Metabel v. União* (STF, Pleno, RE n. 590.809/RS, Rel. Min. Marco Aurélio, j. em 22.10.2014, DJe 24.11.2014)

- *Nispeche da Silva v. Rayes Pereira*
  (STF, Pleno, ARE n. 1.309.642/SP, Rel. Min. Roberto Barroso, j. em 01.02.2024)
- *Portela Santana v. União*
  (STF, Plenário, RE n. 655.265/RS, Rel. Min. Luiz Fux, Rel. para Acórdão Min. Edson Fachin, j. em 13.04.2016, DJe 04.08.2016)
- *Porto Alegre v. Conselho Regional de Contabilidade do Rio Grande do Sul*
  (STF, Rcl n. 54.888/RS, Rel. Min. Nunes Marques, j. em 01.09.2022, DJe 13.09.2022)
- *PriceWaterhouseCoopers v. São Paulo*
  (STF, 2ª Turma, AgRg no RE n. 1.365.583/SP, Rel. Min. Gilmar Mendes, j. em 23.05.2022, DJe 26.05.2022)
- *União v. Associação Pró-Ensino em Santa Cruz do Sul – APESC*
  (STF, Pleno, RE n. 636.941/RS, Rel. Min. Luiz Fux, j. em 13.02.2014, DJe 04.04.2014)
- *União v. Braskem*
  (STF, Pleno, RE n. 955.227/BA, Rel. Min. Roberto Barroso, j. em 08.02.2023)
- *União v. Companhia Agro Industrial de Goiana*
  (STF, 2ª Turma, AgRg na Rcl n. 25.832/DF, Rel. Min. Ricardo Lewandowski, j. em 18.12.2017, DJe 07.02.2018)
- *União v. Petróleo Dois Irmãos*
  (STF, Pleno, RE n. 138.284/CE, Rel. Min. Carlos Velloso, j. em 01.07.1992, DJ 28.08.1992)
- *União v. TBM*
  (STF, Pleno, RE n. 949.297/CE, Rel. Min. Edson Fachin, Rel. para o Acórdão Min. Roberto Barroso, j. em 08.02.2023)
- *Universidade Federal de Goiás v. Alves Lopes*
  (STF, Pleno, RE n. 500.171/GO, Rel. Min. Ricardo Lewandowski, j. em 13.08.2008, DJe 24.10.2008)
- *Universidade Federal de Goiás v. Macedo dos Santos*
  (STF, Pleno, RE n. 597.854/GO, Rel. Min. Edson Fachin, j. em 26.04.2017, DJe 21.09.2017)
- *Venbo v. Rio de Janeiro*
  (STF, Plenário, RE n. 603.136/RJ, Rel. Min. Gilmar Mendes, j. em 28.05.2020, DJe 16.06.2020)
- *Zoghbi v. Presidente do Senado Federal*
  (STF, Pleno, MS n. 28.538/DF, Rel. Min. Marco Aurélio, j. em 23.04.2014, DJe 04.08.2014)

II.II. Superior Tribunal de Justiça

- *Bosquirolli v. IPERGS*
  (STJ, 2ª Turma, AgInt no AREsp n. 853.152/RS, Rela. Mina. Assusete Magalhães, j. em 13.12.2016, DJe 19.12.2016)

- *Fazenda Nacional v. Cotriguaçu*
  (STJ, 1ª Seção, EREsp n. 1.517.492/PR, Rel. Min. Og Fernandes, Relatora para o Acórdão Mina. Regina Helena Costa, j. em 08.11.2017, DJe 1°.02.2018)
- *Fazenda Nacional v. VDA Logística e Transporte*
  (STJ, 1ª Seção, REsp n. 1.945.110/RS, Rel. Min. Benedito Gonçalves, j. em 26.04.2023, DJe 12.06.2023)
- *Franco v. União*
  (STJ, 1ª Turma, REsp n. 1.026.234/DF, Rel. Min. Teori Zavascki, j. em 27.05.2008, DJe 11.06.2008)
- *INSS v. Santos*
  (STJ, 2ª Turma, REsp n. 1.676.027/PR, Rel. Min. Herman Benjamin, j. em 26.09.2017, DJe 11.10.2017)
- *Instituto Federal de Educação, Ciência e Tecnologia do Ceará v. Azevedo*
  (STJ, 1ª Seção, REsp n. 1.888.049/CE, Rel. Min. Og Fernandes, j. em 22.09.2021, DJe 29.09.2021)
- *Itaú v. Romano*
  (STJ, 4ª Turma, AgRg na MC n. 23.595/RJ, Rel. Min. Raul Araújo, j. em 04.08.2016, DJe 12.08.2016)
- *Pettená Filho v. Tribunal de Justiça de São Paulo*
  (STJ, HC n. 274.806/SP, Rel. Min. Rogério Schietti, j. em 14.02.2014, DJe 18.02.2014)
- *Rio de Janeiro Refrescos v. Minas Gerais*
  (STJ, 1ª Seção, AgInt no EREsp n. 2.051.752/MG, Rela. Mina. Regina Helena Costa, j. em 29.08.2023, DJe 31.08.2023)
- *União v. Dimon do Brasil Tabacos*
  (STJ, Corte Especial, EREsp n. 687.903/RS, Rel. Min. Ari Pargendler, j. em 04.11.2009, DJe 19.11.2009)
- *União v. Freire Engenharia*
  (STJ, 1ª Seção, EREsp n. 608.122/RJ, Rel. Min. Teori Zavascki, j. em 09.05.2007, DJe 28.05.2007)
- *União v. Metalgrin*
  (STJ, 1ª Seção, AR n. 4.443/RS, Rel. Min. Herman Benjamin, Rel. para Acórdão Min. Gurgel de Faria, j. em 08.05.2019, DJe 14.06.2019)
- *União v. Sintrajusc*
  (STJ, 1ª Turma, REsp n. 1.458.607/SC, Rel. Min. Napoleão Nunes Maia Filho, j. em 23.10.2014, DJe 03.11.2014)
- *Unimed de Cascavel v. Malikoski*
  (STJ, 2ª Seção, REsp n. 1.822.240/SP, Rel. Min. Paulo de Tarso Sanseverino, j. em 13.10.2021, DJe 27.10.2021)

III English Cases

III.I. Chancery Division

- *Elwes v. Brigg Gas Company* (1886)

III.II. Common Pleas

- *Bole v. Horton* (1673)

III.III. House of Lords

- *Attorney General v. Dean and Canons of Windsor* (1860)
- *Beamish v. Beamish* (1861)
- *Bright v. Hutton* (1852)
- *Donoghue v. Stevenson* (1932)
- *Fairchild v. Glenhaven Funeral Services Ltd.* (2002)
- *Great Western Ry. Co. v. Owners of S. S. Mostyn* (1928)
- *London Tramways Co. v. London County Council* (1898)
- *R. v. Moloney* (1985)
- *Rylands v. Fletcher* (1868)
- *Velley v. Burder* (1837)

III.IV. King's Bench

- *Fischer v. Prince* (1762)
- *Jones v. Randall* (1774)
- *King v. Melling* (1671)
- *Maulay v. Abbot of Whitby* (1281)
- *Rex v. Inhabitants of Underbarrow and Bradleyfield* (1766)
- *Rust v. Cooper* (1777)

III.V. Queen's Bench

- *Bridges v. Hawkesworth* (1851)
- *South Staffordshire Walter Company v. Sharman* (1896)

IV Scotland Cases

Court of Session

- *Glasgow Corporation v. Lord Advocate* (1959)
- *Morgan Guarantee Trust Company of New York v. Lothian Regional Council* (1995)
- *Stirling of Northwoodside v. Earl of Lauderdale* (1733)

The manufacturer's authorised representative in the EU is Springer Nature Customer Service Centre GmbH, Europaplatz 3, 69115 Heidelberg, Germany. If you have any concerns regarding our products, please contact ProductSafety@springernature.com

Printed and bound by CPI Group (UK) Ltd, Croydon, CR0 4YY
30/09/2026
02225608-0014